371·94 RiC

KU-504-715

Autism – The Search for Coherence

of related interest

Asperger's Syndrome
A Guide for Parents and Professionals
Tony Attwood
ISBN 1 85302 577 1

Pretending to be Normal
Living with Asperger's Syndrome
Liane Holliday Willey
ISBN 1 85302 749 9

Asperger Syndrome Employment Workbook
An Employment Workbook for Adults with Asperger Syndrome
Roger N Meyer
ISBN 1 85302 796 0

Enabling Communication in Children with Autism
Carol Potter and Chris Whittaker
ISBN 1 85302 956 4

Parents' Education as Autism Therapists
Applied Behaviour Analysis in Context
Edited by Mickey Keenan, Ken P. Kerr and Karola Dillenburger
ISBN 1 85302 778 2

Behavioural Concerns and Autistic Spectrum Disorders
Explanations and Strategies for Change
John Clements and Ewa Zarkowska
ISBN 1 85302 742 1

A Positive Approach to Autism
Stella Waterhouse
ISBN 1 85302 808 8

Autism: An Inside–Out Approach
An Innovative Look at the Mechanics of 'Autism'
and its Developmental 'Cousins'
Donna Williams
ISBN 1 85302 387 6

Children with Autism, 2nd edition
Diagnosis and Intervention to Meet Their Needs
Colwyn Tevarthen, Kenneth Aitken, Despina Papoudi and Jacqueline Robarts
ISBN 1 85302 555 0

UNIVERSITY OF WALES COLLEGE NEWPORT
LIBRARY AND LEARNING RESOURCES CAERLEON

Autism – The Search for Coherence

*Edited by John Richer
and Sheila Coates*

Jessica Kingsley Publishers
London and Philadelphia

All rights reserved. No paragraph of this publication may be reproduced, copied or transmitted save with written permission or in accordance with the provisions of the Copyright Act 1956 (as amended), or under the terms of any licence permitting limited copying issued by the Copyright Licensing Agency, 33–34 Alfred Place, London WC1E 7DP. Any person who does any unauthorised act in relation to this publication may be liable to criminal prosecution and civil claims for damages.

The right of the contributors to be identified as authors of this work has been asserted by them in accordance with the Copyright, Designs and Patents Act 1988.

First published in the United Kingdom in 2001 by
Jessica Kingsley Publishers Ltd
116 Pentonville Road
London N1 9JB, England
and
325 Chestnut Street
Philadelphia, PA 19106, USA

www.jkp.com

Copyright © 2001 Jessica Kingsley Publishers

Library of Congress Cataloging in Publication Data
A CIP catalogue record for this book is available from the Library of Congress

British Library Cataloguing in Publication Data
A CIP catalogue record for this book is available from the British Library

ISBN 1 85302 888 6

Printed and Bound in Great Britain by
Athenaeum Press, Gateshead, Tyne and Wear

Contents

Part 4 Therapy

Part 5 Services

Part 6 Personal Stories

Introduction

The Search for Coherence

John Richer and Sheila Coates

These are interesting and exciting times for those concerned with people with autism. New ways of understanding the children's problems are being developed, research into underlying physiological mechanisms is yielding fascinating results, the genetic influences are being explored, public awareness is growing and, vitally, therapies are being developed which seem to offer more hope of real improvement for at least some children with autism. At the same time there is concern for the 'autism explosion'; reported cases of autism have increased dramatically in the late 1980s and throughout the 1990s (Rimland 1999, 2000). While some of this increase is due to a broadening of the diagnostic category and better awareness and detection by professionals, most believe that there is a real increase in incidence as well. Only a few other childhood problems have increased so dramatically in recent years, notably allergies (which raises the question of linkage) (van Gent *et al.* 1997).

Autism has, more than most childhood problems, been understood and studied in an enormous variety of ways. There is no widely accepted 'theory of autism', nor an approach to investigating the condition or to its treatment. In the past there was considerable animosity between different schools of thought. Many parents found this confusing and distressing. Yet, talking to and reading about the work of researchers, clinicians and teachers, it is also clear that many are saying and doing compatible things but in different theoretical languages or with different emphases or simply talking about different aspects of the problem: physiology, psychology, education. There is a need to bring these ideas together, building on their positive aspects rather than dismissing because of their weakness, starting to develop a coherence. Like truth, this is a process which will, in the journalists' jargon, 'run and run'. Understanding develops. Also one person's coherence will not necessarily be the same as another's, but the attempt to look over the garden fence and develop a better sense of similarities and differences is worthwhile. This was one of the motivations behind the conference held at Christ Church, Oxford in September 1999 – 'The Search for Coherence from the Fragments of Autism'. Contributors were brought together along several dimensions of apparent difference, the main ones were:

1. Theoretical approaches – e.g. behaviourist and psychoanalytic, psychological and ethological.

2. Place and manner of work – e.g. school, clinic, community, university, hospital, home.

3. Personal perspective and interest – e.g. young person with autism, parent, therapist, teacher, clinician, researcher.

4. Aspects of the problem – e.g. genetics/physiology, social relationships, learning skills.

The last dimension reflects the approach to therapy taken in Oxford. As well as attempting detection as early as possible, we have a three stage approach, although in practice each stage overlaps with the others:

1. Addressing as far as possible the child's physiological problems. Danczak discusses (Chapter 11 in this volume) some aspects of the approaches being developed in a number of centres.

2. Addressing the child's attachment security and early intersubjective communication. The objective is to help the child feel able to engage in intersubjective interactions, albeit simple ones. This is much easier if the child's physiological state is improved. If successful it also makes the next stage easier.

3. Helping the child to develop, to acquire skills and understanding.

This three stage process reflects normal development.

In this book, as in the conference, we kept these stages in mind. Most conference contributors were able to offer papers to this book. The book is organised into six parts.

1. *Mechanisms and processes* – This is the entry point for most people, the children's behaviour, the mechanisms that underly it and the children's development into autistic behaviour and their development after that.

2. *Physiology and medicine* – The underlying physiology and its treatment. (We should have liked to include the conference presentation on genetics, but this was not available.)

3. *Meeting of minds* – This part examines attempts to reach out into the mind of a child with autism, to communicate feelings and thoughts and to develop an intersubjective relationship.

4. *Therapy* – This part continues the theme but the emphasis is on older children or specific behavioural difficulties.

5. *Services* – Developing services for children with autism is vital.

6. *Personal stories* – The last part comprises personal stories by parents, about parents' perceptions and by a young man with autism.

These are not solely conventional scientific accounts, although many individual chapters are. Conventional psychology or psychiatry are sometimes too crude in their measures and too unwilling to look at the real phenomena; accurate recording of the natural phenomena is sometimes sacrificed to methodology acceptable to peers. Sensitive, detailed and intellectually disciplined accounts of individual children's behaviour, or of their reaction to attempts at communication and/or therapy, contain much that should inform scientific as well as practical work.[1] The honest endeavours of sensitive therapists can reveal much, even though it would be dismissed by some 'scientists' as anecdotal. These are the exceptions that prove the rule.[2] For instance the strong version of the interesting Theory of Mind hypothesis is thrown into some doubt by the accounts of some autistic people and by the experience of those interacting and communicating with them, as well as by controlled experiments.

We have also included first person accounts. These are not scientific accounts in the usual sense, but are useful first for their rich and detailed

[1] Direct observation is the starting point of ethology, a branch of zoology, called by Tinbergen (1963) the biological study of behaviour. This has been called 'watching and wondering' by Tinbergen. Complicated apparatus, advanced statistics and obscure jargon are not guarantors of scientific truth or usefulness.

[2] The phrase 'exceptions which "prove" the rule' is, of course, used ironically; the meaning of prove is not 'confirm' but 'test' or 'probe'.

observation, and second because the integration of first and third person accounts is very difficult for children with autism (Richer 1998 and Chapter 3 in this volume). So the experience of people trying to communicate with people with autism is of itself important information.

References

Gillberg, C. and Wing, L. (1999) 'Autism: Not an extremely rare disorder.' *Acta Psychiatr Scand. 99 (6)*, 399–406.

Richer, J. M. (1998) 'Attachment, autism and holding in mind.' Paper presented to the International Society for Human Ethology, Vancover, August.

Rimland, B. (1999) 'The autisn explosion.' *http://www.autism.com/ari/editorials/explosion/html/*

Rimland, B. (2000) 'Cause or coincidence?' *Autism Reasearch Review International 14*, (4), 1.

Tinbergen (1963) 'On the aims and methods of ethology.' *Zeitschrift für Tierpsychologie 20*, 410–433.

van Gent, T., Heijnen, C. J. and Treffers, P. D. (1997) 'Autism and the immune system.' *Journal of Child Psychology and Psychiatry 38*, 337–349.

PART 1

Mechanisms and Processes

CHAPTER I

Editorial

Mechanisms and Processes

John Richer and Sheila Coates

A large amount of research has been devoted to basic questions such as 'What's wrong with autistic children?' 'What is the basic "deficit"?' or, less negatively, 'How are autistic children crucially different from others?' The quantity of research effort, at least in the past, has been out of proportion to the reported prevalence of autism, and says something about the puzzling nature of autism and the perceived wider importance of the problems the children have. As Professor Peter Fonagy once said in passing, 'All interesting questions in psychology come back to autism'. Autistic children challenge us in many ways. They challenge us in some of our notions of what makes humans different from other species: our communication one with another. These include the content of our consciousness and our ability to be empathetic, our social living and our rich use of language, our flexibility, playfulness, adaptability and creativity. All of these are areas where autistic people seem to find great difficulty. They challenge us as parents, carers or therapists, the ordinary loving friendly approaches that are fine with most children simply do not work with autistic children, and often seem to make matters worse. They challenge researchers, especially the community of psychological experimenters since the children so often simply do not cooperate with the experimenters. Finally the children challenge our rigour as scientists, clinicians and carers, since, at least until recently, they have not 'answered back' and given the 'inside story', so they have been the focus of a large number of wild theories!

The history of theorising about autism has had some unfortunate features. Most unfortunate was the early 'blaming' of the 'cold refrigerator' mothers for causing their child's autistic withdrawal. The main effect of this was to cause huge distress to parents who had already lost the child they had been expecting. A subsidiary effect was to oversensitise many to see any research on the children's social behaviour and relationships as *ipso facto* a return to the bad old days of parent blaming. In fact parents know very well that their child's social behaviour and relationships are different and want to understand how and why; this is where autism is most apparent and most devasting to parents and children. The research community then embarked upon a long journey using cognitive deficits models. One of the first was the idea that the children had a 'cognitive language deficit' affecting particular comprehension (Rutter 1968). One of the most recent is they have a 'Theory of Mind (ToM) deficit' (Baron-Cohen 1995; Frith 1989). These deficit models are derived from psychological testing with all the problems inherent in that approach. At their most modest they try to describe a difference between autistic children and others. Most however slip into arguing that the difference they have found between autistic and other children, tested at 3, 5, 8, 12 years, is the 'fundamental' deficit and causes the other problems the child has. It is a way of thinking which has echoes in research looking for bacterial or viral pathogens in illness. Find the pathogen and you have found the cause. While that is not true even for all physical illness, it is certainly not true for the pervasive developmental/behavioural difficulties found in autistic children. The point is so obvious that one feels a bit like the little boy pointing out that the Emperor has no clothes. The 'deficits' that are found can say much that is useful about the differences between autistic and other children at the ages they are measured, and they focus attention on trying to find explanations for these reliably found differ-ences, but they say little about how those differences arose. To state the obvious, in order to study the development of these differences, one needs to study their development from conception onwards, looking at how a child's life unfolds. Given that we are complex biological and cultural beings, this unfolding is likely to be non-linear and interactive and to proceed in ways partly best described by the ideas of catastrophe theory and chaos theory. In addition most processes will be shared with non-autistic children. Autistic children are to be seen as children first, but children who happen also to have autistic behaviour. So much of the understanding of their development will be seeing how they subtly and repeatedly deviate from the developmental paths that most children take, and why the 'homeorhetic' mechanisms (Christopher Ounsted, personal communication) which keep most children on track developmentally operate less well for them, and how they even change their own environments in ways which encourage this different development (e.g. they do not get others interacting much with them; they do not play much).

While the early cognitive deficit theories were unhelpful, the most recent, such as the Theory of Mind deficit ideas, have had a developmental focus, have been useful and fertile and have also allowed people to look at the social relationships of these children without running the risk of being accused of parent blaming. Nevertheless ToM deficits have been found not to be specific to autism nor to occur in all autistic individuals[1]. Mavropoulou (Chapter 8 in this volume) finds from naturalistic observation in school and home that many 'high functioning' autistic children can appropriately use words referring to mental states, and their use varies in a similar way to that of non-autistic children.

As Richer (Chapter 3 in this volume) argues, ToM deficits are part of a wider set of difficulties that these children have and can be partly described as being the result of difficulty in acquiring the skills of the culture. These ideas come from a different approach, ethology, not usually applied in this field (see Richer, Chapter 2 in this voume). This approach is particularly well suited to the study of autistic children (and other human behaviour, but we confine ourselves to autism here). It starts with good direct observation – getting a useful description of the children's behaviour in their everyday environments, the behaviour that demands explanation. Of that behaviour one asks four questions – Tinbergen's 'Four Whys?' (Tinbergen 1963). These concern:

1. Immediate causation – what are the proximate causal factors?

2. Function – what is the behaviour good for?

3. Ontogeny – how did the behaviour develop in the individual?

4. Evolution – how did it evolve?

---

1   This latter finding is not crucial. A reasonable and coherent version of the theory is that the children have difficulties acquiring ToM skills: some never do, but some others acquire a level of skill later. This is what Baron-Cohen (1989) found.

Ethology is a branch of zoology, and like all science it is non-evaluative. Thus the language of 'deficits' is alien to it. Happé takes a step towards this position in her extended abstract in Chapter 6 by focusing on areas in which autistic people do *better* than 'heterotists' (what one autistic person whom she quotes called non-autistic people). She focuses on what she terms the 'weak central coherence' of people with autism – this is their difficulty in seeing the wood for the trees – but she brings a welcome emphasis to their ability to 'see the trees', to pay attention to detail. She speculates that this cognitive style is seen also in some of the relatives of these children and notes the professions they often pursue, such as science, engineering or computing, which require attention to detail.

Her idea of weak central coherence is a variant of a dimension of human difference derived from Jungian psychology (Jung 1921/71) which was proposed many decades ago and which is now measured widely by the Myers-Briggs Type Indicator (MBTI) (Briggs Myers and McCaulley 1985). This test places respondents on one or other side of four dichotomies such that their final profile falls into one of sixteen types. It is noted that all respondents have preferences and abilities on both sides of each dichotomy and that their final score simply reflects how they tend to respond to situations. The dichotomy of interest here is between 'Sensing' and 'iNtuitive' types, abbreviated to **S** and **N**. It refers to how people tend to perceive. Those who tend to fall on the S side focus on the facts and details, which they remember well. They are reliable in the details of their observation. They are realistic rather than imaginative. Intuitive types on the other hand tend to be interested in facts only in so far as they relate to a bigger picture. They are imaginative, future oriented, creative and abstract thinkers. They tend to be optimistic. On the downside, N types can get carried away with ideas and lose sight of the facts. S types can find it difficult to imagine future possibilities, to bring ideas together and see the bigger picture. They tend to be pessimistic. It is fairly clear that Happé's idea of weak central coherence refers to extreme S types. So one aspect of autism can be redescribed as a strong preference for the Sensing style of perceiving. One prediction from this might be that there is a preponderance of S types among the relatives, although the professions Happé notes do not have a large excess of S types in them (Briggs Myers and McCaulley 1985). However, the crucial test would be to offer the test to relatives of autistic children.

Garner and Hamilton (Chapter 7 in this volume) do not find support for the weak central coherence hypothesis from their data. They note that the ideas need to be tested in more situations and more real-life situations. They too argue 'that autism should not be presented as simply a series of deficits, but rather understood as different abilities, or abilities at the extremes of continuums. Such a position appears to be a more true reflection of the qualities of autism.'

ToM hypotheses do not find support from the research of Rowe and Crawford (Chapter 5 in this volume). They argue that the tests based on this hypothesis proved neither sensitive nor specific to autism, at least when tested on adults with learning disabilities, four without Autistic Spectrum Disorder (ASD) (controls), four with ASD (ASD group) and four with developmental frontal lobe syndrome. The frontal lobe group did even less well than the ASD group and both worse than controls on both ToM tasks and tests of 'executive functioning' (tasks requiring sustained attention). They argue that Russell's (1997) proposal that ASDs are primarily disorders of executive functioning accounts for the results better. While caution should be exercised in ascribing primacy to existing differences (see above), it is certainly true that severe attentional difficulties characterise most autistic children, and that the history of many children diagnosed in middle childhood as falling into Asperger Syndrome, is a history of attentional difficulties (Richer, Chapter 3 in this volume).

Rowe and Crawford take the developmental approach by arguing that 'it could be that the timing of the maximal period of autistic pathogenesis predicts neuropsychological outcomes. For example, if deterioration occurs after the secure acquisition of language relating to mental states, it would be predicted that adult ToM functioning would be relatively preserved.' This draws on the developmental principle that the system most affected by stressors is the system which is changing/developing. Many of the differences in severity in autism and patterns of difficulty are probably strongly influenced by this, for instance, from clinical observation, children who seemed to be pursuing a fairly normal sociable development up to a fairly clear point of decline, often, but far from always, seem to have better communicative skills than those who seemed unsociable from birth. The same is found for non-verbal skills, our own extensive assessments of motor development and non-verbal reasoning using the Waldon approach reveals that autistic children who are reported to have been passive and non-communicative from birth are less mature in their motor development than children whose parents report an apparently later onset.

Another factor affecting the course of autism is likely to be the child's security of attachment. Yirmiya and Sigman (Chapter 4 in this volume) importantly show that while all the autistic children they studied would be classified as 'insecure disorganised' in strict scoring of the Ainsworth Strange Situation, a second scoring, ignoring the defining disorganised behaviours, led to a classification which gave the same proportions of secure, insecure ambivalent and insecure avoidant as found in the general population. They argue very interestingly that the attachment motivational system is concerned primarily with personal well-being and safety, with the personal viewpoint of the self. This they argue is not damaged in autism and so the attachment system works as well as in any other child. There is no need to take account of the viewpoint of the other – other minds. The problem for autistic infants comes when that view of the self is normally translated into an Internal Working Model incorporating the viewpoint of the other. They conclude, 'children with autism differentiate between caregivers and strangers and some are securely attached, but their attachment is in the service of the self; it is self-enhancing and does not necessarily take into account the other as a separate self with a separate mind that needs to be related to. Thus children with autism may be displaying attachment at a basic psychobiological level rather than at a more psychological level'. While Yirmiya and Sigman do not assert that insecure attachment is a cause of autism, they do argue that secure attachment seems to be associated with better outcome and thus that part of therapy could be promoting secure attachments in those who seem insecure.

Richer (Chapter 3 in this volume) brings together attachment ideas, difficulties in relating to other minds and general difficulties in becoming a fully paid-up member of the culture (the group mind). He argues that since autistic children can imitate, they have the basic ability to translate between the viewpoint of others and the viewpoint of themselves, between perceiving someone doing something and doing it oneself. However, what they have not done so well is to integrate those two viewpoints, as do most children, through social interaction and play (they do much less of them) or to negotiate the shared conventions (the meanings of words, gestures and so on) with which we communicate subjective states and communicate generally (they tend to be avoidant in the situations in which those meanings are negotiated). He notes the close similarity between the behaviour characteristic of disorganised attachment and the avoidance dominated motivational conflict behaviour of autistic children, and suggests, in line with other attachment theorists, that disruption of the development of social understanding and empathy follows. The difference between autistic children and others is that the disorganisation of perception of the other is argued to derive largely from factors in the (to be) autistic child (probably due in part to attentional difficulties, cf. the executive function hypothesis of Russell 1997) and not from the behaviour of the parents. In other words the children become autistic despite normal parenting. The factors influencing this development are very likely to be multiple and heterogeneous and will include genetics, immune system dysfunction and related nutritional problems. It is interesting, in passing, that the 'epidemic' of reported cases of autism (partly due to better detection and a widening of the category) seems to be paralleled by an epidemic in allergy in children.

This view of autism predicts that the level of ToM abilities would go hand in hand with other social/cultural abilities, which they do. It would also predict that many of the difficulties seen in autism would be seen in other groups too, which they are.

The Search for Coherence requires us to look beyond the area of data, though not to lose touch with it, and to cope with the multifaceted uncertainties of the data and the complexity of human development. Above all it requires an open-mindedness to data and ideas from many sources and a desire to see connections. We hope this book is a small step toward that.

References

Baron-Cohen, S.(1989) 'The autistic child's theory of mind: a case of specific developmental delays.' *Journal of Child Psychology and Psychiatry 30*, 285–97.

Baron-Cohen, S. (1995) *Mindblindness: An Essay on Autism and the Theory of Mind.* Cambridge, MA: MIT Press.

Briggs Myers, I. and McCaulley, M.H. (1985) *Manual: A Guide to the Development and Use of the Myers-Briggs Type Inventory.* Palo Alto, CA: Consulting Psychologists Press.

Frith, U. (1989) *Autism: Explaining the Enigma.* Oxford: Basil Blackwell.

Jung, C. (1971) *Psychological Types.* (Translated by H.G. Barnes and revised by R.F.C. Hall.) Princeton, NJ: Princeton University Press.

Russell, J. (1997) *Autism as an Executive Disorder.* Oxford: Oxford University Press.

Rutter, M. (1968) 'Concepts of autism: a review of research.' *Journal of Child Psychology and Psychiatry 9*, 1–25.

Tinbergen, N. (1963) 'On the aims and methods of ethology.' *Zeitschrift für Tierpsychologie 20*, 410–33.

CHAPTER 2

An Ethological Approach to Autism
From Evolutionary Perspectives to Treatment

John Richer

The ethological approach

Recent decades have seen the approaches and ideas of ethology become more pervasive with fields like evolutionary psychology springing up, although the name ethology has remained largely applied to the study of non-human behaviour. It is one of a number of approaches to the study of human behaviour, and any researcher should use whatever combination of approaches seems best to address the phenomena being investigated. However, I shall focus initially on the ethological approach since it seems to me to be fertile and coherent.

First, what is ethology? Ethology is a branch of zoology and has been defined by one of its early pioneers, Niko Tinbergen (1963), as 'the biological study of behaviour' (see Box 2.1). Two key aspects of the etho-logical approach distinguish it, perhaps more so in past decades than now, from mainstream psychology: evolutionary theory and direct observation of behaviour.

Evolutionary theory

Ethologists have as their background Darwinian evolutionary theory, which embraces the broad sweep of life forms and the struggle for survival by individuals. Dawkins (1976) has described individuals as 'survival machines' for their genes. The theory now includes the fact that we

Box 2.1 Ethology: the biological study of behaviour

Tinbergen characterised the process as 'Watching and wondering':

1. Watching: observing over a long period in as many different situations as possible to get an idea of the range of the animal's behaviour.

2. Wondering:

   - 'Why does that animal do that?' – the 'Four Whys' (see below).

   - 'Isn't that wonderful?' – having a sense of wonder at what the animals do.

Direct observation in the animal's natural environment:

1. Remaining open-minded, but inevitably running though a number of hypotheses in one's mind. Remaining wedded not only to trying to describe behaviour in publicly observable terms (not subjective states), but also to trying to get inside the mind of the animal as an aid to creativity and understanding.

2. Developing a list of 'behaviour elements', where behaviour is defined morphologically (what it looks like, e.g. 'eyebrow raising') or by consequence (what it achieves, e.g. 'approach', 'avoid').

3. 'Split don't lump' – when in doubt whether to put two different behaviours in the same category, err on the side of separating perhaps unnecessarily, rather than lumping together and losing information.

Tinbergen's Four Whys: Four types of answers to the question, 'Why did that individual do that?'

1. Immediate causation – what factors in the animal or its environment influenced the behaviour?

2. Ontogeny – what factors in the animal's history from conception onwards led it to do this behaviour now?

3. Function – what is this behaviour good for? Ultimately, how does it help the survival of that individual's genes?

4. Evolution – how did this type of animal evolve to behave in this way? What is the evolutionary history of this?

In developing a list of behaviour elements, it usually becomes necessary to develop some hierarchical ordering in order to make sense of the complexity and variety of behaviour. A first step is often to try to infer the underlying motivations. This 'motivational analysis' is done by seeing what behaviours seem to occur together in the same time period or tend to occur in the same situation or help achieve the same end.

humans are a culture-creating species. We ascribe minds and consciousness to each other; we are seen as 'survival machines' for the units of cultures, sometimes called 'memes' (essentially an idea or skill) (Dawkins 1976). The survival machine for cultures is now seen as the group, 'we' not just 'I', and selection therefore acts on the group holding the memes. In effect our cultural ability makes our groups, at least for this purpose, into 'super-organisms'.

Direct observation of behaviour

At the other extreme from the abstraction of evolutionary theory, ethologists have always emphasised spending a long time observing and recording a wide range of naturally occuring behaviour in the *natural environment* and trying to make a description of that in *publicly observable* terms.

Early ethological studies

The paper 'The partial non communication of culture to autistic children' (Richer 1978) embraced ideas from both direct observation and evolutionary theory. It argued that autistic children had not absorbed the skills and understandings of their culture as much as other children, and that one factor constraining them was their tendency to avoid social interactions (face to face and joint attention) in which the transfer of culture took place. They could be described as 'dyscultural' children.

Why do autistic children tend to avoid those sorts of interactions? The answer to that needed a detailed examination of their social behaviour and this exemplified the second feature of the ethological approach, the close observation and analysis of naturally occuring behaviour.

It was clear that autistic children were in a state of motivational conflict, in which motivation labelled avoidance or fear, was stronger than in other children and tended to inhibit other motivations such as sociability more than in other children (Richer 1975; Richer and Nicoll 1971). The Nobel Prize winner Niko Tinbergen and his wife Lies came to similar conclusions independently. (Tinbergen and Tinbergen 1972, 1983).[1]

---

1   Buitelaar *et al.* (1991) failed to find an avoidance category of behaviour when they observed autistic children in a playroom. They looked to see whether some of the behaviours we described clustered in time, no such cluster emerged from their Principal Components analysis. They concluded that the children were not predominantly avoidance motivated. In fact their findings were what would be expected from our observations, and their false conclusion illustrates the difficulty that non-ethologists (and it seems the one experienced ethologist in their group) often have when dealing with

One difference between the ethological approach and conventional psychology is that these motivations are defined by how the observed behaviours cluster together, i.e. they seem to occur in the same time intervals, or they are functionally similar in having the same causes and effects. This is the standard ethological approach which starts from the observed behaviour and then out of that develops higher order categories. It is in contrast to the usual psychological approach which starts from higher order categories, such as intelligence, or, as in this volume 'social engagement' (Hyde, Wimpory and Nash, Chapter 24 in this volume), and then tries to find measures for them. This can be very useful as an interim, quick measure for clinical purposes, but as an approach likely to generate reliable scientific understanding, it is unpromising (see Box 2.2).

Some of the behaviours which define avoidance and sociability, and some of the ways that motivational conflict is observed is shown in Boxes 2.3 and 2.4. Autistic children's social behaviour was described as 'avoidance dominated motivational conflict behaviour' (Richer 1975; Richer and Nicoll 1971). Some of the causal factors promoting avoidance included uncertainty or unpredictability in the activity and increasing social intrusion or demand (Richer and Richards 1975). Intrusion increases avoidance up to a point but then avoidance is decreased after intense and prolonged intrusion (Box 2.5).

The type of conflict behaviour changes with the intensity of the underlying fear. Strong fear is associated with unambivalent avoidance, reduced fear with overintense approaches, and low fear with unambivalent approaches. This is an 'inverted J' curve (Figure 2.1).

ethological ideas. First, they measured very few avoidance behaviours and even then used categories which should have been split, e.g. 'non-face' meant looking anywhere except at someone else; this confuses active looking away from others with looking at some inanimate object. Second, in the confines of a small playroom most of the behaviour seen would be conflict behaviour, and maybe sometimes some unambivalent social behaviour. Long periods of pure avoidance behaviour would not be expected to be seen. In much conflict behaviour, avoidance behaviour occurs with other behaviours, so looking in a short time interval will fail to detect an avoidance behaviour category. Large amounts of data and sophisticated statistical techniques may give the appearance of scientific inquiry; unfortunately if the basic data are not properly chosen and the basic questions not properly formulated, the conclusions will be flawed, as was the case with that paper.

Box 2.2 Science and non-science

Blurton Jones (1975) contrasted ethology and psychology thus: 'The lateral thinking inductive approach of ethology can be contrasted with the deductive approach of psychology and its disdain for facts for their own sake.' The 'hypothetico-deductive approach' of psychology makes no apology for proceeding from hypothesis to empirical test. The problem is, what are the hypotheses about? Where do they come from? Partly no doubt because we, as human beings, feel we know a lot about human behaviour, many psychologists have felt it unnecessary to proceed with the laborious business of direct observation, which in any case often seems to yield little that is interestingly new. Partly psychologists set themselves the task of trying to address subjective experience without properly understanding the status of the information they were getting. The result was much psychology of dubious scientific relevance or meaning. Tinbergen (1963) wrote: 'By skipping the direct observation stage that the natural sciences had gone through, psychology was soon losing touch with the natural phenomena'.

Box 2.3 Avoidance and approach behaviours

Avoidance or fear	Sociable
move away, turn away	move towards, turn towards
look away	look towards/gaze fixate
hands over ears/	
eyes, hang head down	
being on the periphery, go still	
fear grin	smile, talk, point, proffer, receive

	Box 2.4 Motivational conflict behaviours	
	Description	**Appearance, in everyday terms**
One motivation 'wins out'		
Alternation	Behaviours of one motivation alternate with behaviours of another	ambivalent, dithering, inattentive
Simultaneous	Behaviours of one motivation appear together	ambivalent, dithering, inattentive
Over-intensity	Behaviour of one motivation appears but too soon/to partial cues, too intensely and too briefly	impulsive and careless
Displacement activities	Behaviour 'irrelevant' to the motivations in conflict appears	fidgeting, fiddling, tics, stereotypes
Aggression, usually redirected aggression		taking it out on someone else
Regression	Behaviour from an earlier stage of development	immature behaviour
Attachment behaviour	Seeks proximity and protection from caregiver	comfort seeking

These two factors interact: autistic children can tolerate more intrusion without avoiding if the social interaction is simple or predictable, but if the activity is difficult the other person needs to be less intrusive to keep the autistic child in the interaction. In other words the threshold for intrusion causing avoidance increases with easy activities.

These findings help explain why autistic children avoid the interactions in which information would normally be communicated. In the typical communication interaction, one person (A) does something towards the other person (B), stops, looks more at B both for the reaction and to signal 'it's your turn now'. B looks away and then replies. Whether

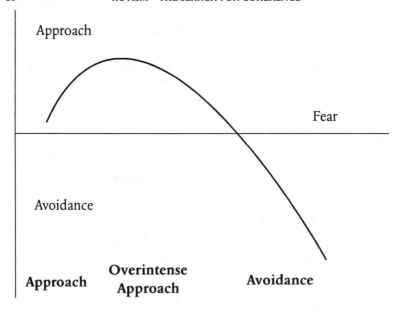

Figure 2.1 The inverted J curve

Box 2.5 Causal factors influencing sociability and avoidance

Increased sociability, decreased avoidance	Decreased sociability, increased avoidance
predictability, easy familiar activities	uncertainty, difficult activities
low social demand or intrusion	medium (normal) social demand or intrusion
high or prolonged intrusion	

---

these are mainly face-to-face interactions or joint attention interactions, they have the same basic characteristics. These include turn-taking, uncertainty at the changeover point for both parties, and a certain pattern of mutual gaze or attention. These characteristics, especially uncertainty and intrusion, tend to promote avoidance in autistic children. At the time they should be replying, they avoid. Sequence analysis of behaviour of teachers trying to engage autistic or non-autistic children in such interactions showed that the autistic children were significantly more likely than the non-autistic children to show avoidance after the teacher made some sociable/communicative approach to them. In other words they avoided when they should have been replying. The structure of the adults' behaviour was the same with each group (Figure 2.2).

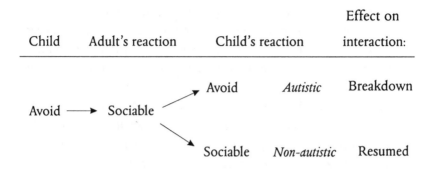

Figure 2.2 Typical interaction sequences in autistic and non-autistic children with their teachers

The result was that the interaction with the autistic children often broke down and there was little negotiation of shared meanings. This breakdown constrained autistic children's acquisition of the skills of their culture: language, understanding subtle social conventions, and so on. While it was not claimed that this was the only cause of the autistic children's 'dyscultural' state, it was a significant one.

When the social anthropologist Geertz (1965) speculated about the hypothetical person without culture he was not, as far as we know, thinking of children or adults with autism. He said:

> Undirected by cultural patterns – organised systems of significant symbols – a man's behaviour would be virtually ungovernable, a mere chaos of pointless acts and exploding emotions, his experience virtually shapeless. (Geertz 1965)

He unwittingly came close to how many people see the experience of children with autism, and how some people, who have recovered sufficiently from their own autism, describe their subjective experience.

This work on social communication has been supported and amplified by the later work of Marian Sigman, Nurit Yirmiya and their colleagues and others albeit working in a paradigm of mainstream psychology and psychiatry and therefore not seen as directly connected, an example perhaps of the fragmentation that leads us to search for coherence.

The development of autistic behaviour

In the companion paper to this (Chapter 3 in this volume) it is argued that autistic children's failure to engage in successful interactions from an early age helps account for many aspects of their social difficulties including their Theory of Mind difficulties and their poor integration of self and other.

This is *not* saying that these processes are sufficient to produce this effect, though they may be, and it is certainly not saying that this is 'the cause' of autism. It is saying that these mechanisms are likely to be important processes in an autistic child's development.

It seems at the moment that the safest position on the causation of autism is that it is multiple and heterogeneous (Kolvin, Ounsted and Roth 1971; Richer 1983; Zappella, Chapter 10 this volume). For the autistic process to get underway probably requires multiple causal factors adding together, and those factors are different in different children, although they end up on similar developmental paths.

Therapy

Heterogeneity of aetiology implies that some therapies might be helpful to only a proportion of autistic children, as seems to be the case. To dismiss some therapies, even to disparage them as 'miracles' (e.g. Howlin 1997), because they benefit only a proportion of children, is to misunderstand the heterogeneity of autism.

Just as when considering the causation of autism we are not looking at a single cause, but at a developmental process of progressively being swept along an autistic developmental path, so when we are looking at therapy we are likewise looking at a number of measures designed to try to remediate ongoing adverse factors, to undo some of the physical and psychological damage that has been done and deflect the child on to a more normal developmental path.

Assessing efficacy is also difficult, not only for the usual reasons such as getting adequate measures of change or appropriate comparison groups, but also because what is said to go on in therapy often describes the intentions or theory of the therapists rather than what actually happens.

A case in point is the Lovaas early intervention programme (see Watkins, Chapter 33, and Lubbock, Chapter 34 in this volume). When a typical Lovaas session is observed from an ethological perspective, a different description of the interaction emerges. It often proceeds as follows:

1. The adult faces the child and intrusively indicates to the child to do something. Outside this context such intrusion would often lead to avoidance unless the activity was very easy for the child. Here it is easy because it has, in the jargon, been 'shaped up' in a number of small steps.

2. Then the adult effusively congratulates, which would also usually lead to avoidance, unless, again, the activity was predictable. Here it is brief.

3. Then the adult turns away to make notes and to decide what to do next. This turning away is a reduction of social intrusion and is done at a time when the situation is less certain (the child does not know exactly what is coming next).

4. Interactions like these are interspersed with 'free play' periods.

The adult is conforming to the pattern of social behaviour that an ethological analysis predicts would be most likely to limit avoidance and increase the chance of staying with the joint activity; there is low intrusion when there is uncertainty, but higher intrusion when there is clarity. A vital part of the success of the Lovaas method is probably that, through repeated successful interactions, children start to develop better relationships and to realise that they can safely respond to demands.

As well as re-interpreting some aspects of the therapy, there are frequently other therapeutic measures being taken at the same time. Talking with parents who have embarked on the Lovaas programme, many have also changed the child's diet or have given mega vitamins or are spending time in intensive play and so on (see Watkins, Chapter 33, and Lubbock, Chapter 34 in this volume).

The key point here is that the written descriptions of therapies, even ones as apparently 'hard nosed' as the Lovaas programme, are incomplete in two senses. First, other interpretations of the 'active ingredients' of the therapy are possible; second, other therapies and changes are proceeding simultaneously. Evaluations of therapies are needed which take these issues into account, and which also look at the heterogeneity of autism and the variety of factors that help a child to progress away from autism, many of which will be insufficient by themselves, but in combination may be helpful.

The Oxford Therapy Programme

This therapy programme is still being developed. It has an early detection aspect. Therapy has three overlapping stages:

1. medical

2. communication and attachment (which is difficult if the child has significant medical or physical problems)

3. development (which is difficult if the child is significantly insecurely attached and if early communication skills and early integration of self and other have not been achieved).

STAGE 1: MEDICAL

Most children do not attract any conventional diagnosis other than autism. Those that do can sometimes be helped (see Zappella, Chapter 10 in this volume). A complex picture of problems emerges including immune system dysfunction, gastrointestinal abnormalities, and impaired detoxification all with effects on brain functioning. Interventions claiming usefulness include eliminating certain foods, supplementation (e.g. Magnesium and B_6, Zinc, essential fatty acids, probiotics), treating candiasis, immune system stimulation, and secretin administration (Langford 2000). Complementary methods (see Danczak Chapter 11 in this volume) have proved helpful to many children. What is clear is that no one medical treatment is helpful to all children, treatments need to be prescribed according to the child's physiological condition, and not simply on the basis that the child has autistic behaviour.

STAGE 2: COMMUNICATION AND ATTACHMENT

This stage has two aspects:

1. Support to parents to help them begin to understand their child and begin to come to terms with the child's problems. Some parents may also need help in their own right to resolve issues from their own past.

2. Developing the skills of parents and other key adults in handling the child. This may include holding the child through tempers (almost always for parents only), animated baby play, joint attention play, attention to the effects of everyday events on the child's attachment security, addressing any sleep and feeding problems. Music in therapy can be helpful (Christie *et al.* 1992; Lewis, Prevezer and Spencer 1996; Prevezer 1998; see also Warwick, Chapter 20, and Newson, Chapter 21 in this volume).

One focus is helping parents to try to take their child's viewpoint – to reach out into the child's mind. Holding (Richer and Zappella 1989; Welch 1983) and Option approaches facilitate this (Kaufman 1976, 1991).

Another focus is the development of ways of facilitating appropriate play. Many parents quickly run out of appropriate play ideas; natural parenting usually involves reacting to one's child's play ideas, not being *proactive* as is usually necessary with autistic children; Janert's work is very helpful here (2000, and Chapter 14 in this volume) as is that of Beyer and Gammeltoft (2000). The work of Zappella and his colleagues is similar to this (Zappella *et al.* 1991). It is in this stage that parents and therapists are trying to help the child integrate self and other (see Richer, Chapter 3, and Yirmiya and Sigman, Chapter 4 this volume).

STAGE 3: DEVELOPMENT

In stage 2, the child is already learning new skills; stage 3 continues this but focusing in addition on skills outside simple social interaction. The aim is for the child to be learning new skills in much the same way as non-autistic children by this stage; however, that is not often achieved and the children need help. Some behaviour modification techniques (such as Lovaas) can be helpful here, as can aspects of the Hanen programme, PECS, TEACCH and other communication aids, Waldon, and so on.[2] Attention must be paid to attachment security, predictability and clarity.

The stages of improvement

The improvement process can be described in many ways. These are two which would both be predicted from the ideas presented here.

---

2   See Awcock and Habgood (1998), Bondy and Frost (1998), Waldon (1984), Keel *et al.* (1997).

STAGES TOWARDS SOCIAL RECIPROCITY.

1. Few interactions.

2. Interactions on the child's terms – adult follows child (cf. Option). The child is developing sufficient confidence to initiate social contact as long as the activity involved is defined by the child and thus simple/predictable.

3. Interaction on adult's terms – child follows adult (cf. Lovaas). Some social confidence has been built up and the adult can now demand compliance as long as it is very clear to the child what is expected.

4. Interaction becomes more reciprocal – as in normal interaction.

STAGES IN THE REDUCTION OF AVOIDANCE/FEAR MOTIVATION

1. Few interactions, avoidance dominated motivational conflict behaviour (autism).

2. Over intense approaches, attention seeking, even aggression. Sometimes this is misinterpreted as deterioration or as challenging behaviour to be discouraged. In fact the child is trying to make more social contact, but the conflict fear leads to overintensity. The adult should aim to welcome the approach but try to help the child to develop more suitable approaches.

3. Normal intensity social approaches.

This is what would be predicted from the 'inverted J' curve (Figure 2.1).

Conclusion

One value of the ethological approach is that it contributes strongly to a detailed understanding of autistic children's behaviour in a way that is both communicable in objective terms and which has clear implications for therapy. Being tied to observable behaviour it enables clinicians to see more clearly the common features in apparently disparate therapies, and thereby helps to generate a more coherent understanding of autism, its treatment and the process of improvement.

References

Awcock, C. and Habgood, N. (1998) 'Early intervention project: evaluation of WILSTAAR, Hanen and specialist playgroups.' *International Journal of Language and Communication Disorders, 33,* 500–505

Beyer, J. and Gammeltoft, L. (2000) *Autism and Play.* London: Jessica Kingsley Publishers.

Blurton Jones, N.G. (1975) 'Ethology, anthropology and childhood.' In R. Fox (ed) *ASA Studies: Biosocial Anthropology*. London: Dent.

Bondy, A.S. and Frost, L.A. (1998) 'The picture exchange communication system.' *Seminars in Speech and Language 19*, 4, 373–388.

Buitelaar, J.K., van Engeland, H., de Kogel, K.H. and van Hooff, J.A.R.A.M. (1991) 'Differences in the structure of social behaviour of autistic children and non autistic controls.' *Journal of Child Psychology and Psychiatry 32*, 995–1016

Christie, P., Newson, E., Newson, J. and Prevezer, W. (1992) 'An interactive approach to language and communication for non-speaking children.' In D.A. Lane and A. Miller (eds) *Child and Adolescent Therapy: A Handbook*. Buckingham: Open University Press.

Dawkins, R. (1976) *The Selfish Gene*. Oxford: Oxford University Press.

Geertz, C. (1965) 'The impact of the concept of culture on the concept of man.' In J.R. Platt (ed) *New Views on the Nature of Man*. Chicago: University of Chicago Press.

Howlin, P. (1997) 'Prognosis in autism: do specialist treatments affect long-term outcome?' *European Child and Adolescent Psychiatry 6*, 55–72.

Janert, S. (2000) *Reaching the Young Autistic Child*. London: Free Association Press.

Kaufman, B. (1976) *Sonrise*. New York: Warner.

Kaufman, B. (1991) *Happiness is a Choice*. New York: Fawcett Columbine.

Keel, J.H., Mesibov, G.B. and Woods, A.V. (1997) 'TEACCH-supported employment program.' *Jounal of Autism and Developmental Disorders 27*, 1, 3–9.

Kolvin, I., Ounsted, C. and Roth, M. (1971) 'Cerebral dysfunction and childhood psychoses.' *British Journal of Psychiatry 118*, 407–414.

Langford, W. (2000) 'A comprehensive guide to managing autism.' In *The Autism File. Special Supplement*. London: The Autism File.

Lewis, R., Prevezer, W. and Spencer, R. (1996) *Musical Interaction: An Introduction*. Ravenshead: Early Years Diagnostic Centre.

Prevezer, W. (1998) *Entering into Interaction*. Ravenshead: Early Years Diagnostic Centre.

Richer, J.M. (1975) 'Social avoidance in autistic children.' *Animal Behaviour 24*, 898–906.

Richer, J.M. (1978) 'The partial non communication of culture to autistic children.' In M. Rutter and E. Schopler (eds) *Autism: Reappraisal of Concepts and Treatment*. New York: Plenum.

Richer, J.M. (1983) 'The development of social avoidance in autistic children.' In A. Oliverio and M. Zappella (eds) *The Behaviour of Human Infants*. New York: Plenum.

Richer, J.M. (1991) 'Changing autistic children's social behaviour: the place of holding.' *Internationaler Kongress 'Festhalten'* Regensburg.

Richer, J.M. and Nicoll, S. (1971) 'A playroom for autistic children and its companion therapy project.' *British Journal of Mental Subnormality 17*, 132–143.

Richer, J.M. and Richards, B. (1975) 'Reacting to autistic children: the danger of trying too hard.' *British Journal of Psychiatry 27*, 526–529.

Richer, J.M. and Zappella, M. (1989) 'Changing autistic children's social behaviour: the place of holding.' *Communication 23*, 35–41.

Tinbergen, E.A. and Tinbergen, N. (1972) 'Early childhood autism: an ethological approach.' *Advances in Ethology 10*.

Tinbergen, N. (1963) 'On the aims and methods of ethology.' *Zeitschrift für Tierpsychologie 20*, 410–433.

Tinbergen, N. and Tinbergen, E.A. (eds) (1983) *'Autistic' Children: New Hope for a Cure*. London: George Allen and Unwin.

Waldon, G. (1984) *Understanding Understandings*. A series of 13 occasional papers. Unpublished manuscript.

Welch, M.G. (1983) 'Retrieval from autism through mother–child holding therapy.' In N. Tinbergen and E.A. Tinbergen (eds) *'Autistic' Children: New Hope for a Cure*. London: George Allen and Unwin.

Zappella, M., Chiarrucci, P., Pinassi, D., Fidanzi, P. and Messeri, P. (1991) 'Parental bonding in the treatment of autistic behaviour.' *Ethology and Sociobiology 12*, 1–11.

CHAPTER 3

The Insufficient Integration of Self and Other in Autism
Evolutionary and Developmental Perspectives

John Richer

Abstract

This chapter brings together attachment ideas, autistic children's difficulties in relating to other minds and their general difficulties in becoming fully paid-up members of their culture of communicating minds. It is argued that since autistic children can imitate, they have the basic ability to translate between perceiving someone doing something and doing it oneself and so to translate between the viewpoint of others and the viewpoint of themselves. However, what they have not done so well is to integrate those two viewpoints, as do most children, through social interaction and play (they do much less of them) or to negotiate the shared conventions (the meanings of words, gestures and so on) with which we communicate subjective states and communicate generally (they tend to be avoidant in the situations in which those meanings are negotiated).

Although the underlying security of attachment relationships seems to be distributed in the autistic group in the same way as in the non-clinical population, there is a close similarity between the behaviour characteristic of disorganised attachment and the avoidance-dominated motivational conflict behaviour of autistic children. In line with other attachment theorists, it is argued that disruption of the development of social understanding and empathy follows from this behaviour. The difference between autistic children and others is that the disorganisation of perception of the other is argued to derive largely from factors in the (to be) autistic child (probably due in part to attentional difficulties) and not from the behaviour of the parents, and this may account for the disjunction between the overt social behaviour and the underlying relationship.

Mind-blindness: an example of wider 'dyscultural' difficulty

In the 1980s an interesting set of ideas emerged under the umbrella of the phrase 'Theory of Mind' (ToM). It was shown by Baron-Cohen and others that autistic children have much poorer 'mindreading' abilities than other children (e.g. Baron-Cohen 1988, 1989, 1995; Frith 1989). The children had difficulty in responding accurately in tasks which required them to take the viewpoint of another. The paradigm task was the false belief task, in which a child can understand that someone else could believe something even though the child knows it was not true. Most children achieve this by about 4 years, most autistic children do not, leading Baron-Cohen to describe them as 'mind-blind'. This was later extended with a number of other ingenious tasks measuring first order theory of mind, as in the basic false belief task, and second order theory of mind, which looks not only at what another person A is thinking but also at what A thinks B is thinking. This ability comes in at about 7 years when children begin to acquire skills of operating in a group and begin to appreciate issues of reputation.

Eisenmayer and Prior discussed these issues in 1991 and more recently Yirmiya and her colleagues (Yirmiya *et al.* 1998) looked at the findings from the large number of theory of mind studies. Failure at theory of mind tasks is not confined to autistic children but seen in children with learning difficulties too. Even the early replications found that between 18 per cent and 28 per cent of autistic children do demonstrate first order theory of mind abilities in false belief tasks. Eisenmayer and Prior (1991) and Happé (1995) reported more recently that up to 60 per cent have been found to pass the first order theory of mind task. Baron-Cohen (1989) reported that a group of autistic children who passed the first order theory of mind task, failed on a second order one – being able to judge the belief that one person had about the beliefs of another. In general those who pass the tests tended to be older, to have higher verbal mental age, to show better pragmatic language skills, and to have a better understanding of abstract concepts and social mores (Eisenmayer and Prior 1991; Yirmiya *et al.* 1998).

The conclusion from all this is that mindreading is part of a wider package of cultural skills. Many autistic children seem to acquire the ability to demonstrate some mindreading abilities but perhaps at a later age than non-autistic children, mindreading difficulties vary in degree among autistic children, and children with better mindreading abilities have better pragmatic abilities and have acquired more cultural/ linguistic concepts generally.

This is the picture of children constrained from acquiring but not necessarily totally unable to acquire the meanings and skills necessary to become a member of the culture, and thus communicate well with other minds. It is a picture of 'dyscultural' children constrained in the ways suggested by Richer, some time before the ToM hypothesis (Richer 1978). Even though autistic children's difficulties with 'mindreading' seem secondary to a general difficulty in acquiring their culture, nevertheless the 'mindblindness' hypothesis has made an important contribution in drawing attention strongly to this area.

Imitation

Necessary for mindreading, for taking the viewpoint of the other, is some ability to imitate. Why? Imitation is not as simple as it might appear. It requires a complex translation from the neural input of seeing what another is doing to the neural output of doing the same (Figure 3.1) (Hinde 1953).

Rizzolatti and colleagues have suggested one locus of this mechanism, in what they call 'mirror' neurons, which fire both on seeing an action and on performing it, and are found in the left inferior frontal cortex (opercular region) and the rostral-most region of the right superior parietal lobule (see Iacoboni *et al.* 1999).

Children are born with this basic ability, and can imitate behaviour such as tongue protrusion or eye widening virtually from birth (Meltzoff and Moore 1977). This ability underlies mindreading and empathy. We are able to understand other people's behaviour in the same way as we understand our own and take into account another person's viewpoint and feelings when planning our own actions.

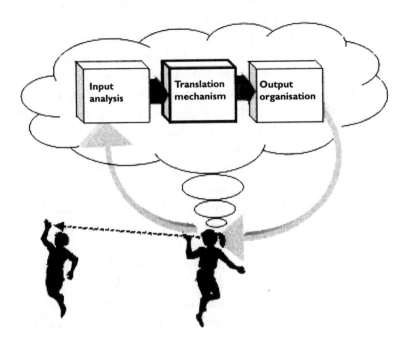

Figure 3.1 The translation involved in imitation

If autistic children are mind-blind to some extent, do they lack this basic ability to imitate? No. The several studies of imitation by autistic children have been the subject of a paper by Whiten and Brown (1998). They noted that autistic children were found to be most successful in imitating actions with objects, less successful in imitating pure body movements and rarely successful in imitating symbolic gestures. They concluded that autistic individuals had the basic ability to imitate, which could be well demonstrated if they were led actively into it with initial promptings in a 'Do as I do' paradigm, but that spontaneous imitation was rare, suggesting 'a lack of motivation or attentional processes which guide normal individuals into spontaneous imitation of certain acts they witness'. Thus the child's motivation, attention and behaviour in social interaction are seen as crucial.

The evolution of 'mindreading'

To get a better picture of human beings' mindreading and the role of imitation in that, it is helpful to take an imaginary step back in evolutionary time. Humphrey (1982, 1986) argued that human beings' large brains evolved not so much to cope with the material environment, but to cope with communication in competition with other humans, the social environment. He suggested that there had been an evolutionary 'arms race' between the ability to deceive others to one's own advantage when communicating, and the ability to see through that deception. The greater information processing capacity of bigger brains gave their owners an advantage. The genes of those who were better at deception and at seeing through deception tended to survive.

It should be added here that this competitive communication is not the only kind. Where interests are shared, where there are cooperative relationships, communications can be sent to benefit the receiver too (Kendon 1991). In some circumstances, such as between parents and children, much communication is of this kind, and it is vital to children's integration into their culture. Often too, the situation is mixed, where individuals are both cooperating and competing (Charlesworth 1992).

At some point in our evolutionary history another change occurred. This was the shift from being a 'behaviourist' to being a 'mentalist' (Figure 3.2).

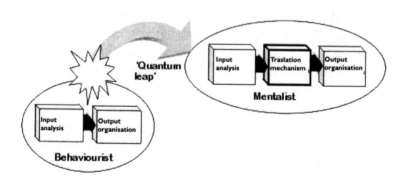

Figure 3.2 Evolutionary quantum leap with the translation mechanism involved in imitaion

Being a mentalist confers great advantages in the 'arms race'. Being able to see what another was thinking (first order ToM), and even what another believed you or a third person were thinking (second order ToM), was a great advantage in competitive interactions.[1] It means that I am able to take the viewpoint of another. I can translate seeing someone doing something in a certain situation to thinking what that person might be thinking, feeling and intending by reference to what *I* might be thinking, feeling and intending if I were in that situation. The translation mechanism of imitation mediates this. Seeing someone doing something can stimulate the possibility of doing it myself. This is most clearly seen in behavioural contagion (you yawn, I yawn) and in empathy. Thus I recruit the large repertoire organising my *own* behaviour to aid my attempt to understand and second guess the other.[2]

The acquisition of mindreading, culture and selfhood

It seems that human infants are not only innately social, but also innately intersubjective (Trevarthen 1980). Rather than use the phrase 'Theory of Mind abilities', I shall use Trevarthen's (1980) less clumsy and more accurate term of 'intersubjectivity'. It refers both to the fact that we share subjective experience and to the process of doing so.

Infants have the emerging capacity to be intersubjective, to read other minds. This capacity requires the ability to imitate which is innate. There is a necessary corrollory to this which is that they must also expect to be mindread by their caregiver. They expect to be in the mind of their caregiver. How might they judge this? In essence, by finding that their needs are met, and by finding that interactions flow well.

From the observer's point of view, this is seen in the contingency, or synchrony, of behaviour between mother and infant (Trevarthen 1977, 1980). Stern (1977) has observed babies with mothers who are sensitive to their moods and synchronous in their behaviour towards their infants

---

1   The advantage of being a mentalist is clearly seen in the work of, for instance, salespeople or negotiators.

2   It is a frequently heard cliché, certainly in the UK, that one can never understand another person's experience unless one has been through the same thing oneself. There is some truth in this, however there is vast effort put into generating vicarious experience, into sharing subjective, first person, experience, not least by storytelling, music, and the Arts generally. This allows individuals to have the benefit of knowledge acquired by many people without taking the risks and effort which would otherwise be required.

and finds that these babies become more sociable, whereas babies of mothers who are less able to be synchronous, become less sociable. Meins (1999) discusses the importance of 'mind-mindedness' in mothers in interacting with their infants. Anat Sher (personal communication) has reported the importance of maternal sensitivity and energy in promoting fastest development in babies: it is the mothers who are good at reading their baby's mind and who energetically but sensitively share the contents of their own mind with their baby, who tend to have babies with the highest developmental scores on tests. Murray and Trevarthen (1985) have shown elegantly and powerfully how 2–3-month-old babies react quickly and with distress to a breakdown in synchrony. They did this by connecting mother and baby by a video link and either having them interact in real time, or asking mother not to react, or playing baby a tape of mother's behaviour earlier, which would not be synchronous with baby's behaviour now. In the latter two conditions babies quickly became depressed and withdrawn.

Trevarthen (1980) describes two key stages in an infant's acquisition of these shared understandings. The first is the stage of primary intersubjectivity which predominates in the first 2 to 4 months. During this time there is much face-to-face interaction between baby and mother. The sensitivity of the mother to baby's needs, and especially the synchrony of the interactions between them which includes the mutual imitation, is argued to reinforce in the baby the idea that there is a person, the mother, who can see into baby's mind, i.e. can see the world as the baby sees it. Here begins the process of combining in the baby's mind the public and private aspects of behaviour, which ends in the easy and automatic taking into account of the other's perspective when acting socially.

The second phase, of secondary intersubjectivity, starts at about 9 months. It is characterised by mother and baby sharing information about a third object. This is joint attention and a key process in the acquisition of language.

Trevarthen (e.g. Burford and Trevarthen 1997) has also noted the importance of playful teasing between child and mother in this process. Teasing is essentially a playful attempt at trying to fool the other person briefly by pretence. In this context, teasing develops and refines the child's mindreading skills by highlighting both difference (pretence/fooling) and similarity (sharing understanding afterwards and enjoying the joke together).

Mental state terms

The acquisition of language referring to mental states is worth looking at more closely, since autistic children have particular difficulty in this area. Harris (1989) sees three abilities as being necessary for this learning: self-awareness, capacity for pretence and ability to distinguish pretence from reality. All these come in at about 18 months. This is also just after the age of the last major brain reorganisation, marked by regressive behaviour, described by van der Rijt-Plooij and Plooij (1992, 1993). They see this reorganisation (at 71–72 weeks) as creating a structure for the development of a sense of self (van der Rijt-Plooij and Plooij, personal communication).

A mental state term connotes two things (Richer 1975a, 1975b).

1. Onlooker's view, the viewpoint of the other, what the state looks and sounds like in someone else. It must connote this if we are to have a shared meaning of the word (Wittgenstein 1953).

2. Agent's view, the viewpoint of the self, what the state feels like. It must connote this if we are to apply it to ourselves.

A child learns the meanings of these terms by first, seeing the behaviour of others to whom the word is applied, and second, having the word applied to themselves and thereby being able to label their own subjective state.

By repeated social experience, self and other, the agent's and onlooker's view, are intimately intertwined. This intertwining is made possible by the translation mechanism of imitation.

Difficulties in acquiring mindreading, culture and selfhood in autism

People with Autistic Spectrum Disorders seem to find this intertwining difficult. An interesting piece of evidence comes from Donna Williams (1996), diagnosed autistic, who writes that in social relationships she is either in 'receive' or 'send' mode. She can either take in information about others, including what they are thinking and feeling (cf. onlooker's viewpoint), or she can act socially (cf. agent's viewpoint), but she has great difficulty doing both together. In her words, there is 'a shutdown in the ability to maintain simultaneous processing of "self" and "other" and this has many drawbacks (Williams 1996). She writes:

> I learned to act as though I had a sense of 'us' and 'we' even if my systems integration problems made it very difficult to consistently process internal 'self' and external 'other' at the same time; an experience that is essential to grasping what 'social' is, and how to be it and why you might want to be. (Williams 1996, p.5)

She describes the consequences of the complete shutdown in the ability to simultaneously process self and other:

> When one is tuned in the other gets tuned out. Here, concepts like 'us' and 'we' and 'company' and 'social' can become very cloudy if not non existent.
>
> All processing capacity may become diverted to processing incoming sensory information and a few or no connections may be made to responding to that information in any outgoing way or even thinking about it. This is the state I call 'ALL OTHER, NO SELF'. When this happens to me it is as if there is only the world, and I do not personally or perceptually (only theoretically in memory and logic) experience my existence whilst experiencing that of someone or something that is external.
>
> On the other hand, incoming information, which has previously been processed, may be responded to at the expense of being able to further process any new incoming information at this time. This is the state I call, 'ALL SELF, NO OTHER'. When this happens to me it is as though there is only me and I only experience my own existence whilst the world, though observable sensorily, is meaningless and insignificant and feels as though it only exists theoretically – like it is all a book that I can return to when I've finished living.
>
> This adaptation has serious drawbacks which, in my experience, include the following:
>
> • Limited or no ability to feel 'social' in spite of the appearance of interaction.
>
> • Appearing to be egocentric purely because of a processing problem that restricts the ability to take account of 'other' at the same time as 'self'.

- Appearing to be a mindless follower purely because of a processing problem that restricts the ability to connect the 'self' when processing 'other'.

- Having to rely upon unconnected (and generally unfelt and unintended) stored responses in the absence of connections that others expect to have been made.

- Limited ability to build up real, felt, closeness or trust (as opposed to the displayed role of closeness or trust) in interpersonal relationships in the way others can.

- Increased chances of social danger through having a limited idea of the intentions or motivations of others in the context in which their actions occur. (Williams 1996, p.129)

The phenomenon that Williams describes is observed most clearly in verbal individuals who have only mild Autistic Spectrum Disorders (ASD). Two types of observation are frequently made.

1. Some people with a diagnosis of ASD can sometimes make good empathetic observations as passive onlookers, but when called upon to act socially tend to become rather awkward and incompetent and unable simultaneously to take in the viewpoint of others in a way which modulates their behaviour.

2. This can vary with stress. In a structured non-threatening setting, talking about non stressful topics, with children with mild Asperger Syndrome, it is often difficult to see any problems in their relating. They are able to talk adequately and sensibly about themselves and others, are sensitive to the viewpoint of others and are able to modulate what they do appropriately. However, when stressed by being either in a less structured, more challenging setting, or with people they regard as threatening, or by addressing significant and stressful topics, their behaviour and what they say changes. They start to behave more impulsively or avoidantly, their speech intonation becomes more characteristically autistic and what they say and do displays extreme egocentricity – a failure to embrace the viewpoint of the other. It is as if their attention narrows to such an extent that their actions do not take into account the viewpoint of others. They frequently, especially if stressed, assume that when some mishap occurred, it was someone else's fault rather than an accident, i.e. they mistake the objective event for the intention. They often seem to fail to see the social context of their actions,

blurting out indiscrete remarks, and failing to keep confidences appropriately are examples. They may entertain a lonely bleak view of the world. They can oscillate between depression and anger. They can be prone to bouts of violence or, when older, of suicidal feelings.[3]

As was stated earlier, a major leap in human evolution was the ability to integrate Self and Other – doing and perceiving – for which a necessary but not sufficient condition was the ability to imitate. People could then recruit their own experience and response planning to the business of understanding, second guessing and responding to others. This conferred great social advantage. Failure to do so confers great social *dis*advantage. The social puzzlement, alienation and incompetence of autistic people is unsurprising given this lack of integration.

The development of human culture, with its intimate sharing of ideas, requires this integration. One way of redescribing a culture is that it is our 'group mind'.[4] Autistic children are culturally 'semi-detached'. They are not quite 'of the same mind'. Unsurprisingly again, they have trouble mindreading.

The inextricable intertwining of ourselves with others has been recognised for a long time. It perhaps entered the culture when there was less emphasis on the group and more on the individual, his thoughts, feelings and rights. As John Donne famously wrote in the early seventieth century:

> No man is an Island, entire of itself, every man is a piece of the continent, a part of the main…any man's death diminishes me, because I am involved in Mankind; And therefore never send to

3   Children and young people with the diagnosis ASD are not the only ones to show this behaviour. It is seen, for instance, in people with the diagnosis of personality disorder. It is seen in a mild form in many individuals under stress who have no formal psychiatric diagnosis. We have also observed in a few relatives of children with an ASD diagnosis a strange difficulty in seeing the social implications of what they say and do. Some may say potentially hurtful or damaging things, or be very insensitive or indiscrete but seemingly without any intent to be unpleasant. It is out of line with their obvious intelligence. It is as if they too have not fully developed the skill of modulating what they say with reference to the likely effect on others and on their own reputation.

4   It has been argued that, in contrast to genetic selection which acts at the level of individuals (individuals are 'survival machines' for genes), the evolution of ideas/ culture/memes, there are many names, is an example of group selection, i.e. the group that holds the adaptive ideas tends to flourish, and the ideas survive because that group which sustains them survives (the group is the 'survival machines' for the culture/ memes/ideas).

know for whom the bell tolls. It tolls for thee. (Donne, *Devotions,* 1624)

Attachment

Intimately connected with these processes are those related to attachment. Parental sensitivity, including the synchrony of behaviour between parent and child, is a feature of children with a secure attachment relationship to that parent (de Wolff and Ijzendoorn 1997).

An attachment relationship is built up between parent and child. This can be secure or insecure to varying degrees according to how much the child trusts that the parent will satisfy its needs. Three types of insecure relationship have been described, ambivalent, avoidant, and disorganised or disoriented. Attachment which is secure or is insecure–ambivalent or insecure–avoidant are seen as *organised* adaptations to particular styles of parenting. Insecure–disorganised, the latest category to be described, focuses on the apparent disorganisation of a stable attachment strategy. Behaviourally, the child seems very confused and shows motivational conflict behaviour similar to that seen in autistic children. This important finding must be put in the context of the relationship between disorganised attachment and the other three categories. Disorganised attachment is generally seen as *orthogonal* to the other three categories. In other words a child can be disorganised *and* secure, or disorganised *and* ambivalent, or disorganised *and* avoidant (Lyons-Ruth and Jacobvitz 1999; Main and Hesse 1990). Disorganisation refers to the intermittent breakdown of the attachment strategy.

In the past, many of these children were categorised as secure. With hindsight this misclassification is especially odd since disorganised insecurity usually arises from the most frightening or confusing experiences, such as abuse (Lyons-Ruth and Block 1996). Main and Hesse (1990) and others looking at the mothers of the disorganised children found that many of these mothers had suffered unresolved trauma and argued that disorganisation arose when the caregiver was frightened or frightening. This was supported by van Ijzendoorn's (1995) meta-analysis showing that there was a significant association between mothers having the Unresolved Adult Attachment Interview classification and the child's attachment relationship to her being Disorganised. Schuengel (1997) videotaped mothers and their children in the Ainsworth Strange Situation and found that mothers of disorganised children had significantly more frightened, frightening and dissociated behaviour.

What might be a baby's experience if the mother's behaviour was like this? If mother was frightened or distracted/disassociated (e.g. having a flashback) her behaviour would be unpredictable and non-contingent. If she was frightening, then the baby would be in great conflict – the figure that children look to for comfort and protection seems to be offering the opposite. So some of the time they might feel attended to and 'held in mind', at other times the synchrony of the interaction would inexplicably break down and they would not feel held in mind. They might wonder where and who they were, and would be confused and disoriented. Their ability to develop mind-sharing skills and learn their culture would be impaired.

Disorganised attachment and development in autism

How does this relate to autism? As Yirmiya and Sigman (Chapter 4 in this volume) have shown, autistic children would be said to be insecurely attached in the disorganised sense, *if* their behaviour in the Ainsworth Strange Situation is scored strictly, but when some of the obvious markers of autism (and disorganisation), such as stereotyped behaviour, are discounted, and when the child's behaviour towards the mother is focused upon, then only a minority of the autistic children fall into the disorganised category. The rest fall into the other attachment security categories in the same proportions as the normal population. Importantly, about half seem to be securely attached. This finding is consistent with clinical observation and with the recent report of Willemsen-Swinkels *et al.* (2000). Two points should be noted. First, the groups of autistic children in these two studies have a mean age over 4 years, considerably older than the 12–18 month olds usually studied in the Ainsworth Strange Situation so the results may not reflect the child's behaviour at this earlier age. Second, the test situation is sometimes modified (Willemsen-Swinkels *et al.* 2000). However, the importance of these differences is unclear. What is clear is that most children with disorganised attachment are not autistic, and most autistic children's underlying attachment relationship with their parents is not disorganised. As Yirmiya and Sigman (Chapter 4 in this volume) note, insecure attachment does not of itself cause autism (although paying attention, when necessary, to the improvement of a child's security of attachment is probably important in treatment). Moreover, although from unsystematically collected clinic data, a few mothers of autistic children have unresolved trauma, there is *no* evidence that this is universal, or even of raised incidence in this group. In addition autistic children do *not* have the objectively recorded experiences of, for instance, Romanian orphans, a few of whom did show autistic features after their extremely deprived and frightening early lives (Rutter *et al.* 1999).

However, attachment ideas may help understand some of the processes which contribute to the development of autistic behaviour and cognitive difficulties. It is my contention that the babies, who do become autistic, experience the sorts of confusions and failure to integrate self and other, similar to the disorganised children, but as a result of the confusion generated largely by their *own* behaviour and information processing, which, tautologically, they experience all the time, rather than confusion generated by the behaviour of others, and sometimes despite the sensitive parenting they receive.

What might this early behaviour be? Children who later become autistic and who never seemed in retrospect to have been developing normally, seem to fall into two groups:

1. a majority who have an easy passive non-initiating temperament

2. a minority who show difficult miserable behaviour.

On top of this many autistic children seem to have motor problems and oddities (Teitelbaum *et al.* 1998).

Many parents report that the children simply did not seem interested in social interaction and were happiest when left alone. Later on they did not enter many joint attention interactions, they were not playful and there was little if any make believe. This is corroborated by home video and other evidence (e.g. Massie 1978a, 1978b). The absence of protodeclarative pointing, make-believe play and joint attention at 18 months is a specific indicator for the later diagnosis of autism at 3 years (Baird *et al.* 2000; Baron-Cohen *et al.* 1992, 1996). Parents whose first child developed autism and who had a second normal child, frequently remark how different their second was, how much more responsive and lively the child was and how much more in contact they felt with the child.

The children who were miserable and inconsolable would have great difficulty in sustaining attention, and like the non-initiating children but for different reasons, they entered few successful primary and secondary intersubjectivity interactions and with similar results. Children who go on to develop Asperger Syndrome often have a history of severe attentional difficulties and a tendency towards avoidant behaviour.

So data from a number of sources, including filmed or videotaped records, and parents' retrospective reports, suggest that the child engaged in many fewer primary and secondary intersubjectivity interactions than other children. The children have not been playful, an important ingredient in social interaction from an early age (Burford and Trevarthen 1997; Janert 2000). Thus they would not have practised the early integration of self and other or negotiated as many of the shared understandings essential for the acquisition of language and other cultural skills. Their abilities in these areas would be reduced, including their ability to take another's perspective into account when deciding their own actions. They simply would not have practised enough at crucial times in their development. This leads to a progressive failure to integrate self and other, action and observation, and thus themselves into their social world by learning the skills for that world.

Conclusions

Autistic children's failure to engage in successful interactions from an early age helps to account for many aspects of their social difficulties including their theory of mind difficulties, and their difficulty in acquiring the skills of their culture, especially social skills. Their problem is not a specific failure to be able to take the viewpoint of others, but a poor *integration of self and other*, such that they have difficulty taking the viewpoint of others into account when planning their own behaviour, and difficulty in responding at all when they are attending to the other's viewpoint.

This is *not* a story about the causes of autism, but about some of the crucial developmental processes which lead to some of the difficulties these children have. It implies that one necessary, though not sufficient (Richer, Chapter 2 in this volume), focus of therapy should be trying to create the conditions in which the early social interactions where self and other are normally integrated can take place.

References

Baird, G., Charman, T., Baron-Cohen, S., Cox, A., Swettenham, J., Wheelwright, S. and Drew, A. (2000) 'A screening instrument for autism at 18 months of age: a 6-year follow-up study.' *Journal of the American Academy Child Adolescent Psychiatry 39*, 694–702.

Baron-Cohen, S. (1988) 'Social and pragmatic deficits in autism: cognitive or affective.' *Journal of Autism and Developmental Disorders 18*, 379–402.

Baron-Cohen, S. (1989) 'The autistic child's theory of mind: a case of specific developmental delay.' *Journal of Child Psychology and Psychiatry 30*, 285–297.

Baron-Cohen, S. (1995) *Mindblindness: An Essay on Autism and the Theory of Mind.* Cambridge, MA: MIT Press.

Baron-Cohen, S., Allen J. and Gillberg, C. (1992) 'Can autism be detected at 18 months? The needle, the haystack, and the CHAT.' *British Journal of Psychiatry 161*, 839–843.

Baron-Cohen, S., Cox, A., Baird, G., Swettenham, J., Nightingale, N., Morgan, K., Drew, A. and Charman, T. (1996) 'Psychological markers in the detection of autism in infancy in a large population.' *British Journal of Psychiatry 168*, 158–163.

Burford, B. and Trevarthen, C. (1997) 'Evoking communication in Rett syndrome: comparisons with conversations and games in mother–infant interaction.' *European Child Adolescent Psychiatry 6*, suppl 1: 26–30.

Charlesworth, W. (1992) 'Co-operation as competition.' Paper presented to the Conference of the International Society for Human Ethology, Amsterdam.

Eisenmayer, R. and Prior, M. (1991) 'Cognitive linguistic correlates of "theory of mind" ability in autistic childen.' In G. Butterworth, P. Harris, A.M. Leslie and H.M. Wellman (eds) *Perspectives on the Child's Theory of Mind.* British Psychology Society Books. Oxford: Oxford University Press.

Frith, U. (1989) *Autism: Explaining the Enigma.* Oxford: Basil Blackwell.

Happé, F.G.E. (1995) 'The role of age and verbal ability in the theory of mind task performance of subjects with autism.' *Child Development 66*, 843–855.

Harris, P.L. (1989) *Children and Emotion.* Oxford: Basil Blackwell.

Hinde, R.A. (1953) 'The term "mimesis".' *British Journal of Animal Behaviour 1*, 7–9.

Humphrey, N.K. (1982) 'Consciousness: a just-so story.' *New Scientist 95*, 474–478.

Humphrey, N.K. (1986) *The Inner Eye.* London: Faber and Faber.

Iacoboni, M., Woods, R.P., Brass, M., Bekkering, H., Mazziotta, J.C. and Rizzolatti, G. (1999) 'Cortical mechanisms of human imitation.' *Science 286*, 5449, 2526–2528.

Ijzendoorn, M.H. van (1995) 'Adult attachment representations, parental responsiveness, and infant attachment: a meta-analysis on the predictive validity of the adult attachment interview.' *Psychological Bulletin 117*, 387–403.

Janert, S. (2000) *Reaching the Young Autistic Child.* London: Free Association Press.

Kendon, A. (1991) 'Some considerations for a theory of language origins.' *Man (n.s.) 26*, 199–221.

Lyons-Ruth, K. and Block, D. (1996) 'The disturbed caregiving system: relationship among childhood trauma, maternal caregiving, and infant attachment.' *Infant Mental Health Journal 17*, 257–275.

Lyons-Ruth, K. and Jacobvitz, B. (1999) 'Disorganised attachment: unresolved loss, relational violence, and lapses in behavioural and attentional strategies.' In J. Cassidy and P.R. Shaver (eds) *Handbook of Attachment: Theory, Research, and Clinical Applications.* New York: Guilford.

Main, M. and Hesse, E. (1990) 'Parents' unresolved traumatic experiences are related to infant disorganised attachment status: is frightened/frightening parental behaviour the linking mechanism? In M. Greenberg, D. Cicchetti and M Cummings (eds) *Attachment in the Preschool Years.* Chicago: University of Chicago Press.

Massie, H.N. (1978a) 'Blind ratings of mother–infant interaction in home movies of prepsychotic and normal infants.' *American Journal of Psychiatry 135*, 11, 1371–1374.

Massie, H.N. (1978b) 'The early natural history of childhood psychosis: ten cases studied by analysis of family home movies of the infancies of the children.' *Journal of the American Academy of Child Psychiatry 17*, 1, 29–45.

Meins, E. (1999) 'Sensitivity, security and internal working models: bridging the transmission gap.' *Attachment and Human Development 1*, 325–342.

Meltzoff, A.N. and Moore, M.K. (1977) 'Imitation of facial and manual gestures by human neonates.' *Science 198*, 75–78.

Murray, L. and Trevarthen, C. (1985) 'Emotional regulation of interactions between two month olds and their mothers.' In T. Field and N. Fox (eds) *Social Perception in Infants*. Norwood, NJ: Ablex.

Richer, J.M. (1975a) 'Agents, onlookers, agreements and intersubjectivity.' Paper read at the Third International Society for Human Ethology conference, Sheffield, UK.

Richer, J.M. (1975b) 'Two types of agreement – two types of psychology.' *Bulletin of the British Psychological Society 28*, 342–345. (Reprinted in D. Child (eds) (1977) *Readings in Psychology for the Teacher*. London: Holt, Rinehart and Winston.)

Richer, J.M. (1978) 'The partial non communication of culture to autistic children.' In M. Rutter and E. Schopler (eds) *Autism: Reappraisal of Concepts and Treatment*. New York: Plenum.

Rijt-Plooij, H. van der and Plooij, F.X. (1992) 'Infantile regressions: disorganisation and the onset of transitions.' *Journal of Reproductive and Infant Psychology 10*, 129–149.

Rijt-Plooij, H. van der and Plooij, F.X. (1993) 'Distinct periods of mother–infant conflict in normal development: sources of progress and germs of pathology.' *Journal of Child Psychology and Psychiatry 34*, 229–245.

Rutter, M., Anderson-Wood, L., Beckett, C., Bredenkamp, D., Castle, D., Groothues, C., Keaveneney, L., Lord, C. and O'Connor, T.G. (1999) 'Quasi-autistic patterns following severe early global privation: English and Romanian Adoptees (ERA) Study Team.' *Journal of Child Psychology and Psychiatry 40*, 537–549.

Schuengel, C. (1997) *Attachment, Loss and Maternal Behaviour: A Study of Intergenerational Transmission*. Leiden: University of Leiden Press.

Stern, D. (1977) *The First Relationship: Infant and Mother*. London: Fontana/Open Books.

Teitelbaum, P., Teitelbaum, O., Nye, J., Fryman, J. and Maurer, R.G. (1998) 'Movement analysis in infancy may be useful for early diagnosis of autism.' *Proceedings of the National Academy of Sciences USA 95*, 23, 13,982–13,987.

Trevarthen, C. (1977) 'Descriptive analyses of infant communicative behaviour.' In H.R. Schaffer (ed) *Studies in Mother–Infant Interaction*. London: Academic Press.

Trevarthen, C. (1980) 'The foundations of intersubjectivity: development of interpersonal and co-operative understanding in infants.' In D. Olson (ed) *The Social Foundations of Language and Thought: Essays in Honour of J.S. Bruner*. New York: Norton.

Whiten, A. and Brown, J.D. (1998) 'Imitation and the reading of other minds: perspectives from the study of autism, normal children and non human primates.' In S. Bråten (ed) *Intersubjective communication and Emotion in Ontogeny: A Sourcebook*. Cambridge: Cambridge University Press.

Willemsen-Swinkels, S.H.N., Bakermans-Kranenburg, M.J., Buitelaar, J.K., van IJzendoorn, M.H., and van Engeland H. (2000) 'Insecure and disorganised attachment in children with a pervasive developmental disorder: relationship with social interaction and heart rate.' *Journal of Child Psychology and Psychiatry 41*, 759–768.

Williams, D. (1996) *Autism: an Inside-Out Approach*. London: Doubleday.

Wittgenstein, L. (1953) *Philosophical Investigations*. Oxford: Blackwell.

Wolff, M.S. de and Ijzendoorn, M.H. van (1997) 'Sensitivity and attachment: a meta-analysis on parental antecedents of infant attachment.' *Child Develeopment 68*, 571–591.

Yirmiya, N., Erel, O., Shaked, M. and Solomonica-Levi, D. (1998) 'Meta-analyses comparing theory of mind abilities of individuals with autism, individuals with mental retardation, and normally developing individuals.' *Psychological Bulletin 124*, 283–305.

CHAPTER 4

Attachment in Children with Autism

Nurit Yirmiya and Marian Sigman

Abstract

Following Bowlby (1969/82), attachment is conceptualised as the 'affectional bond or tie that an infant forms between himself and his mother figure' (Ainsworth, *et al.* 1978). This special bond is associated with concurrent and later social and cognitive abilities in normally developing children. Bowlby suggested that the attachment system is activated when infants are tired or distressed, when there are threats in the environment, and when the attachment figure moves away or is absent. Ainsworth and colleagues designed the Strange Situation procedure to assess the attachment status or working model of relationships of children between the ages of 12 and 18 months with their caregivers. Based on this procedure, in which infants go through a series of separations from, and reunions with, their caregivers, patterns of secure and insecure attachments may be identified. The studies conducted with children with autism, employing various modifications of the Strange Situation procedure, suggest that, similar to other groups of children, about 50 per cent of the children with autism show secure attachment towards their caregivers. The findings that many children with autism reveal secure attachment behaviours is interesting and challenging, given their earlier and later impairments in social behaviour and cognition. The findings are reviewed in relation to attachment theory in general and more specifically, to the development of children with autism.

Attachment in children with autism

According to Bowlby (1969/82) attachment is conceptualised as the 'affectional bond or tie that an infant forms between himself and his mother figure' (Ainsworth *et al.* 1978). This special bond is associated with concurrent and later social and cognitive abilities and well-being in various samples (Weinfield, *et al.* 1999). Bowlby suggested that the attachment system is activated when infants are tired or distressed, when there are threats in the environment, and when the attachment figure moves away or is absent. Bowlby described four phases in the development of attachment: the pre-attachment phase, from birth to 6 weeks; the formation of attachment phase, from age 6 weeks to about 6–8 months; the attachment phase, from 6–8 months to 18–24 months; and a phase of creating internal working models of relationships from age 18–24 months and through the life-span.

Ainsworth and colleagues (Ainsworth and Wittig 1969; Ainsworth *et al.* 1978) designed the Strange Situation procedure to assess the attachment status or working model of relationships of children between the ages of 12 to 18 months with their caregivers. Based on this procedure, in which infants go through a series of separations from, and reunions with, their caregivers, patterns of secure and insecure attachments may be identified. More specifically, four broad categories of attachment, one secure pattern and three insecure patterns, may be assigned based on the infants' behaviour during the strange situation. A secure attachment classification is assigned to infants who show signs of missing the parent during the first separation and even more signs during the second separation. These infants greet their parent actively when reunited; for example, they crawl to the parent at once, seeking to be held. After briefly maintaining contact with the parent these infants settle and return to play. About 65–70 per cent of the infants in samples of typically developing infants are classified as securely attached to their caregivers.

About 20 per cent of the normally developing infants in typical samples are classified as revealing an attachment pattern of insecurity–avoidance type. These infants do not cry on separation but remain focused on the toys or on other aspects of the environment throughout the procedure. Upon reunion they actively avoid and ignore the caregiver by moving away, or leaning away when picked up. They remain unemotional with no expressions of anger. An additional 15 per cent or so of normally developing infants are classified as revealing an attachment pattern of insecurity–ambivalent type. These infants remain preoccupied with the parent throughout the procedure; they may seem actively angry, alternatively seeking and resisting the parent, or they may be passive. They fail to settle or return to exploration upon reunion and continue to focus on the parent and to cry. Main and Solomon (1990) described a fourth category of attachment: insecure–disorganised attachment. These infants display disorganized or disoriented behaviours in the presence of their parent. For example, they may freeze with a trance-like expression with hands in the air; they may rise and then fall prone at the parent's entrance, or cling while leaning away. They may otherwise fit well into the other three classifications.

The different patterns of attachments are conceptualised as responses to different caregiving patterns displayed by the parents. Mothers of children classified as securely attached are more sensitive, expressive and available, and less interfering than mothers of children classified as insecurely attached. Furthermore, mothers of children classified as insecurely attached–avoidant are especially insensitive to their children's signals and seem to dislike physical contact with their children (Weinfield *et al.* 1999).

Research regarding the attachment behaviours and patterns of children with autism towards significant others, and especially towards their mothers, is scarce. This is due, possibly, to the claim once made by leaders in the field of autism, such as Leo Kanner and Bruno Bettelhiem, that autism has a psychogenic origin. This early line of thinking suggested that in many families, parental behaviour contributes to, or is the basis for, autism in the children. For example, when first describing the syndrome of autism in 1943, Leo Kanner wrote that the 'comings and goings, even of the mother, did not seem to register' (Kanner 1943, pp.246–247) and that 'the father or mother or both may have been away for an hour or a month; at their homecoming, there is no indication that the child has been aware of their absence' (p.247). This description immediately suggests that children with autism as Kanner saw them are not attached to their caregivers. This notion that children with autism do not behave in a way that clearly discriminates between caregivers and other adults who are strangers and do not show attachment behaviours towards their caregivers is evident in many clinical descriptions and diagnostic systems including the *Diagnostic and Statistical Manual of Mental Disorders* (American Psychiatric Association (APA) 1980, 1987, 1994).

Thus, two central questions may be asked regarding children with autism and their attachment behaviours and patterns. First and most importantly, do children with autism differentiate between caregivers and other individuals, and second, do they form attachments, secure or insecure, with their caregivers?

Attachment studies with children with autism

Several groups of researchers have investigated the attachment behaviours and/or patterns of attachment in children with autism. Shapiro *et al.* (1987), using a modification of the Strange Situation procedure, investigated the attachment patterns of thirty-six children, fifteen with autism, ten with Atypical Pervasive Developmental Disorder (PDD), three with mental retardation (MR) and eight with a developmental language disorder. The children were aged 30–59 months. They found that eight of the fifteen children with autism, five of the ten children with PDD, one of the three children in the MR group, and one of the eight in the language disorder group were classified as securely attached. Quality of attachment was not associated with mental age (MA) or with severity of symptoms in the group with autism. However, nine of the children with autism who tended to be securely attached revealed a change in their mood so that it was negative at separation.

Rogers, Ozonoff and Maslin-Cole have published a series of papers on attachment behaviours of children with autism. In 1991 these researchers reported on the attachment behaviour of seventeen children with autism or PDD (mean chronological age (CA) of 50.8 months, mean MA of 43.4 months), and a matched group of seventeen children with psychiatric diagnoses other than autism (mean CA of 47.6 months, mean MA of 39.1 months). A modified Strange Situation procedure was employed and continuous rating scales based on the Ainsworth classification were used to code the attachment behaviours of the children. All children clearly differentiated between their mothers and the stranger and no significant differences emerged between children diagnosed with autism and PDD and those diagnosed with other psychiatric diagnoses. For the group with autism and PDD the overall security of attachment score was associated with cognition, gross motor levels and with language but NOT with severity of symptoms as assessed by the Childhood Autism Rating Scale (CARS). None of the associations between the overall security of attachment score and developmental indices was significant for the comparison group.

In their next publication on attachment behaviours in children with autism, Rogers et al. (1993) worked with twenty-one children with autism and eleven children with PDD (mean CA of 46.3 months, mean MA of 33.8 months). Employing the above-mentioned procedures, the researchers found that 50 per cent of the children demonstrated clear evidence of secure attachment behaviour with no difference between children with autism and those with PDD. In another study, Rogers and DiLilla (1990) report that attachment behaviours are not associated with age of onset of social symptoms associated with autism. However, there was a trend for children who developed language prior to age 2 years to have somewhat higher security ratings compared to children who did not develop language prior to this age.

Dissanayake and Crossley (1996, 1997) also investigated the attachment behaviours of young children with autism. In their first paper, they investigated the attachment behaviours of sixteen children with autism (mean CA of 51.6 months), sixteen children with Down syndrome (mean CA of 55.1 months), and sixteen normally developing children (mean CA of 51.1). The three groups were matched on chronological age but not on mental age because only eight participants with autism were verbal in contrast to all of the participants in the comparison groups. Children with autism looked less frequently at their mother, they smiled less and showed her objects less often. In addition, they engaged in less mutual play. However, there were no significant differences in approaching the mother and in physical contact with the mother, such as sitting on her lap. Children in all groups approached their mother, looked at her and faced her more frequently than they did the stranger. Furthermore, there were no significant differences between verbal and non-verbal children with autism on any of the dependent measures.

In 1997, Dissanayake and Crossley published their second paper examining the responses of the children to separations and reunions. They report no differences among the groups in behaviour upon the mothers' departure and return, but the normally developing children were more consistent in their behaviours compared to both clinical groups. Examining possible differences between the eight verbal and eight non-verbal children with autism, they did not find any significant differences between verbal and non-verbal children with autism on separation, but on reunion children with autism who were more verbal reacted more strongly compared to the children who were non-verbal. They approached the mother more and stayed more in close contact with her.

Sigman and Ungerer (1984) studied the attachment behaviours of fourteen children with autism (mean CA of 51.9 months and mean MA of 24.1 months). Social behaviours and proximity-seeking behaviours directed towards mothers and strangers were examined using a modification of the Ainsworth Strange Situation. In both reunions, children with autism directed more behaviours towards the mother compared to the stranger and they showed a specific response to reunion with the mother compared to the stranger. Behaviour towards the mother correlated with symbolic play skills.

Sigman and Mundy (1989) extended this report by comparing the group of children with autism to a group of children with MR and to a normally developing group. They report that the episode had to be terminated sooner for the normally developing children, who became very distressed. Otherwise, there were no significant differences in behaviours during separation from the caregiver. Almost all the children, eleven of the fourteen children with autism, eleven of the fourteen children with MR, and twelve of the fourteen normally developing children showed a clear preference for the mother compared to the stranger during reunion. In a second study, Sigman and Mundy investigated the behaviours of eighteen children with autism, eighteen children with mental retardation, and eighteen normally developing children (mean CA of 53.3, 50.2 and 22.3 months respectively, mean MA of 25.7, 26, 25 months respectively). During separation, eight of the eighteen children with autism, fifteen of the eighteen normally developing children and only one of the children with MR showed distress. During reunion, all groups directed more behaviour towards the caregiver than towards the stranger. Normally developing children exhibited more social behaviour in general; however, there were no differences between children with autism and children with MR.

Finally, Capps, Sigman and Mundy (1994) examined the attachment classifications of nineteen children with autism (mean CA of 48.6 months, mean MA of 24.1) using a modified Strange Situation procedure. These researchers were the first to employ the complete classification system of A (insecure attachment–avoidance), B (secure attachment), C (insecure attachment–ambivalent or resistant), and D (insecure attachment–disorganised). Of the nineteen children, fifteen could be classified as A, B, C or D. All children received an initial classification of D – disorganised attachment pattern. However, when a second sub-classification was assigned, six children were sub-classified as securely attached and the remaining nine children were sub-classified as insecurely attached. No significant differences emerged between the six securely attached and the nine insecurely attached children regarding age, mental age and intelligence. It is interesting to note that the six securely attached children with autism showed no signs of disorganisation apart from repetitive hand and eye movement and odd facial movements that are typically associated with autism. Of the nine insecurely attached children, three were sub-classified as truly disorganised, two were classified as resistant, one as avoidant, and the remaining three were unclassifiable.

Additional comparisons between the six securely attached children versus the nine insecurely attached children revealed that the mothers of the six securely attached children appeared more sensitive and their children initiated more social interactions and had higher scores on receptive language. Finally, the six securely attached children exhibited non-verbal requesting behaviours directed towards the mother and experimenter more frequently and were more responsive to bids for joint attention of the experimenter than the insecurely attached children.

Conclusion

The above-mentioned studies demonstrate without a doubt that children with autism clearly differentiate between caregivers and strangers. Moreover, children with autism are able to form secure attachments with their caregivers. Similar to other groups of children, about 50 per cent of the children with autism show evidence of secure attachment with their caregiver. Furthermore, secure attachment is associated with various developmental competencies and perhaps with greater parental sensitivity but not with severity of symptoms.

Two main issues may be raised regarding these findings. One issue relates to understanding the intact attachment evident for about 50 per cent of children with autism, given their pervasive developmental difficulties. The second issue relates to possible differences between children with secure attachment patterns versus those with insecure attachment patterns. The question raised here is whether attachment status may operate as a protective or a risk factor for children with autism. We now turn to discussing these two issues.

The finding that the attachment classifications of children with autism are not dissimilar to those of other children may be somewhat surprising given the development of children with autism, which is characterised by gross impairments in social behaviour. During the earlier, pre-attachment phase, the most apparent impairment seen in children with autism is in joint attention behaviours (Mundy 1995; Mundy and Sigman 1989a, 1989b; Sigman and Capps 1997); during the later phase, that of internal working models, there are well-documented impairments in Theory of Mind (ToM) abilities (Yirmiya, et al. 1998). Given the great difficulties that these children experience in their social behaviour, how can we understand and incorporate the fact that most of them show secure attachment patterns with their caregivers?

We would like to suggest that children with autism show the most difficulty with behaviours that necessitate a working model of the self and of the other and their interdependence. In contrast to behaviours that necessitate taking into account both the self and the other, behaviours that are motivated by the self, and that do not necessitate taking into account the other as a separate person, are not as difficult. Thus, during the pre-attachment phase children with autism experience the most difficulties in joint attention behaviours and fare better on non-verbal behaviours that involve requesting and social turn-taking (Mundy 1995; Mundy and Sigman 1989a, 1989b; Sigman and Capps 1997). Joint attention, in contrast to requesting and social turn-taking behaviours, requires some notion of the other as a separate self; the act involves self and other, and requires a reflective self. Similarly, ToM abilities by definition require taking into account the other as a separate person with her/his own state of mind. In contrast to both joint attention and ToM abilities, the classic Strange Situation procedure involves behaviours that are motivated by the self and are self-directed. There is no need to take into account the other as a separate mind. The Strange Situation, designed initially for normally developing children, does not offer a dynamic assessment of a relationship but rather focuses on what is perceived to be the outcome of a relationship – the child's attachment pattern. As such, it appears to enable an assessment of the attachment patterns of children with autism and reveals that 50 per cent of these children show secure attachments that are indicative of responsive and sensitive parenting. The Strange Situation is designed to assess just that; it is not an assessment of the children's ability to take the parents' state of mind into account, only their 'knowledge' of whether their parents are there for them to depend on. The motivation of the children is to relieve the self from distress and their behaviour during the strange situation procedure reflects whether they typically can, or can not, count on their caregiver to help them in doing so.

The attachment patterns examined in the Strange Situation typically develop during the first year of life and continue to develop into more complex models for most children. However, for most children with autism these attachments do not continue to develop into the final stage of forming internal working models of the other, which characterises most 'normal' or normative modes of relationships. Thus, children with autism differentiate between caregivers and strangers and some are securely attached, but their attachment is in the service of the self; it is self-enhancing and does not necessarily take into account the other as a separate self with a separate mind that needs to be related to. Thus children with autism may be displaying attachment at a basic psychobiological level rather than at a more psychological level (Kraemer 1992).

The second issue relates to our understanding of the reported associations among secure attachment classifications and various developmental outcomes. Although causality cannot be inferred, it is important to note that some of the data suggest that children with secure attachment classifications function linguistically and cognitively better than children with insecure attachment classifications. It may be that these assets enable the formation of more desirable attachment patterns, or vice versa. A study examining the family environment and the attachment status of children with autism in a longitudinal design is currently in progress in Professor Sigman's laboratory. The data from this study may clarify the role of family and individual characteristics in the development of attachment behaviours of children with autism and offer some information regarding directionality. We know that for normally developing children, attachment classifications are associated with later developmental outcomes such that children with secure attachment patterns at an earlier age fare better socially and cognitively later on compared to children with insecure attachment patterns. Thus, attachment status (and the parental behaviour associated with it) operates as a protective or a risk factor in children's lives. Furthermore, the attachment classification of normally developing children to their parents is associated with the pattern that they tend to develop towards their out-of-the-home caregiver and peers (Howes 1999). Thus, there is no reason why attachment classification for children with autism should not operate in a similar way, as a protective or a risk factor for other domains of development. Secure attachment does not cure autism and insecure attachment does not cause autism. Yet parental availability and sensitivity which leads to the formation of secure attachment may enable the child with autism to develop more optimally than if the parental behaviour is less sensitive and the attachment status is characterised as insecure. The same is true for other caregivers as well; sensitive and responding caregiving may enable a better prognosis. Future research should examine whether educational and intervention programmes that take into account the attachment paradigm and foster caregiving behaviours associated with secure attachment classifications (e.g. Howes and Ritchie 1998) can be helpful for parents and professionals caring for children with autism and for the children themselves.

References

Ainsworth, M.D.S., and Wittig, B. A. (1969) 'Attachment and exploratory behavior of one-year-olds in a strange situation.' In B.M. Foss (ed) *Determinants of Infant Behavior*. London: Methuen.

Ainsworth, M.D.S., Blehar, M.C., Waters, E. and Wall, S. (1978) *Patterns of Attachment*. Hillsdale, NJ: Erlbaum.

American Psychiatric Association (APA) (1980) *Diagnostic and Statistical Manual of Mental Disorders, 3rd edn. (DSM-III)*. Washington, DC: APA.

American Psychiatric Association (APA) (1987) *Diagnostic and Statistical Manual of Mental Disorders, 3rd rev. edn. (DSM-IIIR)*. Washington, DC: APA.

American Psychiatric Association (APA) (1994) *Diagnostic and Statistical Manual of Mental Disorders, 4th edn. (DSM-IV)*. Washington, DC: APA.

Bowlby, J. (1969/82) *Attachment and Loss. Vol. I, Attachment*. London: Hogarth Press.

Capps, I., Sigman, M. and Mundy, P. (1994) 'Attachment security in children with autism.' *Development and Psychopathology 6*, 249–261.

Dissanayake, C. and Crossley, S.A. (1996) 'Proximity and sociable behaviors in autism: evidence for attachment.' *Journal of Child Psychology and Psychiatry 37*, 149–156.

Dissanayake, C. and Crossley, S.A. (1997) 'Autistic children's responses to separation and reunion with their mothers.' *Journal of Autism and Developmental Disorders 27*, 295–312.

Howes, C. (1999) 'Attachment relationships in the context of multiple caregivers.' In J. Cassidy and P.R. Shaver (eds) *Handbook of Attachment: Theory, Research, and Clinical Applications*. New York: Guilford.

Howes, C. and Ritchie, S. (1998) 'Changes in child-teacher relationships in a therapeutic preschool program.' *Early Education and Development 9*, 411–422.

Kanner, L. (1943) 'Autistic disturbances of affective contact.' *Nervous Child 2*, 217–250.

Kraemer, G.W. (1992) 'A psychobiological theory of attachment.' *Behavioral and Brain Sciences 15*, 493–511.

Main, M. and Solomon, J. (1990) 'Procedures for identifying infants as disorganized/disoriented during the Ainsworth Strange Situation.' In M.T. Greenberg, D. Cicchetti and E.M. Cummings (eds) *Attachment in the Preschool Years*. Chicago: University of Chicago Press.

Mundy, P. (1995) 'Joint attention, social-emotional approach in children with autism.' *Development and Psychopathology 7*, 63–82.

Mundy, P. and Sigman, M. (1989a) 'The theoretical implications of joint attention deficits in autism.' *Development and Psychopathology 1*, 173–183.

Mundy, P. and Sigman, M. (1989b) 'Specifying the nature of the social impairment in autism.' In G. Dawson (ed.) *Autism: New Perspectives on Diagnosis, Natures, and Treatment*. New York: Guilford.

Rogers, S.J. and DiLalla, D. (1990) 'Age of symptom onset in young children with pervasive developmental disorders.' *Journal of the American Academy of Child and Adolescent Psychiatry 29*, 863–872.

Rogers, S.J. Ozonoff, S. and Maslin-Cole, C. (1991) 'A comparative study of attachment behavior in young children with autism or other psychiatric disorders.' *Journal of the American Academy of Child and Adolescent Psychiatry 30*, 483–488.

Rogers, S.J., Ozonoff, S., and Maslin-Cole, C. (1993) 'Developmental aspects of attachment behavior in young children with pervasive developmental disorders.' *Journal of the American Academy of Child and Adolescent Psychiatry 32*, 1274–1282.

Shapiro, T., Sherman, M., Calamari, G. and Koch, D. (1987) 'Attachment in autism and other developmental disorders.' *Journal of the American Academy of Child and Adolescent Psychiatry 26*, 480–484.

Sigman, M. and Capps, L. (1997) *Children with Autism: A Developmental Perspective*. Cambridge, MA: Harvard University Press.

Sigman, M. and Mundy, P. (1989) 'Social attachments in autistic children.' *Journal of the American Academy of Child and Adolescent Psychiatry 28*, 74–81.

Sigman, M. and Ungerer, J. (1984) 'Attachment behaviors in autistic children.' *Journal of Autism and Developmental Disorders 14*, 231–244.

Weinfield, N., Sroufe, A.L., Egeland, B. and Carlson, E. A. (1999). 'The nature of individual differences in infant–caregiver attachment.' In J. Cassidy and P.R. Shaver (eds) *Handbook of Attachment: Theory, Research, and Clinical Applications*. New York: Guilford.

Yirmiya, N., Erel, O., Shaked, M. and Solomonica-Levi, D. (1998) 'Meta-analyses comparing theory of mind abilities of individuals with autism, individuals with mental retardation, and normally developing individuals.' *Psychological Bulletin 124*, 283–305.

CHAPTER 5

Neuropsychology of 'Mind'

Dermot Rowe and Linda Crawford

Abstract

This largely clinical descriptive study was designed to complement previous research in learning disability concerning Autistic Spectrum Disorders. A deficit in Theory of Mind has been widely reported in Autistic Spectrum Disorders. ToM is defined as the ability to perceive another person's mental state, and involves a spectrum from knowing what someone else might be able to see to how they might feel. More recent research has argued in favour of poor executive function, termed 'dysexecutive function' in Autistic Spectrum Disorders as the underlying cause of ToM problems. Dysexecutive function (impaired performance on frontal lobe tasks assessing higher order functioning, particularly skills such as inhibition of pre-potent responses, planning, feedback control and goal-directed behaviour) has been strongly associated with frontal lobe syndrome. This study aimed to address the presence or absence of ToM deficits in adults with dysexecutive syndromes of developmental origin, by presenting two ToM tests and a battery of executive function tasks to four adults with an Autistic Spectrum Disorder, four adults with developmental frontal lobe syndrome, and four adults with a learning disability (controls). The results suggest that problems with ToM were at least as severe in the developmental frontal lobe syndrome group as in the Autistic Spectrum Disorder group. This case series supported the view that ToM deficits are neither sensitive nor specific for Autistic Spectrum Disorders.

Introduction

The Theory of Mind (ToM) hypothesis of autism is the leading hypothesis from a number that have attempted to understand and empirically explain the characteristic socialisation, communication and imagination impairments observed in individuals with autism (Wing and Gould 1979). This intuitively appealing hypothesis, which rests substantially on its attempts to explain social impairment, states that autistic individuals have a developmentally impaired ability to understand mental states and to attribute mental states to others. Underlying aetiological factors, for example, genetic and/or neurodevelopmental, may interact with neuropsychological mediating mechanisms to give rise to the observable behaviour exhibited by individuals with an Autistic Spectrum Disorder (Bailey, Phillips and Rutter 1996).

Previous research investigating the ToM deficit in autism has primarily compared the performance of individuals with autism on ToM tests to individuals with a learning disability of unknown aetiology, individuals with Down Syndrome, or to individuals with other diagnoses associated intellectual impairment, such as specific language impairment. However, these studies are limited in terms of their generalisability for a number of reasons. The majority of the studies have used heterogeneous groups that have included children and adults with mixed aetiologies, and despite the underlying biomedical aetiology of individuals with Autistic Spectrum Disorders being likely to differ (e.g. approximately 50% of autistic individuals will have an underlying aetiology such as Rett Syndrome, Tuberous Sclerosis Complex, Fragile X Syndrome, or other). Similarly, in line with the performance of normal children on ToM tests, an individual's developmental level has been found to influence ToM capacity (Eisenmayer and Prior 1991).

Furthermore, methodological weaknesses, for example, relatively poor group matching on IQ assessments, such as on the WISC-R (Weschler Intelligence Scale for Children, Revised) or WAIS-R (Weschler Adult Intelligence Scales, Revised) or on verbal assessments (as both IQ and verbal IQ have been suggested to be a predictor of performance on ToM tests) have made comparison of results difficult. There are numerous ToM tests currently used in empirical studies, such as false belief, deception, or desire tasks. Therefore, comparability between studies assessing ToM is limited if different ToM tests are used in assessment (Yirmiya *et al.* 1998).

Impaired ToM performance by autistic individuals has also been described in terms of dysexecutive function. Dysexecutive function is an umbrella term associated with poor performance on tests assessing frontal lobe functioning (Hughes, Leboyer and Bouvard 1997). Poor executive functioning has been reported in a variety of developmental, neurological and psychopathological disorders (Hughes, Russell and Robbins 1994; Ozonoff 1997), including autism (Russell 1997). In addition to type of aetiology, an individual's performance on executive functioning tests may also vary due to the severity and localisation of neurological impairments across conditions, as well as the timing of the onset of dysexecutive function during development. Research limitations, including a relatively poor definition of what specific cognitive abilities actually constitute 'executive function' ability have, however, left this whole area subject to considerable debate (Ozonoff 1997).

Thus the aim of this study was to investigate the specificity of the ToM hypothesis to the autistic syndrome, as well as the influence of dysexecutive function on ToM performance. Four adults with autism were assessed on both ToM and executive function tests, and their performance was compared to that of four adults with developmental frontal lobe syndrome (who have dysexecutive function by definition) and four learning disabled adults who had neither autism nor developmental frontal lobe syndrome.

Method

Four adults (three males and one female; mean age = 26 years) with mild learning disability and Autistic Spectrum Disorder, and four adult males (mean age = 29.25 years) with mild learning disability and developmental frontal lobe syndrome (organic personality disorder of developmental origin, frontal lobe type) were chosen from the Oxfordshire Learning Disability NHS Trust database to participate in the study. All individuals had previously been assessed by specialist learning disability psychiatrists, and had ICD-10 compatible diagnoses. The frontal lobe syndrome group all underwent brain MRI scanning which confirmed frontal pathology in each case, consistent with the clinical history for aetiology of the syndrome (head injury, hypoxia or severe hypoglycaemia in each case).

The control group consisted of four males (mean age = 26 years) with mild learning disability who were neither frontal nor autistic and were chosen from the Trust's general database of adults with a learning disability, not just those in receipt of psychiatric services. Only people with mild learning disability (ICD-10), confirmed on the Wechsler Adult Intelligence Scale, were approached, as more severe intellectual impairment would preclude participation in the tests. All those approached consented to take part in the study.

Each participant completed four assessment instruments, presented in the same order to each individual. First, the Sally–Anne false belief task (Frith 1989) which required the participant to be able to infer that Sally would look for the ball where she left it before leaving the room, as opposed to giving a pre-potent response of where Anne hid it when Sally left the room. Second, a fact belief task which consisted of a sketch of a boy looking at a box containing sweets on a table, with the participant having to say what the boy could see. Third, the Behavioural Assessment of the Dysexecutive Syndrome (BADS: Wilson *et al.* 1996), which is an assessment of executive function. The order of assessment of the BADS sub-tests were the Rule Shift Cards Test, Key Search Test, Zoo Map Test, Temporal Judgement Test, Action Programme Test, and the Modified Six Elements Test. Finally, the Luria three-step test (Luria 1979) which is a simple motor test of frontal function involving a sequence of hand movements.

Results

Performance on the ToM tests (i.e. the false belief and fact belief task) differed between groups. All four individuals in the control group passed both of the ToM tests. Two of the four individuals with an Autistic Spectrum Disorder passed the false belief task, and three passed the fact belief task. For individuals with frontal lobe syndrome of developmental origin, none out of four passed the false belief task and one passed the fact belief task.

Performance on the executive function tasks also differed between groups. All individuals in the control group scored relatively better on the BADS (mean = 13.25/30) than the Autistic Spectrum Disorder group (mean = 7.25/30) and the developmental frontal lobe syndrome group (mean = 6/30). All four controls passed the Luria's three-step test, whereas two out of four individuals with an Autistic Spectrum Disorder passed, and no individuals with frontal lobe syndrome of developmental origin passed.

Failures on the false and fact belief tasks were defined as universally due to an inability to inhibit pre-potent responses and bear in mind the perceptual set of another individual. All low scores on the BADS were accounted for by inability to go beyond very simple executive functioning tests (for example, card sorting). All cases of failure on Luria's three-step test were due to inadequate sequencing of hand movements despite repeated previous modelling of the correct method.

Discussion

This was essentially a preliminary and clinical descriptive study. The results must be interpreted with caution owing to the low numbers involved, although this is a common state of affairs in the literature relating to Autistic Spectrum Disorders. Adult participants with Autistic Spectrum Disorders were recruited which is quite unusual in the literature and gives some idea about the natural history of ToM and executive function beyond adolescence. People with frontal lobe syndrome of developmental origin provided a useful comparison group in terms of possessing poor executive functioning but not having previously been described in terms of ToM. The ToM tests were sufficiently simple for adults with a learning disability to attempt, however some of the executive function tasks would have been predictably difficult for adults with a global intellectual disability. Hence it may be more helpful to think in terms of relative rather than absolute dysexecutive function.

The results of this study support the burgeoning literature that ToM deficits are neither sensitive nor specific for Autistic Spectrum Disorders. The results support the view that learning disability alone is not necessarily associated with severe dysexecutive function and may be in keeping with adequate ToM. However, the results give some credence to the view that the primary neuropsychological deficit in Autistic Spectrum Disorders is one of executive function (Russell 1997). As such, problems with verbal encoding in particular may give rise to the epiphenomenon of poor ToM. Inconsistent ToM deficits in Autistic Spectrum Disorder populations would be predicted from this model, and it could be that the timing of the maximal period of autistic pathogenesis predicts neuropsychological outcomes. For example, if deterioration occurs after the secure acquisition of language relating to mental states, it would be predicted that adult ToM functioning would be relatively preserved. A less intuitively appealing hypothesis is that poor ToM, as a primary deficit, leads to impaired executive functioning. Other experimental paradigms are required to address this. Recent research has also shown interest in examining perceptual abilities and deficits in individuals with autism in order to account for the superior cognitive skills in some individuals that the executive function theory does not adequately account for. Some authors have advocated ToM as a rather modular capacity, possibly with fairly circumscribed neuroanatomical affiliates (right orbito-frontal cortex; see Baron-Cohen *et al.* 1994). However, given the diversity of neuropsychological demands for various ToM tasks, considerable parallel processing, involving multiple distributed cortical networks, seems more plausible. Such a view is more in keeping with contemporary views of cognitive neuroscience and owes less to some Cartesian 'ghost in the machine'.

Acknowledgements

We would like to thank all those who participated in this study. We would also like to thank Professor Peter Halligan for his helpful advice and guidance, and Mr Richard Cooke for his artistic contribution.

References

Bailey, A., Phillips, W. and Rutter, M. (1996) 'Autism: towards an integration of clinical, genetic, neuropsychological, and neurobiological perspectives.' *Journal of Child Psychology and Psychiatry 37*, 1, 89–126.

Baron-Cohen, S., Ring, H., Moriarty, J., Schmitz, B., Costa, D. and Ell, P. (1994) 'Recognition of mental state terms: clinical findings in children with autism and a functional neuroimaging study of normal adults.' *British Journal of Psychiatry 165*, 640–649.

Eisenmayer, R. and Prior, M. (1991) 'Cognitive linguistic correlates of "theory of mind" ability in autistic children.' In G. Butterworth, P. Harris, A.M. Leslie and H.M. Wellman (eds) *Perspectives on the Child's Theory of Mind.* British Psychological Society Books. Oxford: Oxford University Press.

Frith, U. (1989) *Autism: Explaining the Enigma.* Oxford: Blackwell.

Hughes, C., Leboyer, M. and Bouvard, M. (1997) 'Executive function in parents of children with autism.' *Psychological Medicine 27*, 209–220.

Hughes, C., Russell, J. and Robbins, T.W. (1994) 'Evidence for executive dysfunction in autism.' *Neuropsychologia 32*, 477–492.

Luria, A.R. (1979) *Higher Cortical Functions in Man.* London: HarperCollins.

Ozonoff, S. (1997) 'Components of executive function in autism and other disorders.' In J. Russell (ed) *Autism as an Executive Disorder.* Oxford: Oxford University Press.

Russell, J. (ed) (1997) *Autism as an Executive Disorder.* Oxford: Oxford University Press.

Wilson, B.A., Alderman, N., Burgess, P.W., Emslie, H. and Evans, J.J. (1996) *Behavioural Assessment of the Dysexecutive Syndrome.* Bury St. Edmonds: Thames Valley Test Company.

Wing, L. and Gould, J. (1979) 'Severe impairments of social interaction and associated abnormalities in children: epidemiology and classification.' *Journal of Autism and Developmental Disorders 9*, 11–30.

Further reading

Baron-Cohen, S. and Goodhart, F. (1994) 'The "seeing-leads-to-knowing" deficit in autism: the Pratt and Bryant probe.' *British Journal of Developmental Psychology 12*, 397–401.

Benson, G., Abbeduto, L., Short, K., Bibler-Nuccio, J. and Maas, F. (1993) 'Development of theory of mind in individuals with MR.' *American Journal on Mental Retardation 98*, 427–433.

Charman, T. and Baron-Cohen, S. (1995) 'Understanding photos, models, and beliefs: a test of the modularity thesis of theory of mind.' *Cognitive Development 10*, 287–298.

Cooper, M. (1997) 'Autism.' In O. Russell (ed) *The Psychiatry of Learning Disabilities.* London: Gaskell.

Dennett, D. (1991) *Consciousness Explained.* Harmondsworth: Penguin.

Frith, U., Happé, F. and Siddons, F. (1994) 'Autism and theory of mind in everyday life.' *Social Development 3*, 108–124.

Gillberg, C. and Coleman, M. (1992) 'The biology of the autistic syndrome'. In *Clinics in Developmental Medicine 126,* 2nd edn. London: McKeith.

Happé, F.G.E. (1994) 'An advanced test of theory of mind: understanding of story characters' thoughts and feelings by able autistic, mentally handicapped, and normal children and adults.' *Journal of Autism and Developmental Disorders 24*, 129–154.

Hughes, C. and Russell, J. (1993) 'Autistic children's difficulty with mental disengagement from an object: its implications for theories of autism.' *Developmental Psychology 29*, 498–510.

Ozonoff, S., Pennington, B.F. and Rogers, S.J. (1991) 'Executive function deficits in high-functioning autistic individuals: relationship to theory of mind.' *Journal of Child Psychology and Psychiatry 32*, 1081–1105.

Perner, J., Frith, U., Leslie, A. and Leekam, S.R. (1989) 'Exploration of the autistic child's theory of mind: knowledge, belief and communication.' *Child Development 60*, 689–700.

Tager-Flusberg, H. and Sullivan, K. (1995) 'Attributing mental states to story characters: a comparison of narratives produced by autistic and mentally retarded individuals.' *Applied Psycholinguistics 16*, 241–256.

Yirmiya, N., Erel, O., Shaked, M. and Solomonica-Levi, D. (1998) 'Meta-analysis comparing theory of mind abilities of individuals with mental retardation, and normally developing individuals.' *Psychological Bulletin 124*, 283–307.

Yirmiya, N., Solomonica-Levi, D., Shulman, C. and Pilowsky, T. (1996) 'Theory of mind abilities in individuals with autism, Downs Syndrome, and mental retardation of unknown etiology: the role of age and intelligence.' *Journal of Child Psychology and Psychiatry 37*, 1003–1014.

Zubris, D.K. (1994) 'Comparison of knowledge of self and other in children with autism, children with other developmental disabilities and pre-schoolers without disabilities'. Unpublished doctoral dissertation, George Washington University, Washington, DC.

CHAPTER 6

Why Success is More Interesting than Failure

Understanding Assets and Deficits in Autism

Francesca Happé

Autism is a devastating disorder of social and communicative development, affecting at least one in a thousand children and adults. In recent
years, there has been a considerable advance in understanding the nature
of these social difficulties, which appear to spring from a failure to
represent thoughts and feelings – sometimes called 'mind-blindness'.
What 'mind-blindness', and indeed all deficit accounts of autism, fail to
explain is why people with autism are often so unusually good at certain
things. Take, for example, the young man with autism who draws like a
master although unable to fasten his coat or add 5 and 5. Or the girl with
autism who has perfect pitch and can play any tune by ear after only one
hearing. Or the boy with autism who can tell you, within seconds, what
day of the week any past or future date will fall upon. Or, less spectacularly
but more commonly, the child who can construct jigsaw puzzles at
lightning speed, even picture-side down, or the adult who despite
generally low ability recalls the exact date and time of your last visit,
perhaps twenty years ago. How can we explain these abilities?

There are at least two possible interpretations of such superior performance. The first is that these individuals are actually of high intelligence,
and that these 'islets of ability' actually reflect the true intelligence level –
which must be underestimated, in that case, by standard assessments. It is
possible that children with autism score so poorly on standard IQ assess-

ments because social insight is crucial both developmentally and on-line in IQ tests. In other words, we acquire knowledge and skills primarily through interaction with other people – and even IQ assessments involve some degree of 'mindreading'.

Alternatively, the surprising skills in individuals with autism may reflect the workings of a very different sort of mind – a different information processing style. Take, for example, the finding that perfect pitch is very common in even musically naive children with autism. It has been suggested that perfect pitch is relatively easy for normal children to acquire before the age of 6 years or so, when a shift occurs from processing features (notes) to processing relations among features (melody). Might people with autism retain a feature-based, rather than global, processing style throughout their lives?

There is now good evidence for a detail-focused processing style in autism. This has been referred to as 'weak central coherence'. Central coherence is the term coined by Uta Frith for the normal tendency to process information in context for meaning, to integrate information to get the 'big picture', usually at the expense of the parts. For example, after reading this you will (I hope) remember the gist, but will probably forget the actual words you read. People with autism often do the opposite – recall the exact words but fail to get the meaning! Their processing appears to be piecemeal and detail-focused – the normal drive towards meaning and gestalt is weak.

Children and adults with autism show weak central coherence, or detail-focused processing, at a number of different levels. At the perceptual level, for example, people with autism (even of low IQ) are very accurate in judging visual illusions – where surrounding context induces misperception in ordinary people. At the visuo-spatial level, people with autism excel at the Embedded Figures Test, finding small shapes hidden in bigger designs with consummate ease. On verbal tasks, too, people with autism process parts rather than wholes – so they may finish a sentence like 'The sea tastes of salt and…' with 'pepper', or 'You can go hunting with a knife and…' with 'fork'!

This type of detail-focused processing, or weak coherence, appears to be a cognitive style not deficit, associated with advantages as well as disadvantages. This is reinforced by findings from an ongoing study of the relatives of children with autism. Autism has a strong genetic component, but it is not as yet clear which genes are involved, nor what traits they might affect in non-autistic individuals who carry them. Our study focuses on skills and assets that might characterise the relatives of those with autism. In particular, it seems that many fathers of boys with autism also show weak central coherence, mirroring their son's performance assets and deficits despite high IQ and achievement. Many of these fathers excel in professions where the ability to focus on small details helps, such as science, engineering or computing.

Central coherence, then, may form a continuum of cognitive style, from 'weak' to 'strong' – with ordinary people falling somewhere along this continuum, and people with autism (and their relatives?) falling at the extreme 'weak' end. Weak coherence, like strong, brings both assets and deficits. The challenge for the future is to uncover the cognitive and brain mechanism of coherence better to understand autism. In the mean time, recognition of the many things that people with autism are good at is a positive step. Hans Asperger, one of the first clinicians to describe and name Autism Spectrum Disorders, believed that a bit of autism was necessary to be a good scientist (he also saw autism as 'an extreme form of maleness'!). As one able man with autism said, those of us who do not have autism can also be described as belonging to a 'syndrome' – he called us 'heterotists'. One definition of a heterotist is a person who can't spot a piece of thread on a patterned carpet. The theory of weak central coherence reminds us that not only do people with autism find difficult what we find easy, automatic and intuitive, but also they find easy what many of us find difficult.

Further reading

Overviews and reviews

Frith, U. and Happé, F. (1994) 'Autism: beyond "theory of mind".' *Cognition 50*, 115–132.

Happé, F.G.E. (1994a) *Autism: An Introduction to Psychological Theory.* London: UCL Press/Psychology Press.

Happé, F.G.E. (1994b) 'Annotation: psychological theories of autism. The "theory of mind" account and rival theories.' *Journal of Child Psychology and Psychiatry 35*, 215–229.

Happé, F.G.E. (1999) 'Autism: cognitive deficit or cognitive style?' *Trends in Cognitive Sciences 3*, 216–222.

Specific academic papers

Frith, U. and Snowling, M. (1983) 'Reading for meaning and reading for sound in autistic and dyslexic children.' *Journal of Developmental Psychology 1*, 329–342.

Happé, F.G.E. (1994c) 'Wechsler IQ profile and theory of mind in autism: a research note.' *Journal of Child Psychology and Psychiatry 35*, 1461–1471.

Happé, F.G.E. (1995) 'The role of age and verbal ability in the theory of mind task performance of subjects with autism.' *Child Development 66,* 843–855.

Happé, F.G.E. (1996) 'Studying weak central coherence at low levels: children with autism do not succumb to visual illusions: a research note.' *Journal of Child Psychology and Psychiatry 37,* 873–877.

Happé, F.G.E. (1997) 'Central coherence and theory of mind in autism: reading homographs in context.' *British Journal of Developmental Psychology 15,* 1–12.

Heaton, P., Hermelin, B. and Pring, L. (1998) 'Autism and pitch processing: a precursor for savant musical ability.' *Music Perception 15,* 291–305.

Jolliffe, T. and Baron-Cohen, S. (1997) 'Are people with autism and Asperger syndrome faster than normal on the Embedded Figures Test?' *Journal of Child Psychology and Psychiatry 38,* 527–534.

Mottron, L. and Belleville, S. (1993) 'A study of perceptual analysis in a high-level autistic subject with exceptional graphic abilities.' *Brain and Cognition 23,* 279–309.

Mottron, L., Belleville, S. and Ménard, A. (1999) 'Local bias in autistic subjects as evidenced by graphic tasks: perceptual hierarchization or working memory deficit?' *Journal of Child Psychology and Psychiatry 40(5),* 743–755.

Plaisted, K., O'Riordan, M. and Baron-Cohen, S. (1998) 'Enhanced visual search for a conjunctive target in autism: a research note.' *Journal of Child Psychology and Psychiatry 39,* 777–783.

Plaisted, K., Swettenham, J. and Rees, L. (1999) 'Children with autism show local precedence in a divided attention task and global precedence in a selective attention task.' *Journal of Child Psychology and Psychiatry 40,* 733–742.

Pring, L., Hermelin, B. and Heavey, L. (1995) 'Savants, segments, art and autism.' *Journal of Child Psychology and Psychiatry 36,* 1065–1076.

Shah, A. and Frith, U. (1983) 'An islet of ability in autistic children: a research note.' *Journal of Child Psychology and Psychiatry 24,* 613–620.

Shah, A. and Frith, U. (1993) 'Why do autistic individuals show superior performance on the Block Design task?' *Journal of Child Psychology and Psychiatry 34,* 1351–1364.

Snowling, M. and Frith, U. (1986) 'Comprehension in "hyperlexic" readers.' *Journal of Experimental Child Psychology 42,* 392–415.

Tager-Flusberg, H. (1991) 'Semantic processing in the free recall of autistic children: further evidence for a cognitive deficit.' *British Journal of Developmental Psychology 9,* 417–430.

CHAPTER 7

Evidence for Central Coherence

Children with Autism do Experience Visual Illusions

Iain Garner and David Hamilton

Abstract

Previous work suggests that individuals with autism show inferior performance when perceiving illusions. Happé (1996) interprets this as showing
that they have weak central coherence. This study shows that individuals
with autism can recognise illusions and in some cases more strongly than
non-autistic groups. Discussion of these contradictory results and implications for the theory of weak central coherence are presented.

Introduction

Perceptual anomalies are frequently reflected in autobiographical
accounts of individuals with autism (Grandin, 1984; Williams, 1992).
These accounts report a range of anomalies within perception. The quality
that appears to link all these experiences is that they are traumatic. It
should also be noted that unlike many qualities of autism these anomalies
are not in any obvious or immediate way socially bound and form part of a
group of non-social deficits (see Bryson, Wainwright-Sharp and Smith
1990; Courchesne *et al.* 1994). These non-social deficits include restricted
repertoire of interests, a desire for sameness which reaches obsessional
levels, enhanced rote memory, focus on sections of objects and islets of
ability. It would seem reasonable to suggest that these deficits are cognitive
in nature and reflect differences in the way information is cognitively

manipulated. In order to gain a full understanding of autism, it is necessary to examine these non-social aspects.

Happé (1996), following on from earlier work (Frith 1989; Frith and Happé 1994; Happé 1994), has provided a body of research that addresses the issue of perceptual anomalies within autism. Central to this research is the theory of weak 'central coherence'. This theory suggests that individuals with autism tend to process local rather than global information and fail to process this information in context, thus leading to a fragmented experience of the world. In certain contexts this approach to perceptual processing would prove advantageous such as spotting embedded figures and the rapid reproduction of unsegmented block designs. Research has shown the enhanced performance of individuals with autism at these tasks providing initial support for the weak central coherence theory (Jolliffe and Baron-Cohen 1997; Shan and Frith 1993).

Using six common visual illusions Happé (1996) demonstrated that the individuals with autism show low susceptibility to illusions. She argued that this was evidence of weak central coherence as visual illusions require global and contextual processing of information. If such processing were not engaged in, illusions would not be experienced. Further to this Happé demonstrated that artificially separating the illusions by pre-segmenting the images, so reducing their effectiveness, did not influence the autistic sample but did cause the control sample to succumb to fewer illusions. Again this indicates that the global nature of the perceptual experience did not influence how participants with autism experience the illusion. This research suggests that individuals with autism experience weak central coherence at low levels of perceptual processing.

The aim of the present study was to establish a greater degree of accuracy in assessing the susceptibility to illusions, thereby measuring indirectly the relative strength of central coherence in autistic and typically developing children. Earlier research has been based on an 'all or nothing' model, visual illusions being either seen or not seen. Using a computerised measure of visual illusion (CMVI) the study aimed to ascertain the point at which (or the extent to which) an illusion is experienced.

Method and development of CMVI

Participants

In this study 120 primary school children between the ages of 4 and 7 took part, along with nine participants with autism. Children with autism were included in the study only if their standard score on the Peabody Picture Vocabulary test (PPVT) was greater than 70 (Table 7.1). This reduced the likelihood that autism was confounded with learning difficulty.

Table 7.1. Profile of participants with autism (age data in years:months)			
	Mean	**SD**	**Range**
Age	11.1	4.2	5.11–17.11
PPVT	9.3	2.8	6.0–13.0
Standard Score	90.0	13.67	72–114

Materials

A computerised measure of visual illusion was developed to show exactly when an illusory image was experienced. Greater insight into exactly when an illusory image was experienced would allow more detailed comparisons between autistic and non-autistic populations.

The software exploited two illusions: the Muller-Lyer figure and Kanizsa triangle. These two illusions were chosen because they represented the extremes of experience of visual illusions within Happé's (1996) study of visual illusions, the Muller-Lyer illusion being experienced by most (88 per cent) and the Kanizsa triangle being experienced by very few (8 per cent) autistic participants. The software was designed to be completely mouse driven and the visual images were stripped down to their basic elements, so as not to present any information that was unnecessary to experience the visual illusions.

The Muller-Lyer image is presented along with two training tasks. It was felt that these training tasks were needed to gain knowledge of the participants' ability to judge the exact mid-point of two extremes in a task not expected to induce a distortion of perception. Knowledge of this is needed to interpret the illusion task and assess the person's ability to judge the location of the mid-point.

CMVI

Computerised Measure of Visual Illusions

Figure 7.1 The lines trainer task from the CMVI

The image in Figure 7.1 shows the line training task. Participants were asked to place the central line in the middle of the two extremes. This was achieved using the keys on the mouse, the right key moving the line to the right, the left key to the left. The same procedure was used with a circle training task. The circle task has the same basic features as the line task but the vertical lines are replaced with small circles. This makes the selection of the centre point slightly more difficult as the centre point of the circle has to be assessed as well as the mid-point of the two extremes.

CMVI

Computerised Measure of Visual Illusions

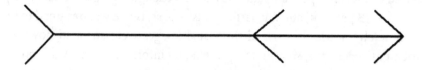

Figure 7.2 The Muller-Lyer illusion task from the CMVI

The diagram in Figure 7.2 shows how the Muller-Lyer illusion was used in this study. Rather than the more usual two parallel lines, one with inward facing arrowheads and one with outward facing arrowheads, a single line with contra facing arrowheads was used. Due to the effect of the illusion the centre is perceived to be left of the actual mid-point.

CMVI

Computerised Measure of Visual Illusions

Figure 7.3 The Kanizsa triangle task from the CMVI

The Kanizsa triangle task required the participants to bring the three corner inducing points together using the mouse right key. Pressing the key brings all three corner points together (Figure 7.3). This occurs uniformly so that the shape of the figure is maintained while the distance between the elements is reduced. Participants were requested to manipulate the figure slowly and to stop as soon as an image was created (i.e. when they experienced the illusory triangle).

The CMVI was designed to record automatically the point at which the participant placed the mid-point or experienced the illusory triangle. Participants were unaware of the performance recording process and were given no impression of responses being correct or incorrect during the study.

Procedure

Each participant took part in a quiet area within his or her usual learning environment. The participant was first requested to place the centre shape at the middle of the two extremes, first for the two trainer tasks and then the illusion task. Participants were then asked to move the three corner shapes of the Kanizsa illusion together and stop immediately if another shape appeared.

Results

Results are shown in Table 7.2.

Age	N	Line		Circle		Illusion	
		Mean	SD	Mean	SD	Mean	SD
4	31	72.42	52.37	66.61	79.92	66.19	44.24
5	27	69.81	43.56	45.00	31.01	84.07	62.64
6	31	40.81	23.84	32.42	20.57	67.90	40.62
7	31	35.81	23.84	35.16	25.45	67.42	41.19
Autistic	9	7.78	5.65	5.56	3.91	43.88	21.61

Table 7.2 The results of the trainer tasks and the Muller-Lyer illusion task

Note. Figures refer to error scores for the two trainer tasks and illusion task (measured in VDU pixels away from the actual centre point).

Improvement of accuracy with age of the non-autistic populations for non-illusory tasks

ACCURACY ON LINE TASK

Statistical analysis of the line task showed a significant difference between the groups and that the autistic group performed the task better than any other group (F = 9.58, df 4 / 124, P<0.00). It should also be noted that there was a developmental trend within the four age groups, with the 4 year olds performing least well and the 7 year olds performing best.

ACCURACY ON CIRCLE TASK

The autistic participants' performance on the circle task was shown to be significantly better than the 4 and 5 year olds but no difference was noted with the 6 and 7 year olds (F = 4.39, df 4 / 124, P<0.002). Again a developmental trend can be seen in the performance of on this task across the four age groups.

ACCURACY ON ILLUSION TASK

Analysis of the illusion task showed that there was no significant difference between the four age groups and the autistic population (F = 1.43, df 4 / 124, P<0.05). Also no significant developmental trends were noted across the age groups.

Table 7.3 Results for the Kanizsa triangle illusion.			
Age	N	Mean	SD
4	31	424.51	439.72
5	27	382.22	405.55
6	31	557.41	520.71
7	27	406.45	362.22
Autistic	9	897.78	753.16

Note. Figures in the table refer to the point at which participants perceived the Kanisza's illusion during the final CMVI task (measured in VDU pixels points away from the convergence point of the three corner inducing shapes – at this point an actual triangle was formed).

The very large standard deviations in Table 7.3 indicate that the responses from the groups are far from homogeneous. Statistical analysis of these data reveal that there was a significant difference between the groups, with the autistic group experiencing the illusory triangle significantly earlier than all other groups bar the 6 years, where no difference was shown (F = 2.64, df 4 / 124, P>0.05).

Discussion

The theory of weak central coherence would suggest that individuals with autism would perform less well on tasks that require global processing of information. Any figure that requires an illusory image to be induced from a series of parts requires global processing; Kanizsa triangle demands this. From the above analysis it can be shown that the group with autism are able to perceive the illusory triangle when the inducing corners are further apart than any of the other groups. This indicates an ability to process information at a global level, and at a level of central coherence that, in this context, is stronger than the non-autistic groups. In light of this evidence, the proposition of universal weak central coherence must be questioned.

This result runs counter to Happé's (1996) earlier research, which showed a very poor performance on the Kanizsa illusion. There are a number of methodological differences between the studies that may partly explain the differing results. First, the majority of Happé's autistic participants also had mild learning difficulties at a level which may have had confounding effects on the results. Second, Happé's research used static pictures of the illusions, whereas this research had moving elements to it. In the present study, the movement of the three inducing corners of the triangle may have aided the global processing and cued central coherence. Third, the Kanizsa triangle image used in this study was abridged in that it contained the inducing circle corners but not the second triangle's right angle corners. It is possible that autistic children are more likely to engage in local processing when presented with relatively complex visual stimuli.

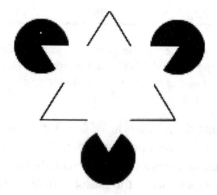

Figure 7.4 The full Kanizsa triangle – note the three additional corner inducing angles

This reduction in the amount of information to be globally processed may have enhanced the success of the process. In Figure 7.4 the right angle inducing corners aid the perception of the illusory contours when viewing the ordinary Kanizsa triangle. Their absence from the CMVI triangle may also explain the relatively poor performance of the non-autistic groups when inducing the illusory triangle. Further study using these inducing corners should be undertaken to address these points. However, it cannot be ignored that the participants with autism demonstrated that they were able to experience the illusion and implement central coherence. To ensure that they had actually experienced the illusory triangle and not just stopped responding, each participant was requested to trace the outline of the figure they saw on screen with their finger. Using this method all the autistic participants demonstrated they had cohered a triangle from the corner inducing circles. It is worth noting that although all the autistic participants did experience the illusory triangle the intra-group variation was quite dramatic, as noted by the large standard deviation. However, all autistic participants experienced the triangle and most experienced it well before the non-autistic participants indicating a varied but enhanced ability.

The implications of this result must be examined with reference to the associated theories. There are a number of theories that attempt to explain the phenomenon of visual illusions (Day 1994; Gibson 1979; Gregory 1980). Of particular interest here is Day's unified theory of perception. Within this theory Day (1994) argues that veridical and illusory perception is controlled via the same basic mechanism and that all perception is essentially the coherence of relatively disparate information. For example, the proprioceptive information feedback from the muscles is involved with judgement of visual distance. Hence the ability to judge depth requires central coherence. Coherence is exploited at all stages of perception according to Day. The Muller-Lyer illusion for example is a product of the judgement of interapical length and overall length and the resolution of any conflict this causes. The illusory experience of the Muller-Lyer is due to the overall extent of the inward arrow shape being less than the outward arrow shape, resulting in the interapical length appearing shorter. This means that in order for the illusion to be experienced, as it was here and in Happé's (1996) study, participants must have cohered the differing information together. The perceptual compromise needed to experience the illusion is evidence for coherence. Hence, individuals with autism can cohere information. What must be addressed, however, is whether such an ability is relatively weak.

The results from the Kanizsa triangle indicate an enhanced ability at inducing the illusory triangle in the autistic population. This means that the autistic population is able to bring together the disparate parts and reach a meaningful (if illusory) conclusion before the non-autistic participants. Such a result would seem to indicate enhance coherence abilities. However, the ability to cohere was demonstrated within relatively atypical conditions, that is, the coherence was demonstrated within a single perceptual modality. Most perceptual experiences are intermodal and exploit information from many senses. The Kanizsa illusion and the Muller-Lyer are a product of the visual correlates alone. Thus the results can be interpreted as participants with autism being able to cohere within a perceptual modality and even having superior functioning at unimodal coherence. The ability to cohere at the intermodal level cannot be directly commented upon.

Embedded Figures tests (EFT) have been recognised as an area where individuals with autism perform better than non-autistic populations (Jolliffe and Baron-Cohen 1997; Shan and Frith 1993) and this has been explained via weak central coherence. This explanation must be questioned in light of this study. EFT tests are also unimodal and effectively demonstrate the opposite ability to the visual illusions results. That is EFTs demonstrate reduced ability to cohere and visual illusions demonstrate enhanced ability to cohere. These results need not be interpreted as directly contradictory, it is possible that coherence, weak or otherwise is a cognitive preference or style. Happé (1999) has raised this notion of coherence as cognitive style and certainly the idea that coherence is a continuum and individuals with autism are at one extreme appears to be appropriate. If this is the case the ability at EFT may represent the preferred or more able approach to the environment but the visual illusions demonstrate that the skills to cohere are not absent. This explanation reframes the notion of 'weak' within weak central coherence, the weakness is potentially as a result of preference for local processing not the result of an inability to cohere in this way. The consequences of such a position are considerable when methods of intervention are considered, for example, teaching a new ability requires a notably different approach to encouraging the utilisation of a dormant ability. In conclusion the idea that weak central coherence dominates all perceptual experience of individuals with autism is incorrect. Autistic populations have demonstrated cohering abilities. However, cohering abilities have not been demonstrated across perceptual modalities and this type of cohering is common in 'real world' perceptual processing. Study of coherence at a multimodal level must form a priority for further research, if its possible relationship with perceptual trauma is to be fully investigated. This research has also highlighted the issue that autism should not be presented as simply a series of deficits, but rather understood as different abilities or abilities at the extremes of continuums. Such a position appears to be a more true reflection of the qualities of autism.

References

Bryson, S.E., Wainwright-Sharp, J.A. and Smith, I. (1990) 'Autism: a developmental spatial neglect syndrome?' In J.T. Enns (ed) *The Development of Attention: Research and Theory.* Amsterdam: Elsevier/North Holland.

Courchesne, E., Townsend, J.P., Akshoomoff, N.A., Yeung-Courchesne, R., Press, G.A. and Murakami, J.W. (1994) 'A new finding: impairment in shifting attention in autistic and cerebellar patients.' In S.H. Broman and J. Grafman (eds) *Atypical Cognitive Deficits in Development Disorders: Implications for Brain Development.* Hillsdale, NJ: Erlbaum.

Day, R.H. (1994) 'The foundations of veridical and illusory perception.' In S. Ballesteros (ed) *Cognitive Approaches to Human Perception.* Hillsdale, NJ: Erlbaum.

Frith, U. (1989) *Autism: Explaining the Enigma.* Oxford: Blackwell.

Frith, U. and Happé, F.G.E. (1994) 'Autism: beyond "theory of mind".' *Cognition 50,* 115–132.

Gibson, J.J. (1979) *The Ecological Approach to Visual Perception.* Boston, MA: Houghton Mifflin.

Grandin, T. (1984) 'My experiences as an autistic child and review of related literature.' *Journal of Orthomolecular Psychiatry 13,* 144–174.

Gregory, R.L. (1980) 'Perceptions as hypotheses.' *Philosophical Transactions of the Royal Society of London,* Series B no. 290, 181–197.

Happé, F.G.E. (1994) *Autism: An Introduction to Psychological Theory.* London: UCL Press.

Happé, F.G.E. (1996) 'Studying weak central coherence at low levels: children with autism do not succumb to visual illusions. A research note.' *Journal of Child Psychology 37,* 7, 873–877.

Happé, F.G.E. (1999) 'Autism: cognitive deficit or cognitive style?' *Trends in Cognitive Sciences 3,* 6, 216–222.

Jolliffe, T. and Baron-Cohen S. (1997) 'Are people with autism and Asperger syndrome faster than normal on the embedded figures test?' *Journal of Child Psychology 38,* 5, 527–534.

Shan, A. and Frith, U. (1993) 'Why do autistic individuals show superior performance on block design test?' *Journal of Child Psychology and Psychiatry 34,* 1351–1364.

Williams, D. (1992) *Nobody Nowhere.* London: Doubleday.

CHAPTER 8

Autistic Children's Talk about Mental States at School and Home

An Empirical Investigation

Sophia Mavropoulou

Theoretical background

Currently, experimental research has offered evidence that there is a minority of individuals with high-functioning autism who perform successfully on advanced theory of mind tests (Baron-Cohen 1989, Bowler 1992; Happé 1994; Ozonoff, Pennington and Rogers 1991a, 1991b). On the other hand, naturalistic research suggests that children with high-functioning autism are 'noticeably deficient' in their ability to talk about cognitive mental states at home (Tager-Flusberg 1992). Nevertheless, this naturalistic study examined exclusively the autistic child's mental state language, without paying attention to issues related to the interaction between the child and others. It also has to be noted that this study did not examine whether or not these children showed a basic theory of mind ability in a test setting. This leaves unanswered the question of whether high-functioning autistic persons with basic theory of mind abilities still have persisting problems in real life situations?

There is a paucity of research on whether children with high-functioning autism apply (or fail to do so) their social understanding in different contexts. This is a significant gap given the evidence that the normal development of a theory of mind occurs through the transactional experience between caregivers and children (Bruner and Feldman 1993) and given the hypothesis on the adverse effects autistic children's avoidant behaviour in social interactions on their acquisition of social and cultural skills (Richer 1978, and Chapters 2 and 3 in this volume).

The research questions of this study were:

1. Do children with high-functioning autism talk about their own and others' mental states in the naturalistic contexts of school and home and if so how?

2. Is there evidence that familiar others at home and in school encourage or inhibit able autistic children's talk about their own and others' mental states?

Methodology

Participants

The target group comprised seven children with high-functioning autism (HFA) attending the same class in a special school for autistic children in the northern part of England. The comparison group included eight children with moderate learning difficulties (MLD) from a special unit in the same area. The two groups of children were of similar chronological, verbal and non-verbal mental age (Table 8.1). Verbal ability was assessed with the Short Form of the British Picture Vocabulary Scale (BPVS) (Dunn, *et al.* 1982). Non-verbal ability was measured with Raven's (1956) Coloured Progressive Matrices.

Table 8.1 Descriptive characteristics of the two groups of children			
	HFA (n=7)	**MLD (n=8)**	**T-test**
$\overline{X}$CA	11.95	12.43	t=0.47, p=0.99
SD	3.54	3.31	
$\overline{X}$VMA	7.88	7.2	t=0.68, p=0.57
SD	2.76	2.11	
$\overline{X}$NVMA	8.78	6.50	t=1.96, p=0.10
SD	2.98	1.33	

Procedures

At school, two kinds of sessions were audio-recorded and transcribed:

1. group sessions (offering opportunities for discussions, e.g. 'describe what you did at the weekend' and activities, e.g. 'how to make a conversation')

2. curriculum sessions (e.g. maths, English).

The total amount of recorded 'group' sessions was 137 mins for the children with HFA and 118 mins for the children with MLD. The total amount of recorded 'curriculum' sessions: 197 mins for the target group and 33 mins for the comparison group.

At home, six children with HFA and three children with MLD were observed during three visits, each a week apart. It was more difficult to obtain the cooperation of families with children with MLD; four families refused to give their consent for home visits, because they had been involved with other research in the past. Therefore, the amount of data collected from the comparison group was less than the target group.

The number of utterances was corrected for the different lengths of the observation sessions using the formula: $N = \dfrac{a \times b}{c}$ where a = the number of mental state utterances by children with high-functioning autism, b = the total amount of recorded time of group sessions for the group with moderate learning difficulties, and c = the total number of recorded time of group sessions for the group with high-functioning autism.

Method of analysis

All transcripts were analysed in two ways. First, all transcripts were searched for lexical terms that referred explicitly to four psychological states:

1. Perception (e.g. 'look', 'hear')

2. Desire (e.g. 'want', 'need')

3. Emotion (e.g. 'hug', 'cry')

4. Cognition (e.g. 'remember', 'know').

The second aim was to look for conversational turns in which references to psychological states were made. A conversational turn was defined as one speaker's utterance followed by another speaker's utterance. Each conversational turn was coded in terms of:

1. Speaker – adult (parent or teacher) or child
2. Listener – adult or child or children
3. Whose psychological state was being referred to – self, other, both
4. Pragmatics (as follows).

Teachers' and parents' utterances were classified in four categories:

1. *Didactic/ controlling:* efforts to control the behaviour of the child (e.g. 'If you were listening, you would know').
2. *Commentary:* identification of one's mental state (e.g. 'I know what's happening', 'What I want to do is...').
3. *Questioning:* making a question about a mental state (e.g. 'What have you liked to do in school this week?').
4. *Directing/guiding behaviour:* giving instructions for a task (e.g. 'Try to think of something').

Children's utterances were coded under five categories of pragmatic context:

1. *Self-interest:* drawing attention to one's own needs (e.g. 'I need a tissue').
2. *Sophisticated:* explaining one's actions (e.g. 'He's dreaming all day').
3. *Commentary:* simple comments (e.g. 'I feel like you, Gail. I don't like the cold').
4. *Describing a mental state:* giving information to the teacher as a response to her request (e.g. 'I haven't heard about that').
5. *Questioning/clarifying:* asking a question about a mental state (e.g. 'What do you mean?').

Results

This section will focus only on the findings from the two sets of naturalistic evidence in relation to the aims of this study:

1. Do children with high-functioning autism talk about their own and others' mental states in the naturalistic contexts of school and home and if so how?

2. Is there evidence that familiar others at home and in school encourage or inhibit able autistic children's talk about their own and others' mental states?

Table 8.2 Summary of results		

Context: H = home, Sg = group time in school,
                   Sc = curriculum time in school,
                   S = both school contexts
Speaker: P = parent, T = teacher, C = child		

>or< gives the direction of difference, followed by the significance level		

Use of psychological state terms

HFA children only

	Sg v H	v Sc	P v T
Perception	–	>.05	–
Desire	<.05	>.001	–
Emotion	–	>.001	–
Cognition	–	–	<.001

Comparison of groups

	At School	At Home
	HFA v MLD	HFA v MLD
Perseption	–	–
Desire	–	–
Emotion	>C.001	>P, C.001
Cognotion	<T.001	<P.001
	>C.001	<C.001

Pragmatics

HFA group on;y

	Adult T v P	Child H v S
Didactic	–	–
Commentary	–	>.001
Questioning	–	>.001
Describe a mental state	–	<.001
Guiding	>.001	–
Refer to own mental state	–	>.001
Refer to adult's mental state	–	>.01
Refer to child's mental state	–	<.05

The results relevant to these questions are summarised in Table 8.2.

It was clear from this study that the HFA group children did use mental state terms, though some, emotion terms, were used with a lower frequency than the comparison group of children, and some, cognitions, were used with a higher frequency.

The use of these terms by the HFA group varied with the context in unsurprising ways. For example, more 'desire' terms were used at home, fewer mental state terms other than 'cognition' were used in the curriculum sessions at school. They referred to their own and the adult's mental states more at home than at school, but to other children's more in school.

The finding that the HFA group children used more emotion words than the MLD group children perhaps indicates that HFA children have a higher emotional maturity.

Conclusion

These findings show that high-functioning autistic children do use mental state terms and that their use varies unsurprisingly with context. Larger studies with more data from comparison groups would need to be undertaken to support this conclusively. The findings need to be set alongside those of Tager-Flusberg (1992), whose children were younger. It is likely that there is a considerable variation in the use of mental state terms in autistic children and that this varies with age (i.e. many acquire their use but at a later age than normal children) and with other verbal and pragmatic skills. This is consistent with the position that there are constraints on the acquisition of the understanding and use of mental state terms in autistic children, but that there is not an absolute deficit, such as a complete inability to read other minds, which would rule out any appropriate use of mental state terms.

There have been attempts to teach autistic people specifically to 'mindread' (e.g. Howlin, Baron-Cohen and Hadwin 1999; Ozonoff and Miller 1995). The findings give support to attempts to help autistic children learn mental state terms and similar semantics and pragmatics by focusing on the processes which constrain their acquisition.

References

Baron-Cohen, S. (1989) 'The autistic child's theory of mind: a case of specific developmental delay.' *Journal of Child Psychology and Psychiatry 30*, 285–298.

Bowler, D.M. (1992) '"Theory of mind" in Asperger's syndrome.' *Journal of Child Psychology and Psychiatry 33*, 877–893.

Bruner, J. and Feldman, C. (1993) 'Theories of mind and the problem of autism.' In S. Baron-Cohen, H. Tager-Flusberg and D. Cohen (eds) *Understanding Other Minds: Perspectives from Autism.* Oxford: Oxford University Press.

Dunn, L., Dunn, L., Whetton, C. and Pintilie, D. (1982) *British Picture Vocabulary Scale.* Windsor: NFER-Nelson.

Happé, F. (1994) *Autism: An Introduction to Psychological Theory.* London: UCL Press.

Howlin, P., Baron-Cohen, S. and Hadwin, J. (1999) *Teaching Children with Autism to Mind-read: A Practical Guide.* Chichester: Wiley.

Ozonoff, S. and Miller, J. (1995) 'Teaching theory of mind: A new approach to skills training for individuals with autism.' *Journal of Autism and Developmental Disorders 25*, 415–433.

Ozonoff, S., Pennington, B.F. and Rogers, S.J. (1991a) 'Executive function deficits in high-functioning autistic individuals: relationship to theory of mind.' *Journal of Child Psychology and Psychiatry 32*, 1081–1105.

Ozonoff, S., Pennington, B.F. and Rogers, S.J. (1991b) 'Asperger's syndrome: evidence of an empirical distinction from high-functioning autism.' *Journal of Child Psychology and Psychiatry 32*, 1107–1122.

Raven, J. (1956) *Coloured Progressive Matrices.* London: H.K. Lewis.

Richer, J.M. (1978) 'The partial non communication of culture to autistic children.' In M. Rutter and E. Schopler (eds) *Autism: a Reappraisal of Concepts and Treatment.* New York: Plenum.

Tager-Flusberg, H. (1992) 'Autistic children's talk about psychological states: deficits in the early acquisition of a theory of mind.' *Child Development 63*, 161–172.

PART 2

Physiology and Medicine

CHAPTER 9

Editorial

Approaches to the Physiology of Autism

John Richer and Sheila Coates

There is clear evidence for a strong genetic contribution to the aetiology of autism (Le Couteur *et al.* 1996). So far family studies have not revealed which genes make this contribution, but as Bailey (1999) noted, a major value of this work is in identifying which proteins are likely to be involved in increasing the risk of autism. The physiological systems that those proteins influenced can then be focused upon.

The genetic influences in autism need to be seen as just that, influences. The early twin studies showed clear concordance for autism, but equally there were monozygotic twins who were not concordant. All behaviour is a product of genetic and environmental influences, the interesting question is what are the processes which lead to a particular behaviour. It is useful to remember the distinction made many years ago by the ethologist Robert Hinde, between environment *stable* and environment *labile* behaviours (Hinde 1970). The stable behaviours are those which occur in animals with a wide variety of environmental histories (i.e. strongly influenced by genes), the most labile behaviours are those which require very particular environments (i.e. strongly influenced by environmental factors).

It is likely that the aetiology of autism is both multiple (requiring many causal factors acting together) and heterogeneous (different sets of causes in different children) (Kolvin, Ounsted and Roth 1971; Richer 1983).

Zappella draws attention in Chapter 10 to the heterogeneity of conditions, such as epilepsy, associated with autism, and how treating those conditions can sometimes improve the autism itself. He argues for heterogeneity of treatment programmes, and that while there may be common features in the treatment of autistic behaviour and the children's social and cognitive difficulties, it is likely that many other aspects of treatment will differ from child to child and evaluation of treatment regimes needs to take this into account. It is important to develop ways of diagnosing the individual child's problems and fitting treatment to that rather than offering the same treatment just because the child is autistic.

Danczak's approach embraces these ideas in Chapter 11. His treatment regime is tailored to the child. His approach also embraces complementary as well as conventional methods. While he has a working hypothesis that a major factor in the aetiology of autism is a failure of the immune system, with knock on effects on many bodily systems including the brain, gut and liver, his treatment is focused on restoring normal gut functioning using complex homeopathic remedies and probiotics.

Danczak's approach fits well with the idea that treatment aims to shift the child's physiology from its (pathological) state, of which numerous indicators have been found, to a more normally functioning state. While the possibility of coincidence/placebo must always be borne in mind, the success, or partial success, of some treatments, each with a few autistic children, can be understood as the treatment being sufficient to shift that child's physiology towards a more normal state, to varying extents, whereas as with other children the same treatment may be insufficient. The mixed results (significant improvement in some, some positive effects in some, no apparent effect in others) obtained with, for instance, secretin, DMG, dietary changes and mega vitamins can be seen in this way. Each can add a little to the jigsaw and should not be dismissed.

It is also likely that improving autistic children's physiology is only the first step in their treatment, their relationships and learning still need to be addressed (see Richer, Chapter 2 in this volume).

References

Bailey, A. (1999) 'Genetics.' Paper presented to the conference *The Search for Coherence from the Fragments of Autism.* Oxford, September.

Hinde, R.A. (1970) *Animal Behaviour.* New York, NY: McGraw Hill.

Kolvin, I., Ounsted, C. and Roth, M. (1971) 'Cerebral dysfunction and childhood psychoses.' *British Journal of Psychiatry 118*, 407–414.

Le Couteur, A., Bailey, A., Goode, S., Pickles, A., Robertson, S., Gottesman, I. and Rutter, M. A. (1996) 'A broader phenotype of autism: the clinical spectrum in twins.' *Journal of Child Psychology and Psychiatry 37*, 785–801.

Richer, J.M. (1983) 'The development of social avoidance in autistic children.' In A Oliverio and M. Zappella (eds) *The Behaviour of Human Infants.* New York: Plenum.

CHAPTER 10

Early Intervention in Autistic Disorders

Michele Zappella

Different packages of treatments for 'one' condition, named autism

Early intervention in autism is a central topic for at least two reasons.

1. There is a strong need to help the toddler and give a guidance to the family and to the nursery.

2. It is often claimed that early intervention goes together with a better outcome.

Presently many young children with autism receive a diagnosis by the age of 2 to 3 years with criteria which correspond to international agreements (ICD-10 and DSM-IV, ABC, CARS, ADI[1] and others). However, the type of intervention varies to a considerable extent. The number of treatments which are proposed is great and always increasing and this fact represents a cause of confusion and may be a disadvantage for both parents and the child: Howlin (1997) and Trevarthen (1998) have listed about twenty different treatments, and others could be added.

The approaches which apparently support these varied therapies tend to consider autism as one condition, although probably determined by

---

[1]   ICD-10 – International Classification of Diseases 10; DSM-IV – Diagnostic and Statistical Manual 4; ABC – Autism Behaviour Checklist; CARS – Childhood Autism Rating Scale; ADI – Autism Diagnostic Interview.

different genetic disorders (International Molecular Genetic Study of Autism Consortium 1998; Philippe *et al*. 1999) and individual differences are taken into account, particularly the great variability in the abilities present. The various methods tend often to be considered as discrete packages, but their evaluation rests on controlled studies of 'autism', as if the groups were homogeneous. Some approaches dismiss the possibility of positive results, i.e. of a complete cure of autism, others claim more or less brilliant results. Among the latter Lovaas (1987), through the use of behavioural treatments, claimed a recovery rate close to 50 per cent for those young children with autism where treatment was prolonged to many hours per day. More recently with an approach called 'floor therapy', based on affective reciprocal interactions plus the eventual use of augmentative use of pictures and signs, Greenspan and Wieder (1997) claimed a 58 per cent of 'good to outstanding' results: children who evaluated with the CARS 'shifted into the non-autistic range'. Positive results were reported by Birnbrauer and Leach (1993) and by others (Rogers 1996). On the other hand the supporters of the TEACCH method do not aim for normality and are usually critical of more optimistic claims.

Some approaches propose a meticulous structure of the day. Others give more flexible and general suggestions and attempt to integrate approaches which aim to support language and social skills in the natural environment (Harris 1998; Harris and Handleman 1994). Emphasis on tayloring the intervention to the client as a unique person, not as belonging to a specific subgroup or disorder, tends to characterise these approaches.

In evaluating these methods we can consider the advantages and disadvantages of each 'package', or, alternatively, see more in depth which can be the most relevant inspiring principles existing in some of them. For example, the idea of reinforcing strong areas, of giving a visual structure and of supporting emerging areas are probably the more valuable aspects of the TEACCH method. Some of these are present also in other approaches. In addition there are some interesting recurring findings in early intervention studies: for example, in three different reports there is a rapid recovery which doubles the rates of normal development (Hoyson, Jaieson and Strain 1984; Rogers and Di Lalla 1991; Zappella 1996). This rapid improvement at the beginning of treatment was found in 32 per cent of the cases in my series and only a minority of these had an entirely positive final result. Rapid recoveries with a normal outcome have been described in adoptees coming from profoundly deprived institutions and showing initially an autistic behaviour and can be considered an evidence of social deprivation. In the children with autistic disorders we are considering now, however, such an analogy would be simplistic and inadequate and there are different kinds of explanations which will be discussed below.

A specific intervention for each disorder and set of disabilities

A different approach is based on considering autism as composed of different syndromes, including those with peculiar developmental courses, and different sets of disabilities. Early intervention should start with a diagnosis concerning the specific disorder and the present set of disabilities. This requires caution on behalf of the professional: both the word autism and the profound difficulty in communication that goes with it represents a threat to the emotional balance of parents and to the structure of the family. This is one of the reasons why the first visit conducted by the specialist is likely to have a strong impact on the family and should aim both to start an accumulation of knowledge on the child's conditions, abilities and disabilities, and to open a communication with him/her and his/her family.

There are at least two aspects in the diagnosis of autism in young children. One approach is based on an observation conducted at a distance. Another approach includes both observing at a distance and also observing within close tactile often playful interaction with the clinician.

In this age group eye, hearing and sometimes tactile avoidance are common and a number of types of interaction such as friendly, exploratory, playful and comfort seeking may be very reduced or absent at a first observation conducted from a distance, but may be revealed and fostered by a number of interactions conducted by the examiner. Ethologists have long been showing that these types of behaviour may be inhibited, for example, if nobody fosters them, and this may well be the case in a family frightened by the odd and very difficult behaviour of their affected child, or revealed and eventually reinforced by the imposition of strict regimes.

It is the job of the professional to look into this aspect of behaviour and try to activate the child's prosocial behaviour. Some toddlers with autism are disturbed by a loud voice and the specialist should ask parents: if this is not the case, the specialist can suddenly call the child by name with a high, bright, friendly voice and the child may turn unexpectedly towards the specialist with a look of curiosity to the surprise of the parents. The specialist may then ask the child to come closer, which can occasionally occur. Subsequently the mother can be asked to take the child on her lap and start to take the child's hands, stroke them on the child's cheeks and vice versa, while talking in a slow, expressive way. There are a number of tactics which can be used here, many copied from early mother–child interactions.

The aim of this approach is at least twofold: it helps to reduce the fear in the child and in the parents and it reveals more extensively some aspects of the approach behaviour which can be the basis for obtaining more cooperation from the child on other tasks. A few-years-old child with an autistic disorder has very little symbolic representations, if any, and the child's cognitive abilities correspond to a sensori-motor level: the professional who interacts with the child at this level will be able to motivate the child to interact and cooperate, and also to assess if the child, for example, understands words, to what extent the mouth or hands can be used, etc. From the first contact with the family the diagnosis of autism is not the only factor to be considered, two others are:

1. The type of relationship the examiner establishes with the child and the family.

2. An initial understanding of what kinds of disabilities are present (i.e. verbal auditory agnosia, disorders of coordination, etc.). Elements suggestive of a disorder which follows a specific course should also be considered. The diagnosis of Autistic Disorders should be supported by a careful and complete medical evaluation and by a number of laboratory evaluations, including EEG, neuroimaging, chromosomal and metabolic studies, possibly selected in view of the specific clinical problem a young child will pose.

Early intervention: medical aspects

However, once the diagnosis of autism is done, we are only at the beginning of an appropriate assessment of what kind of autistic disorder we are dealing with.

Probably the first thing to suspect and to assess, starting with the medical history of the child, is connected with the presence of a disorder which can be treated medically. Though rare, the possibility of a *Landau–Kleffner Syndrome (LK)* should be suspected in toddlers who, after a normal development including an adequate development of language and of symbolic abilities lose within a few weeks or months most of their language, both in understanding and speaking. Some of these children show an autistic behaviour. This regression usually follows epileptic fits but it may occur without them. A sleep EEG should resolve this question by showing, in LK cases, the presence of prolonged bursts of spike and slow waves and/or temporal focuses.

In these cases pharmacological treatments (valproate, steroids) can be of considerable help (Bishop 1985) and in some cases be successful in completely removing both the autistic behaviour and the language defect. Occasional brilliant results have been reported in other epileptic disorders (Deonna *et al.* 1995).

A similar approach, albeit different in the prognosis, concerns children who show *flexion spasms with hypsarrhythmia*. In both cases pharmacological intervention is the first step, to be followed by rehabilitation measures which may concern language therapy or other developmental procedures.

About half of those children with autism who also develop epilepsy do so in the first years of life: these include cases amenable to a positive control of the fits as well as rare cases such as those described by DeLong and Heinz(1997) as *early-life bilateral hippocampal sclerosis*, often associated with episodes of status epilepticus.

It is important to look at whether the child belongs to the general subgroup of *Autistic Disorders with Deterioration (AD-D)*. This can be assessed partly through taking a history from the parents, and in many cases this information can be supplemented through the observation of home videos. In these cases sleep EEGs have shown a prevalence of abnormalities almost double that in children where there was evidence of an early autistic disorder in the first months of life (Tuchman and Rapin 1997). The presence of these abnormalities can inform medical treatment. Recent evidence, obtained from magnetoencephalography (Levine *et al.* 1999), suggests that in AD-D epileptic discharges may be even more frequent and include features, in part at least, analogous to LK.

The relevance of a medical treatment in the above conditions varies and it may be very beneficial in some cases of Landau–Kleffner Syndrome and supportive in other cases.

Similar considerations can be given for those clinical syndromes where a metabolic defect is the core of the disorder, causing both autism and mental retardation. Presently *phenylketonuria* (PKU) and autism are only an exceptional observation in most western countries after the introduction of neonatal screenings. In contrast *Purine Autism* is a disorder which is amenable to a treatment with oral pyrimidine or with a purine restricted diet and/or allopurinol (Page *et al.* 1997). This condition should be suspected in children with marked developmental delay, especially in language, ataxia, impaired fine motor control, hyperactivity, seizures and autism and checked by the evaluation of the uric acid in their urines.

Pre- and post-natal infections (rubella, cytomegalovirus, herpes simplex) have been suggested as possible causes of autism: among the rubella cases a significant number of cases had a favourable outcome at follow-up (Chess 1977).

Early onset mood disorders, revealing themselves with symptoms of autistic behaviour, and usually with significant family loading for these conditions, can be treated with the corresponding drugs. DeLong, Teague and McSwain Kamram (1998) have treated with fluoxetine a group of selected children of this kind with excellent or good results, especially in language abilities. In these cases drug therapy was supported by the evidence of asymmetrical metabolism of serotonin between the two hemispheres, reduced on the left one in subjects with autism (Chugani *et al.* 1997). The DeLong studies fit my personal experience, confirming significant improvements by treating in a similar way (i.e. through antidepressant and mood regulators drugs) autistic children with a family history loaded with mood disorders and with a clinical course of cyclic, profound changes of their mood. With this treatment in some cases a child may lose all autistic features, reveal normal intellectual abilities, and remain a child with chronic depression and eventually social phobia or an essentially manic child. In most cases, however, these children reach adolescence with an odd, peculiar personality, gifted with witty attitudes and with some imagination, unusual for children with vestiges of autism, and more consistent with traits of mood disorders. The management of their behaviour includes, especially when they are young, a developmental guidance, while a rigid structure of their lives would be inappropriate.

In addition one encounters at times *blind children with autism,* often with a profound disturbance of the sleep cycle: in these cases *melatonin* often helps to recover this important biological rhythm.

If we consider the above conditions amenable to an early medical therapy we can realise that improvement can be obtained in many of these cases and in a few the result can be a complete reversal of the clinical picture with a resulting normal outcome. It must be noted that the drugs used for these different conditions are profoundly different in their action on neurotransmitters and success in therapy is related to their specific action. This principle, i.e. the possibility that some cases with an appropriate, specific treatment, are amenable to improvement and in rare cases even to complete recovery, is easily accepted on medical grounds, and should be kept in mind as a possible model also in connection with other types of interventions based on human interactions.

Early intervention: based on human interactions

In almost every case, including those mentioned above, however, early intervention in autism is predicated on relational ideas.

In a limited percentage of cases a number of neurological syndromes can occur: these include Tuberous Sclerosis, Hypomelanosis of Ito, Down Syndrome, Williams Syndrome, Fragile X, etc. These disorders, and also other malformations of the central nervous system evident, for example, at the MRI[2], are more frequent in children with a low IQ. Although they may show some peculiarity in child's behaviour(see, for example, Fragile X and Williams Syndrome), they do not usually represent *per se* the basis of a specific early intervention.

Here we have, instead, two main referral points.

On one side we must consider the weight of *specific disabilities.* These include:

1. *language and communication, socioaffective and repetitive modalities* (see ICD-10 and DSM-IV)

2. in most cases with *retardation*

3. especially in those who do not speak, often accompanied by *disorders of coordination*

2   MRI – Magnetic resonance imaging.

4. in addition, they go together with more or less *profound perturbations* of the psychological development both in terms of *primary and secondary intersubjectivity,* of *directed interaction* and of *cooperation,* and in terms of abnormalities of a number of prosocial activities which are better evaluated on ethological grounds.

On the other hand we have to notice the *course of the disorder* which in some cases follows specific patterns. The cyclic pattern of early onset mood disorders has already been mentioned. In addition there are other disorders which may be amenable to a successful treatment on relational grounds. These are the *Dysmaturational Syndrome with early onset Familial Multiple Complex Tics, reversible autistic behaviour with outcome in attention deficit disorder with hyperactivity* and those *autistic behaviours following early institutionalisation.* Let us consider the first one. I found no descriptions of these children in the literature and I have therefore to rely only on my experience, which includes, at the side of numerous cases seen as outpatients and inpatients, twenty-four children described in the literature, twenty-three of whom were males, all with complex motor tics (in some cases both motor and vocal) of various severity, frequently present in one or both parents and eventually in other relatives. Attention Deficit Hyperactivity Disorder (ADHD) is frequent among first degree males. They have a normal development in the first year of life and a regression with autistic behaviour and retardation in their second year: as a consequence at 2–3 years of age their abilities are below the norm. Difficulties in motor coordination of the mouth and in the fine movements of the hands may also coexist. These children have a normal physical appearance and are normal at various laboratory tests such as EEG, chromosomes, metabolic studies, MRI (Zappella 1994a, 1996, 1999, 2000).

These children were treated with an unconventional approach based on intense cuddling and movement, a therapeutic approach outlined in the following section which allows them to change profoundly and reveal a number of abilities both in terms of prosocial activities and cooperation. The intervention is subsequently carried on daily by relatives and by others (in the nursery, by therapists), and the young child will rapidly recover a number of other abilities in various areas. Progress, however, may be slower in coordination and language and only by 5 or 6 years of age traces of autism are completely cancelled and intellectual abilities recovered at a normal level. These children turn out usually to be affected by ADHD accompanied by chronic tics and occasionally by Obsessional

Compulsive Disorder (OCD). In some cases a full Tourette Syndrome represents the final outcome. These cases should be distinguished from other autistic disorders where Tourette Syndrome is a comorbid feature (Baron-Cohen *et al.* 1999) and, until the child in due time reveals important positive changes, the diagnostic evaluation should remain cautious. The nature of this disorder, which includes a probable relevant genetic component, is unknown but a peculiar type of gene-environment interaction concerning the present way of raising children has been suggested (Zappella 2000).

This syndrome is apparently frequent and represented 12.1 per cent of an outpatient population of young children with autism (Zappella 1999).

A note can be made in this respect on the success, claimed in the past, for the holding therapies in autism: the claimed percentage of success was close to 10 per cent (Prekop 1984; Zappella 1987), similar to the percentage of the dysmaturative syndrome in outpatient's populations of children with autistic behaviour and in point of fact some of the successfully treated cases belonged to this subgroup (Zappella 1999). Some of these, now outdated techniques, could favour intimacy and motivation for cooperation, and in the early 1980s they were probably the main approach able to help children belonging to the dysmaturative syndrome.

Children with autistic behaviours following early institutionalisation can also be successfully treated through developmentally oriented approaches (Rutter *et al.* 1999).

At the other extreme there is the *Preserved Speech Variant of the Rett Complex (PSV)* (Zappella 1992; Zappella, Gillberg and Ehlers 1999). These are only girls and recent studies have shown in some of them the presence of a MECP2 mutation in chromosome X (De Bona *et al.* 2000). The course of their disorder includes an apparently adequate development in the first year of life, followed by a sequence of profound interactional disturbances, losing the use of their hands and developing stereotypic washing-like activities. This disorder is structured into four stages: early onset stagnation, rapid regression, pseudostationary period, late motor deterioration. This condition can be suspected early for some differences with classic Rett Syndrome: namely, normal head circumference, normal spine, a few words preserved. When they become older they attain a stereotyped and repetitive speech and recover some ability in the use of their hands. At 2–3 years of age these girls may still be in the second stage of their disorder and in this case early intervention may be limited to recovering some degree of social interaction and response to music. When they move towards the beginning of the third stage the disability in their motor coordination and the autistic symptoms are severe and the neurobiologic disability cannot be modified by relational interventions. In this stage treatment should support them where they are weak, in helping them to increase their communication through the tools of the Augmentative and Alternative Communication as well as stimulate them where they are strong and, for example, introduce music with their active participation. In the subsequent course of the disorder some speech therapy can eventually be of help as well as a developmental guidance. Some structuring of home and school with the aid of pictures can also be of help. In this case the prognosis is profoundly different and treatment aims at improving communication and the quality of life.

In both examples, the favourable and the unfavourable disorders, environment has an impact on the child's conditions. It may profoundly alter the course of the dysmaturative syndrome, and, though it will not alter the sequence of stages in PSV, it may help the child to communicate better and improve the quality of her life.

In many cases of autism, however, a developmental course of the kinds described is not seen. Analysis of their behaviour suggests different profiles which require a differential therapeutic approach.

Here the number of different situations is great and the following examples may be appropriate guidelines of the general strategy which can be suggested.

If we consider the first of the group of symptoms described in ICD-10 (or in DSM-IV), relating to socioaffective disturbances, we often get in touch with toddlers with autistic behaviour who will walk into the office with a considerable gaze avoidance. At times they may make a lot of fuss by refusing to walk in and/or showing a strong degree of body avoidance. Hearing avoidance is usually among the first symptoms referred by parents. Looking at them from a distance they do not show friendly, explorative and playful behaviours. Cooperation is often very reduced or absent. The children may be hyperactive or hypoactive, they often do not talk or they may be able to say only a few words repetitively. In terms of the development of relationships these toddlers may be less able than a few-weeks-old baby. They have lost any sense of rhythm in the relationship, of ability to take turns and to share common meanings. At this stage, work on two-way interaction is a priority and mimics the early 'primary intersubjectivity' interactions between mother and infant described by Trevarthen (1979). In this way the therapist usually starts the interaction with the child and then coaches the parent to have the child on the lap, talking slowly with a lively expressive face, trying to get an eye-to-eye interaction and searching for a common emotional tune in order to be first an 'echo' of the child and then introducing variants. In some cases children will accept this type of interaction and get involved with it, giving appropriate affiliative responses or engaging in simple activities such as sticking out their tongue, pinching the nose, biting a finger. During this interaction, which makes both the toddler and the parent more and more lively and happy and aims at getting the parent in an emotional state congruent to that of the child, the parent often tickles and touches the child's body in a jolly, attention-getting way. Exploration, play and affiliation are elicited.

The aim of recovering the rhythm of the relationship is a central one for both the child and the parent. It should be carefully elicited starting from the level of acceptance the child shows. In some children, where avoidance is pronounced, this interaction may start by a delicate touching and light scratching of the back and then proceed to more advanced stages of interaction. In this way the children begin to relate, starting from a simple level of interaction, consistent with their present abilities. At the same time the parents recover the 'phantasy' of their child and the ability to pass it on to the child, an essential prerequisite of intimacy and tenderness at every age. In this way parents become more sensible to the needs of their children. This type of interaction favours in normal babies the development of a sense of identity, imitation, maturation of feelings, security, language and creativity and it is probable that, in part at least, some of these abilities can be reinforced in these young children. We often observe that it is more easily followed by cooperation in many cases.

Children can also be intruded upon through some of their many activities and, since toddlers often like to run around, the parent takes the child by the hand and runs with the child quickly. The child follows and shows signs of pleasure. Then suddenly the adult takes the child on his or her lap near a table and physically prompts the child in an activity such as, for example, building a tower of cubes which the child has so far refused to do.

The problem of motivating the child is a central one and other toddlers may be motivated by other types of physical activities or by music or, if they are hyperselective to colours, by exposure to computer diskettes with colour devices which may be the starting point of introducing them to different activities. In this context the voice of the adult, which can become at times brilliant and high, at others unexpectedly low, can also be a powerful tool of activation.

Parents are also instructed to consider some of the items included in the checklist of a developmental scale (for example, the Portage Guide for Early Education (White and Cameron 1987)) as a general indication of activities which can be suggested to the child. The request is made to parents to engage intensively, one or both of them, with the child with the above activity for about an hour per day. This limited period of time should be sufficient to create every day an intense, planned type of sequential interaction. It helps both parent and child to develop sensitivity to each other and success with each.

The above approach has an ethological foundation which suggests that some systems of movements (i.e. affiliation, attachment, exploration of the other, etc.) may facilitate each other. It attempts to allow those adults who belong to the daily life of the children to interact with them on a level corresponding to their real cognitive development, essentially sensori-motor, to motivate them with adequate tactics and in this context to allow them to act on reality, know it better and develop their cognitive, communicative and further abilities. We call it Emotional Activation with Reciprocal Corporeal interaction (EARC: Zappella 1996, 1998). It is highly successful in the dysmaturational syndrome, described above, but it can be of help in a number of other situations. It is often implemented by the use of gestures in order to increase communication and by pointing to objects, photographs, pictograms. It gives the family a major therapeutic role but it usually goes together with an integration of other therapies, especially speech therapy. The approach suggested for the nursery is similar, but it is more focused on cooperative work conducted in small groups of children. In the nursery the child is mainstreamed and followed by a special teacher. After a few weeks or months a toddler may change and show important improvements in preverbal interactions but as well as having limited expressive language significant difficulty understanding other people's verbal language may become evident. In these cases care is taken to have adults and other children express themselves with an extensive use of gestures, by pointing to objects, by speaking slowly and in an expressive way. Pointing to figures, structuring short expressions through them can be achieved with a variety of tools, including Picture Communication

System and Bliss. A variety of boards can also be used to organise communication for the purposes of daily life. With these and other instruments Alternative and Augmentative Communication (AAC) becomes the main approach to improve the conditions of these children (Cafiero 1995, 1998).

Both the family and the nursery are helped by an organised pattern of the day with times for play, for music, for more specific cognitive abilities. The structure of the day is viewed as a form of communication and is more or less flexible according to the needs of the child.

In other children *verbal auditory agnosia* can reveal itself through a different clinical picture when, for example, accompanied by reduced socioaffective abilities and severe mental retardation. In these cases the neurobiological constraints may make these children less amenable to a behavioural change than in the example described above and, in addition to AAC, it may be appropriate to introduce a more rigorous structure with visual cues in order to help the child's understanding. The same considerations may apply to a non-verbal child with intensive hyperselectivity and repetitiveness.

In contrast we may have a toddler who develops with considerable *prosocial abilities* in terms of affectionate, friendly and playful behaviours associated with a superficial cocktail-party speech but *with considerable difficulties in verbal comprehension and elements of hyperlexia*. In these cases the toddlers are already able to master abilities connected with primary intersubjectivity and directed interactions with them should follow a different pattern. A programme can be organised with a special visual structure for reading stories at a higher level of comprehension, representing them concretely with puppets (or with other children), work with a minicomputer and a number of structured interactions at a spoken level with relatives and peers to increase social and linguistic abilities.

The tools of the intervention may be very different: in some cases work on primary intersubjectivity may profoundly change children's conditions, in others the neurobiological constraint will not allow a notable improvement, while in other children it would be inappropriate because the child has already mastered these abilities.

It is well known that *lack of joint attention* is a recurrent abnormality in autism and careful work on pointing, as described by Newson (Chapter 21 in this volume), is of paramount importance. Less care has been paid in the literature to *difficulties in oral and/or manual motor coordination* which are

frequent (Gibbs *et al.* 1999) and consistent with the presence of fine abnormalities of the cerebellum found in most neuropathological observations
(Bauman and Kemper 1997). In these cases, speech therapy work on the
coordination of the mouth is important and it can be appropriately implemented daily by short child–parent interactions modelled on holding for
pleasure where the parent gets into a vocal synthony with the child and
then gives the child a slightly different feedback, helping to duplicate
syllables and to structure words. The close face-to-face interaction,
especially if played in a nice, amusing way, can be of help to the child to
model the mouth and expressions in an appropriate way (Zappella 1987).
In these cases the use of low technology auxiliary helps, such as big Macs,
switches, etc., may be of great help in revealing and supporting the
abilities of these toddlers.

Many young children with autism have good visual abilities and
elements of a visual structuring of daily activities, either in the form of
images, photos, or initially with objects, also with the aim of an
autonomous organisation can be very helpful.

The use of images and colours can be of help in structuring a play environment where the toddler can be helped to organise himself in a more
autonomous way.

It must be added that the treatment of autistic children requires
creativity and invention on the part of the therapists as I have described in
another contribution (Zappella 1994b).

Another relevant point is concerned with the main actors of rehabilitation. At an early age *the family* plays a central role: it is therefore important
to consider the emotional condition of the family and of its components.
Feelings of alarm, fear, shame, sadness and rage may concern both parents
and can easily be followed by depression, especially in the mothers, by
diminished positive interactions between the parents, leading to disunion
and eventually separation, and by a marked reduction of social interactions outside the family. Social isolation of the family is often a consequence, and is often accompanied by a greater economic burden, which in
turn may be followed by a variety of unfortunate patterns. The social class
and the type of culture to which the family belongs may also have major
relevance. Many families, especially those coming from the economically
most advanced part of the country, feel excluded from the prevailing
culture of present society, based as it is on competition. A child with an
autistic disorder may often mean the end of a successful career for parents

and a poor outlook for their child. The risk of a profound disintegration of the family is a major one for the efficacy of every early intervention. The relationship with professionals from the first visit onwards is vital in order to improve the emotional atmosphere of the family, to start a new communication with the child and to coach parents in replicating it and to reinforce communication between parents and with the wider community. The need of therapeutic interventions, for example, for depression of one or both parents may be necessary. In this way early intervention aims at the same time to help the toddler directly and to support the family and its internal and external communication.

Thus there is great heterogeneity in the aetiology and presentation of autistic disorders and in the way each child develops over time. Some key points in early intervention are as follows:

1. making use of many elements of early infant–parent relationships to improve social interaction and relationships

2. the development or recovery of abilities, following a developmental sequence

3. giving a human and a visual structure

4. above all, communication at a preverbal, gestural level and at a verbal level.

A precise profile for the intervention should be geared on the profile of the child's disabilities, those specific to autistic disorders as well as those which frequently occur with it (for example, disorders of coordination).

Rehabilitation and pedagogic approaches can be enriched by an appropriate and specific use of drugs. Early intervention in autism has been the object of an extensive literature and of a number of therapies. The present possibility to distinguish among different subgroups in terms of dysfunctional versus neurological disorders, of disorders characterised by a specific course versus more stable disorders and in terms of specific disabilities may well increase the possibility of more adequate treatments. The evidence reported in this chapter suggests, for example, that only a few young children with autistic behaviour, belonging to precise subgroups and syndromes, can eventually reach a favourable outcome and that it is the quality, not the full day intensity, of the intervention that helps them. If these conclusions are confirmed, it will be appropriate to modify those statements in favour of the 'intensity' of early programmes.

Finally it is also worth noting that some of the special methods for the treatment of autism are closely similar to those used elsewhere: for example, Elizabeth Newson's and John Richer's approaches have much in common with what we are doing in Siena. The use of their methods should bring similar advantages to children, for example, belonging to the dysmaturative syndrome, who, in contrast, would probably not benefit from other approaches organised on a rigid, monotonous structuring of life based on repetitive activities.

It may well be that in the near future there will be a confluence, and at the same time a clear distinction, of therapeutic approaches, tailoring early interventions to the specific disabilities and conditions of the child. This would certainly be to the advantage of the child with autistic disorder and, more extensively, of the child's family.

References

Baron-Cohen, S., Scahill, V.L., Izaguirre, J., Hornsey, H. and Robertson, M.M. (1999) 'The prevalence of Gilles de la Tourette syndrome in children and adolescents with autism: a large scale study.' *Psychological Medicine 29*, 1151—1159.

Bauman, M.L. and Kemper, T.L. (1997) 'The neurobiology of autism.' Baltimore, MD: Johns Hopkins University Press.

Birnbrauer, J.S. and Leach, D.J. (1993) 'The Murdoch early intervention program after 2 years.' *Behaviour Change 10*, 63–74.

Bishop, D.V.M. (1985) 'Age of onset and outcome in "acquired aphasia with convulsive disorder" (Landau-Kleffner Syndrome).' *Developmental Medicine and Child Neurology 27*, 705–712.

Cafiero, J.M. (1995) 'Teaching parents of children with autism picture communication symbols as a natural language to decrease level of family stress.' (doctoral dissertation, University of Toledo, 1995). Dissertation Abstracts International, University Microfilms, no. 9540360.

Cafiero, J.M. (1998) 'Communication power for individuals with autism.' *Focus on Autism and Other Developmental Disabilities 13*, 113–121.

Chess, S. (1977) 'Follow up report on autism in congenital rubella.' *Journal of Autism and Childhood Schizophrenia 7*, 69–81.

Chugani, D.C., Musik, O., Rothermel, R., Behen, M., Chakraborty, P., Manguer, T., da Silva, E.A. and Chugani, H.T. (1997) 'Altered serotonin synthesis in the dento-thalamo-cortical pathways in autistic boys.' *Annals of Neurology 42*, 666–669.

De Bona, C., Zappella, M., Hayek, G., Meloni, I., Vitelli, F., Bruttini, M., Cusano, R., Loffredo, P., Longo, I. and Renieri, A. (2000) 'Preserved speech variant is allelic of classic Rett syndrome.' *European Journal of Human Genetics. 8*, 325–330.

DeLong, G.R. and Heinz, E.R. (1997) 'The clinical syndrome of early life bilateral hippocampal sclerosis.' *Annals of Neurology 42*, 11–17.

DeLong, G.R., Teague, L.A. and McSwain Kamram, M. (1998) 'Effects of fluoxetine treatment in young children with idiopathic autism.' *Developmental Medicine and Child Neurology 40*, 551–562.

Deonna, T., Ziegler, A., Malin-Ingvar, M., Ansermet, F. and Roulket, E. (1995) 'Reversible behavioural autistic-like regression: a manifestation of a special (new?) epileptic syndrome in a 28-month-old child. A 2-year longitudinal study.' *Neurocase 1*, 1–9.

Gibbs, J., Cogher, L., Savage, L. and Smith, M. (1999) 'Specific language impairment and autism.' *Developmental Medicine and Child Neurology 41*, Supplement 81.

Greenspan, S.I. and Wieder, S. (1997) 'Developmental patterns and outcomes in infants and children with disorders in relating and communicating: a chart review of 200 cases of children with autistic spectrum diagnoses.' *Journal of Developmental and Learning Disorders 1*, 87–141.

Harris, S.L. (1998) 'Behavioural and educational approaches to the pervasive developmental disorders.' In F.R. Volkmar (ed) *Autism and Pervasive Developmental Disorders*. Cambridge: Cambridge University Press.

Harris, S.L. and Handleman, J.S. (1994) *Preschool Education Programs for Children with Autism*. Austin, TX: Pro-Ed.

Howlin, P. (1997) 'Prognosis in autism: do specialist treatments affect long-term outcome?' *European Child and Adolescent Psychiatry 6*, 55–72.

Hoyson, M., Jaieson, B. and Strain, P.S. (1984) 'Individualized group instruction of normally developing and autistic-like children: a description and evaluation of the LEAP curriculum model.' *Journal of the Division of Early Childhood 8*, 157–171.

International Molecular Genetic Study of Autism Consortium (1998) 'A full genome screen for autism with evidence for linkage to a region on chromosome 7q.' *Human Molecular Genetics 7*, 571–578.

Levine, J.D., Andrews, R., Chez, M., Patil, A.A., Devinsky. O., Smith, M., Kanner, A., Davis, J.T., Funke, M., Jones, G., Chong, B., Provencal, S., Weisend, M., Lee, R.R and Orrison, W.W. (1999) 'Magnetoencephalography patterns of epileptiform activity in children with regressive Autism Spectrum Disorders.' *Pediatrics 104*, 405–418.

Lovaas, O.I. (1987) 'Behavioural treatment and normal educational and intellectual functioning in young autistic children.' *Journal of Consulting Clinical Psychology 55*, 3–9.

Page, T., Yu A., Fontanesi, J. and Nyhan, W.L. (1997) 'Developmental disorder associated with increased cellular nucleotidase activity.' *Proceedings of the National Academy of Sciences USA 94*, 11601–11606.

Philippe, A., Martinez, M., Giulloud-Bataille, M., Gillberg, C., Rastam, M., Sponheim, E., Coleman, M., Zappella, M., Aschauer, H., van Malldergerme, L., Penet, C., Feingold, J., Brice, A., Leboyer, M. and the Paris Autism Research International Sibpair Study (1999) 'Genome-wide scan for autism susceptibility genes.' *Human Molecular Genetics 8*, 805–812.

Prekop, J. (1984) 'Erfolgsrate der Therapie durch "Festhalten".' *Der Kinderartz 6*, 1170–1175.

Rogers, S.J. (1996) 'Early intervention in autism.' *Journal of Autism and Developmental Disorders 26*, 243–246.

Rogers, S.J. and Di Lalla, D.L. (1991) 'A comparative study of the effects of a developmentally based preschool curriculum on young children with autism and young children with other disorders of behaviour and development.' *Topics in Early Childhood Special Education 11*, 29–47.

Rutter, M., Andersen-Wood, L., Beckett, C., Brerdenkampt, D., Castle, J., Groothues, C., Kreppner, J., Keayeney, L., Lord, C., O'Connor, T.G. and the English and Romanian Adoptees (ERA) Study Team (1999) 'Quasi-autistic patterns following severe early global deprivation.' *Journal of Child Psychology and Psychiatry 40*, 537–549.

Trevarthen, C. (1979) 'Communication and co-operation in early infancy: a description of primary intersubjectivity.' In M. Bullowa (ed) *Before Speech: The Beginnings of Human Communication*. London: Cambridge University Press.

Trevarthen, C., Aitkin, K., Papoudi, D. and Robarts, J. (1998) *Children with Autism*. London: Jessica Kingsley Publishers.

Tuchman, R., and Rapin, I. (1997) 'Regression in pervasive developmental disorders: seizures and epileptiform electroencephalographic correlates.' *Pediatrics 99*, 560–566.

Volkmar, F.R. and Nelson, D.S. (1990) 'Seizure disorders in autism.' *Journal of the American Academy of Child and Adolescent Psychiatry 29, 127–129*.

White, C. and Cameron, M. (1987) *Portage Early Education Programme*. Windsor: NFER-Nelson

Zappella, M. (1987) *I bambini autistici, l'holding e la famiglia*. Rome: Nuova Italia Scientifica.

Zappella, M. (1992) 'The Rett girls with preserved speech.' *Brain and Development 14*, 98–101.

Zappella, M. (1994a) 'Bambini autistici che guariscono: l'esempio dei tic complessi familiari.' *Terapia di Famiglia 46*, 51–62.

Zappella, M. (1994b) 'Shared emotions and rapid recovery in children with delayed development.' *The Clinical Application of Ethology and Attachment Theory, Occasional Papers no. 9.* Association for Child Psychology and Psychiatry.

Zappella, M. (1996/1998) *Autismo Infantile: studi sulla affettività e le emozioni.* Rome: Carocci. Span. trans: Autismo Infantil, Fundo de Cultura Economica, Mexico, 1998.

Zappella, M. (1999) 'Familial complex tics and autistic behaviour with favourable outcome in young children.' *Infanto (Brasil)*, in press.

Zappella, M. (2000) 'A dysmaturational syndrome: early onset complex tics, reversible autistic behaviour with outcome in attention deficit with hyperactivity.' *Developmental Medicine and Child Neurology* (submitted).

Zappella, M., Gillberg, C. and Ehlers, S. (1999) 'The preserved speech variant: a subgroup of the Rett complex. A clinical report of 30 cases.' *Journal of Autism and Developmental Disorders 28*, 519–526.

CHAPTER II

Complementary Medicine in Autistic Disorders

Results from the Application of a Working Hypothesis

Edward Danczak

Abstract

The treatment of Autistic Spectrum Disorders is helped by trying to understand the underlying causes. Many differing causes have been suggested including food allergy, infections, brain damage, poisoning, metal deficiencies, vaccine damage and vitamin deficiencies.

Studies of brain circulation suggest that there is an impairment of activity over the fronto-parietal areas which would be expected to limit function in speech, perception, coordination and motor skills.

Selection of treatment depends on the recognition of the underlying cause, which appears to be a heritable failure of the immune system and the metabolic effects of that failure. This is supported by twin and family studies, together with direct evidence from the children.

Signalling hormones from the disturbed immune system interfere with brain cell function, and due to deficiencies in the immune system responses to common antigens are reduced, reflecting low T cells and in turn lower production of antibodies.

Deficiencies of metals such as Zinc and Magnesium compound this because much of immune cell activity is dependent upon them.

Phenol sulphyltransferase (PST) deficiency leads to poor detox management; toxic Sulphite is not converted to sulphate. In the presence of Sulphite, acquisition of immune tolerance is disturbed.

Treatment in this programme is directed towards restoring normal gut function, using complex homeopathic medicines and probiotics. Improvement in liver function is achieved by reducing the load on PST by diet, and by replacing minerals in deficiency. Gut function is impaired by mineral deficiency so reabsorption of toxic metabolites and food substances is reduced by using active laxatives.

Twenty children were diagnosed using DSM protocols in clinics in India, Pakistan, USA, UK, Egypt, UAE and Saudi Arabia.

Results from these twenty treated children showed that fifteen had Sulphite in the urine, before treatment, but after six months of treatment there was a complete absence of Sulphite in 60 per cent and a significant fall in 13 per cent. This was associated with positive behavioural changes including reduced hyperactivity, more referring gaze, and better social interaction, faster speech acquisition, better use of computational skills, improvements in perceptive development, and improved hand–eye coordination.

Physical symptoms such as night sweats were reduced. There were fewer attendances for ear, nose and throat (ENT) and upper respiratory tract infection (URTI) problems. Weight and height increased reflecting improved bowel function, diarrhoea and constipation resolved and continence improved.

Confounders include behavioural intervention, concurrent drug treatment, drug interactions, and placebo response.

Introduction: a working hypothesis for underlying physiological dysfunctions in autism

The results of treatment applying the working hypothesis outlined in this chapter suggest that management of the underlying biochemistry and immune disorder can be associated with improvement in functional activity and behaviour. To treat these conditions requires some understanding of the underlying disorders, and management of these appears to offer some help. The use of complementary medicines can be helpful in the biochemical management of Autistic Spectrum Disorders.

Over 175 autistic children have attended my practice; their progress is being monitored and they are in various stages of recovery. This chapter refers to a group of twenty children in 1997–8 who were entered into the study simultaneously and followed up together over a period of six months.

What is the cause?

There is no single answer. The search for an effective treatment has been undermined by the desire to find a *single* effective treatment. To date there has been none.

Among suggested causes has been food allergy (Egger *et al.* 1985) and candida infection (Shaw and Chaves 1996) suggesting an incompetent immune system. Immune cell loss, with inadequate numbers of lympho-cytes and poor immunoglobulin production supports this (Gupta *et al.* 1998). A form of poisoning has been suggested when children with lead poisoning were seen to have significant behavioural changes (Marlow *et al.* 1983). Other heavy metals such as mercury will produce changes in behaviour and mental retardation (Rea 1996). Brain mapping by Egger has shown that fronto-parietal circulation is impaired, consistent with poor speech development and perceptive disorders leading to poor com-munication. Motor development and coordination function is also impaired with evidence of poor hand–eye coordination and a likely sensory ataxia.

How do we make a choice in treatment?

Treatment in all medical activity should be directed towards the underlying causes of illness. It is no good for example treating the symp-tomatic cough of bacterial pneumonia while ignoring that the underlying infection will respond to antibiotic treatment.

What is the underlying cause?

There seems to be a heritable failure of the immune system complicated by the metabolic effects of that failure.

Twin studies are helpful, showing a concordance in identical twins of close to 70 per cent (Bailey *et al.* 1995). In my own practice I have a number of identical twins with autism. It is important to recognise, however, that despite being identical, the severity of autism appears to be different in each of the children reflecting some environmental effects upon the gene expression.

Indirect evidence of immune incompetence is indicated by family histories where there is an increased incidence of atopy (asthma and eczema), irritable bowel particularly in the mother, autoimmune conditions such as SLE (systemic lupus erythematosus), and immune arthritis such as rheumatoid arthritis. Grandparents frequently have a strong history of multiple joint arthritis. In my own practice I have more children with parents with Crohns disease than I would have expected.

The concentration of the gene pool for atopy together with dietary changes suggests that the risk of developing Autistic Spectrum Disorders is likely to be increasing with over 4 million atopic individuals in the population at present.

Direct evidence in the child includes glue ear, with recurrent Otitis media events, having numerous courses of antibiotics, recurrent upper respiratory tract infections are common and food reactions have been noted frequently by parents discovering their child reacts badly with deterioration in symptoms on exposure to common foods such as wheat or milk. There is frequently a history of persistent diarrhoea with episodic constipation (Goodwin and Cowen 1971; Mann and Truswell 1998).

What immune incompetence?

Studies have focused upon three areas, the signalling link between immune cells, the presence of immune cells and the production of immunoglobulins.

The immune system signals between its parts by the use of interleukins which are numbered peptides and which have specific inflammatory and pro-inflammatory activity. Il2, Il6 and Tumour necrosis factor are particularly raised in concentration indicating an active immune process. Biopsy of the bowel has shown a failure of white cell activity suggesting an interference in antigen (foreign body) consumption.

Interleukins can interfere with brain cell function. Tumour necrosis factor impairs astrocyte cell membrane function with evidence of calcium channel failure which is incidentally dependent upon Magnesium (Koller, Thiem and Siebler 1996).

Lymphocytes are grouped into T and B cell types. T cells effectively run the immune system and have different numerical classification prefixed CD. CD4, helper cells, have been shown to be low in 7 out of 45 children and in the same children CD8 killer cells are low in 16 out of 45 (Gupta *et al.* 1998).

As a result of this, it would be expected that the production of immune responses to challenge will be adversely affected. The response to mumps was reduced in 29 out of these 45, to candida by 12 out of 45 and tetanus by 16 out of 45. In my own practice a child being monitored for immune status lost his immunity to tetanus over a six-month period.

What else is low?

Frequently Zinc is low, and this has importance in both the immune system and in healing. There are over 150 enzyme processes dependent on Zinc (Mann and Truswell 1998).

It is a co-factor in immune enzymes; Thymulin for example favours T cell activity, with differing concentrations helping both CD4 and CD8 cells. This will thus affect resistance to infection (Prasad 1998).

Zinc is involved in cell repair. It has a positive effect on the migration of epithelial cells. Topical zinc was used for many years to promote wound healing. Over 90 per cent of atopic individuals are short on Zinc.

In the digestive tract Zinc has direct effects on taste and smell. For many years until sophisticated laboratory tests were available, detection of Zinc deficiency involved a simple taste test; the patient was given a strong tasting substance, no taste was recognised. Zinc was then given and the test repeated; the successful recognition by taste and smell confirmed the Zinc deficiency which had been present. Autistic children appears to enjoy very strongly flavoured foods. Zinc is also important in fat metabolism (Mann and Truswell 1998).

Poor Zinc levels appear to be related to increase in gut infection. Diarrhoea exacerbates Zinc depletion since it is very rich in Zinc. The normal pancreas secretes a Zinc rich digestive juice. Homeopathic VEGA machine testing frequently shows the pancreas as a stressed organ. It is possible that Secretin given therapeutically causes large amounts of digestive juices to be made which by virtue of the amount of Zinc present has a protective effect on the gut and will help in gut healing. The peptidase enzymes which are responsible for breakdown of casein and gluten in the bowel are both zinc dependent (Reichelt *et al.* 1994). Zinc has been shown to be of value in behavioural disorders (Lewith *et al.* 1996).

Magnesium is particularly important in cell membrane and pump activity, and is important in ATP management. It is of proven value in behavioural disorders (Pfeiffer *et al.* 1995).

Liver function is reflected in detoxification metabolism; a specific area of interest is the enzyme system phenol Sulphyl transferase (PST). This group of enzymes is the principal route through which excess neurotransmitters are broken down such as adrenaline. A deficiency in this enzyme system is frequently associated with hyperactivity and attention deficit (O'Reilly and Waring 1993). It was thought at one time that this may be an indicator for autism but has been shown to be obtunded in schizophrenia, irritable bowel, migraine and asthma. In the presence of an incompetent PST enzyme system there is a reduced level of immune tolerance.

Detoxification depends on centrilobular access in the liver via the portal vein. The release of interleukins from the gut may produce a mild hepatitis with limitation of uptake of substrate into the centrilobular areas where the detox enzymes are concentrated. Thus in addition to an absolute deficiency of PST, which may be exacerbated by food substances such as Tartrazine which interferes with PST activity and Molybdenum (co-factor) deficiency there is a relative deficiency caused by access problems.

A ready measure of this enzyme system's competence is the presence of Sulphite in the urine.

Can this enzyme failure be treated?

By reducing the level of gut disturbance and consequent release of interleukins, the access to the centrilobular area of the liver should be increased. If foods are excluded which load this enzyme system and which may impede its effectiveness, then more enzyme should be available to break down catecholamine. Removing food substances which have a smiliar basic structure to adrenaline like compounds would be expected to help. This group of foods contains phenolic base structured chemicals and would be expected to load the PST enzyme system. Reducing the food phenolic chemical load is an extensive and laborious dietary management scheme.

Using a smaller group of foods within this group, such as the salicylate group of foods is helpful. It does have the advantage of removing food colourants (Weiss 1986) and highly allergenic foods such as tomatoes

(Egger *et al.* 1985) and introducing potato chips. McDonald's is one of the first places my patients become familiar with!

In addition increasing gut throughput will prevent reabsorption of toxins and toxic metabolites. This is standard management when there is a reabsorption process affecting the large bowel.

Probiotics

Nutrition of gut mucosa depends upon the presence of a normal population of gut commensals. In autistic children there is an abnormality of gut population with relative excess of candida species. Acidophilus bacteria may have a supportive role in enhancement of B interferon production (Plummer 1992). Supportive prescription of probiotics is thus indicated.

Conventional medical intervention

In orthodox approaches Nystatin, Lactulose, food avoidance, and drug intervention such as Ritalin and Haloperidol have been used.

By contrast in this technique no psychotropic drugs are given, and in fact very few parents arrive in my UK practice with their children on Ritalin or Haloperidol.

Outline of treatment

Investigation

Because investigations are funded by parents, investigations are kept to a minimum. A hair sample is taken for mineral analysis (Wecker *et al.* 1985) and sent to Biolab in London who have analysed in excess of 70,000 samples and have good retest reliability.

A urine sample is analysed for Sulphite and D Glucaric acid which reflects the detoxification functions.

Investigations using a VEGA machine, a modified form of electroacupuncture, are performed.

Diagnosis

All twenty children had been diagnosed previously using DSM protocols in clinics in India, Pakistan, USA, UK, Egypt, UAE and Saudi Arabia.

Treatment résumé

For all children hair and urine samples are taken at the beginning of treatment.

A complex homeopathic medicine is given in drop form, together with a probiotic containing two species of Lactobacillus, and E Coli (not pathogenic no. 0157). Following hair sampling metal replacement is undertaken with dosage larger than the RDA for the size and weight. An isopathic homeopathic medicine Phenol C30 is given to desensitise the child to remaining food phenolics in the body and diet (Lewith *et al.* 1996).

A low salicylate diet is introduced.

Results

Hair sample analysis showed the following minerals in deficiency in order of frequency: Zinc 100 per cent, Magnesium 60 per cent, Selenium 35 per cent, Manganese 30 per cent and Chrome 15 per cent.

Table 11.1 shows comparative results over three measurements taken at three monthly intervals for urinary Sulphite and D Glucaric acid.

All children with raised D Glucaric acid levels had Sulphite in the urine although the reverse is not true. There were children with low D Glucaric acid levels with positive urinary Sulphite.

There were seven children with raised D Glucaric acid levels indicating liver stress. Of these six returned to the normal range on this protocol. One had a rise in D Glucaric acid but this was not associated with a Sulphite rise.

Looking at the Sulphite group there were fifteen children (75 per cent) who were Sulphite positive which in nine went to zero (60 per cent). There was a substantial fall in two (13 per cent) and no change in three (20 per cent). One child had an increase in Sulphite concentration (6 per cent).

After the first three months of mineral support if no appreciable fall in Sulphite was seen liquid Molybdenum was given as a daily supplement in addition to the metals.

What behavioural changes were seen?

There was a reduction or absence of hyperactivity and improved attention. These were reflected principally in improved sleep and concentration.

	D-Glucaric acid			Sulphate		
Table 11.1						
Abnormal Levels:	*Borderline 8.5+ Increased 12.5+ Marked 30.0+*			*Over 0*		
Test date	*July 97*	*Oct 97*	*Feb 98*	*July 97*	*Oct 97*	*Feb 98*
Child No.						
11423	14.4	4.1	6.0	2.5	4	1.5
11434	6.0	2.4	4.7	nil	nil	nil
11436	20.6	5.7	10.7	18.5	6	nil
11418	18.3	9.2	8.4	10.5	nil	2.5
11422	9.8	3.4	10.2	7	1	nil
11405	4.0	2.7	5.2	5	4	nil
11413	7.2	4.9	3.8	nil	1.5	2.5
11431	2.9	7.6	2.9	4	nil	nil
11649	10.4	3.2	3.7	1	1	nil
11432A	6.2	2.8	3.8	4	3	nil
11432 Ai	15.2	1.4	2.8	16	2.5	4.5
11410	12.9	6.4	16.8	16	1.5	nil
11417	11.3	5.1	8.9	nil	nil	nil
11428	7.6	9.2	11.7	16	nil	nil
11433	4.8	2.5	–	nil	nil	–
11435	12.7	4.5	4.1	5	nil	nil
11411	4.5	7.9	10.2	nil	nil	nil
11408	11.4	5.0	10.6	1	3	1.5
11416	7.8	3.1	4.2	9	2	3.5
11421	18.2	4.7	4.0	2	7	nil

Summary				
D Glucaric acid		**Sulphite**		
Before treatment:				
Raised concentration:	7	Sulphite:	positve	15
			negative	5
After treatment:				
Fall to normal	6	Zero reading	9	60%
Rise	1	Fall	2	13%
		Unchanged	3	20%
		Increase	1	6%

Table 11.1 Urinary Sulphite and D Glucaric acid measures.

Referring gaze improved, together with social interaction such a parallel play and interaction with other children. Language acquisition improved, together with computational skills such as mathematics. Perceptive development was noticeable with children exploring sensory aspects such as carpet stroking or running water where previously afraid of it. Improved hand–eye coordination was seen with one high-functioning child being invited to join the school cricket team.

Did all children achieve the same recovery level?

Children were at different ages, and the disease process had been present for different periods and in different degrees of severity.

Infections and gut function improved. There was a reduction or absence of night sweats. Attendances for ENT and URTI were reduced. Weight and height increased consistent with bowel function improvement. Continence improved with absence of diarrhoea and constipation.

Confounders

Among the group were children receiving Lovaas therapy. One of the children had been managed with a combination of Ritalin, Phenergan and Haloperidol producing akathisia a recognised side-effect of Haloperidol excess. Removal of these medicines led to a rapid resolution of the akathisia and agitation caused by Phenergan. Hyperactivity is a recognised side-effect of Phenergan in children.

The possibility of placebo effects must always be borne in mind, especially in autism where, because of the severity of this illness, parents are desperate to find improvement. The meaning of some behavioural changes must also be carefully considered, for instance avoidance of eye contact in some of the societies the children came from is a sign of deferential respect and so increase in eye contact cannot be relied upon as a marker for clinical improvement.

Conclusion

The results of the treatments on these twenty children, taken together with the emerging results from a larger number of children, suggest that this treatment and the working model are worth pursuing, especially considering the speed and economy with which the improvements are achieved. Clearly, controlled trials are needed, but these early results are promising and consistent with other developments in the field.

References

Bailey, A., Le Couteur, A., Gottesman, I., Bolton, P., Simonoff, E., Yudza, E. and Rutter, M. (1995) 'Autism as a strongly genetic disorder: evidence from a British twin study.' *Psychological Medicine 25*, 1, 63–77.

Egger, J., Carter, C.M., Graham, P., Gumley, D. and Soothill, J.F. (1985) 'Controlled trial of oligoantigenic diet treatment in the Hyperkinetic syndrome.' *Lancet* 540–545

Goodwin, M.S. and Cowen, M.A. (1971) 'Malabsorption and cerebral dysfunction: a multivariate and comparative study of autistic children.' *Journal of Autism and childhood Schizophrenia 1*, 1, 48–62.

Gupta, S., Aggarwal, S., Rashanravan, B. and Lee, T. (1998) 'Th1-and Th2-like Cytokines in CD4+ and CD8+ T cells in autism.' *Journal of Neuroimmunology 85*, 1, 106–9.

Koller, H., Thiem, K. and Siebler, M. (1996) 'Tumour Necrosis Factor-alpha increases intracellular calcium and induces a depolarisation in cultured astroglial cells.' *Brain 116*, (pt 6), 2021–2027

Lewith, G.T., Kenyon, J.N. and Lewis, P. (1996) *Complementary Medicine: An Integrated Approach.* Oxford: Oxford University Press.

Mann, J.I. and Truswell, J.S. (1998) *Essentials of Human Nutrition.* Oxford: Oxford University Press.

Marlow, M., Errera, J. and Jacobs, J. *(1983) 'Increased lead and cadmium burdens among mentally retarded children and children with borderline intelligence.' American Journal of Mental Deficiency 87*, 5, 477–483.

O'Reilly, B.A. and Waring, R. (1993) 'Enzyme and sulphur oxidation deficiencies in autistic children with known food/chemical intolerances.' *Journal of Orthomolecular Medicine 4*, 198–200.

Pfeiffer, S.I., Norton, J., Nelson, L. and Shott, S. (1995) 'Efficacy of Vitamin B6, and magnesium in the treatment of autism: a methodology review and summary of outcomes.' *Journal of Autism and Developmental Disorders 25*, 485–493.

Plummer (1992) *Lactic Acid Bacteria and their Role in Human Health.* Birmingham: BioMed Publications.

Prasad, A.S. (1998) 'Zinc and immunity.' *Journal of Molecular and Cellular Biochemistry 188*, 1–2, 63–69.

Rea, W. (1996) *Chemical Sensivity Volume III.* London: CRC Press.

Reichelt, K.L., Knivsberg, A.M., Nodland, M. and Lind, G. (1994) 'Nature and consequences of hyperpeptiduria and bovine caseinomorphs found in autistic syndromes.' *Developmental Brain Dysfunction 7*, 71–85.

Shaw, W. and Chaves, E. (1996) 'Abnormal urine organic acids associated with fungal metabolism in urine samples of children with autism.' *Consensus Report of the DAN Group.* San Diego, CA: Autism Research Institute.

Wecker, L., Miller, S.B., Cochran, S.R., Dugger, D.L. and Johnson, W.D. (1985) 'Trace element concentrations in hair from autistic children.' *Journal of Mental Deficiency Research 29* (pt 1), 15–22.

Weiss, B. (1986) 'Food additives as a source of behavioural disturbances in children.' *Neurotoxicology 7*, 197–208.

Additional source material

Autism Research Institute, 4182 Adams Avenue, San Diego, California, USA, CA92116.

Baker, S.M. and Pangborn, J.B. (1995) 'Clinical Assessment Options for Children with Autism and related Disorders.' DAN Conference, Dallas, January.

Passwater, R.A. and Cranton, E.M. (1983) *Trace Elements, Hair Analysis and Nutrition.* New Canaan: Keats Publishing Inc.

PART 3

Meeting of Minds

CHAPTER 12

Editorial

Meeting of Minds

John Richer and Sheila Coates

Autistic children's difficulty in the meeting of minds goes to the heart of the condition. The difficulties that autistic children have in reaching out to others, and others have in reaching out into the minds of the children, are the daily experience of all who are with them. They 'live in a world of their own', i.e. not ours. One offshoot of this experience has been the idea that these children are 'mind-blind', that they have a specific difficulty in seeing the viewpoint of others, something necessary for human communication. While interesting and fruitful, this idea, like so many from experimental psychology, has proved to be too narrowly focused. Specific difficulty in seeing the viewpoint of others is neither specific to autism nor present in all autistic people. The difficulty is part of a wider difficulty in acquiring the skills of the culture (e.g. language, social signals) with which communication, and so the meeting of minds, can take place. The meeting of minds is extremely difficult, but is the goal towards which most parents and other adults strive.

In Chapter 13 Sheila Coates emphasises the importance of developing trusting communicating relationships with a child, before much meaningful education can proceed. As with the development of the intersubjective relationship between babies and their caregivers, this may involve simple playful interaction, following a child's interest to develop a shared attention as, for instance, in the Option approach, or helping a child to follow an adult's direction, as in the Lovaas programme. Both involve the adult closely monitoring the emerging mutual interaction and relationship.

Play, discussed by Janert (Chapter 14) and by Sherratt (Chapter 15), has the potential for achieving this end, since it focuses on what the child is attending to and sharing that activity. With most non-autistic children, play is an effective form of learning and of developing and maintaining relationships. The play activity, chosen as it is by the child, is 'top of mind' for that child at that moment. If the adult can sensitively tune in to that interest (see what is in the child's mind) and, even better, challenge and add to that activity (share what is in her or his mind with the child) a meeting of minds takes place and the child's development is taken forward and the relationship enriched.

However, playing with autistic children is very difficult. The children, unlike most children, do not initiate play activities or try to involve the adult. Instead the adult has to do the 'unnatural' thing and initiate play. This often fails since the activity is misjudged, it is not in the child's mind. Most adults quickly run out of play ideas, and are discouraged by the failure of the interaction. Both Janert and Sherratt in this volume and elsewhere argue for the value of play in the meeting of minds and offer many play ideas.

Otter and Masefield discuss the controversial topic of Facilitated Communication (FC) in Chapter 16. It is not to be seen as a 'treatment' but FC has held out the prospect that there can be a meeting of minds with autistic children whose minds were previously thought to be unreachable. However, FC has been strongly criticised as being only a 'clever Hans' phenomenon, and clear experimental evidence produced to show that the facilitator, not the child, is actually answering the questions. Most people have therefore dismissed the communication achieved via FC as illusory. With a number of children and facilitators this is probably true. However, the experience with this technique has led a number of teachers and clinicians to believe that sometimes there may be genuine communication from the child.

Otter and Masefield have carefully and sensitively explored FC for a long period. Their work demonstrates the value of close careful observation and respectful interaction, by people who know their children intimately (and not just in a hit and run way as experimental subjects). They wanted to see if there was any value in this technique. Their conclusion is that for many autistic children it has value, and that there are collateral benefits, but considerable discipline, care and respect are necessary if this meeting of minds is really to take place.

CHAPTER 13

The Relationship IS the Thing

Sheila Coates

I contribute as a teacher, who for more than twenty years has been trying to explore what creates an effective learner–teacher partnership with an autistic child.

As a headteacher I have tried to support staff so that they can be confident in their efforts to explore the learning tools which create an effective partnership. Most teachers are used to a framework, an agreed syllabus or a method for learning. In normal development the tools for such learning are established by the time a child enters the nursery or pre-school phase. As teachers we can only 'shape' the experience a child has already acquired. For some children there are voids in the early 'experience gathering' parts of development. Before learning can begin we have to address these. They are particularly evident for the child with autism in the following areas:

1. shared interpersonal attention which develops through the attachment processes

2. joint attention shared with an object or pursuit —

3. the ability to act directly on one's own surroundings in a meaningful ongoing way.

In early child development 'shared attention' forms a channel for the child and primary caregiver (usually baby and mother) to give and take, mutually explore, and develop subtle reciprocal understandings. It is now recognised that children with autism have an impaired capacity for this shared attention, or they may develop it and lose it (Trevarthen *et al.* 1996).

Mutual gazing, rough and tumble, word play, sophisticated joking/ punning/computer games, may be among the tools employed in the teacher's search to find a point of joint attention, of shared interest, of mutuality. Anne Alvarez (1992) in her work with Robbie describes the extreme search for a lifeline to reach an autistic child. Without a point of contact it is impossible to begin a learner–teacher dynamic. *Connecting with the child*

In a shared activity a teacher might follow approaches such as the Options approach, or Intensive Interaction, where the focus is on the teacher following the child's interest and so engaging in the child's reality. Conversely the applied behaviour approaches – TEACCH, SPELL, Lovaas – help the child to follow adult direction. Both types of approaches are effective. The necessary ingredient in both methods is the capacity of the adult to monitor the emerging mutual interaction and relationship. This is very like the development of the relationship between baby and mother. Mother assumes understanding by the baby but compatible with what baby can understand. A process develops into mutual understanding, shared meaning. The timings, pace and direction of these interchanges have been clearly demonstrated as in Elizabeth Newson's papers (Newson, this volume).

In the current English education system, desired outcomes have to be specified in advance. A child with autism may take a convoluted and unconventional route to change. This may require imagination, design and years of patience to accomplish and neither method nor outcome can be precisely specified in advance. Take the child who learnt to read using the Beatles song titles: no place for phonics or word building for this child. Take the child where staff suggested he might learn to 'greet people' as a target but then the next target was to 'stop' the same child greeting anyone unconditionally.

How can we help children enough to share with us what they know and understand, and also what they want to know! We can use speech, signing, augmented communication, rhebus/PECS: the choice is daunting. The available route to communication for any child may be only as good as the communicator. Niko Tinbergen and close colleague Dr John Richer helped to support our early understanding of observation and the description of behaviour. However, to understand the structure of an autistic child's behaviour sometimes seems impossible. Nevertheless I am struck by the quality of observation and intuition which staff translate into subtle changes of their own behaviour, or the environment. This contrasts at the other extreme with the pursuance of a teaching/therapy 'by numbers' approach, following rigid guidelines. At its best this can give a framework within which a closer relationship can be negotiated; more commonly however real communication is missed. The potential for observing behaviour, reflecting on its function, and adapting accordingly, promotes the magic of communication.

Good observation and intervention can take place only if the staffing allows for the diligence required to observe children with autism. The capacity to observe and describe in detail has to be a major justification for a high pupil–person ratio. In many instances the moment of realisation, a revelation, is fleeting, not obviously relevant to the present situation and can be in danger of not being shared again. From the non-verbal to highly verbal child the same moments of contact can be missed.

If a close communicating relationship can be established, the child's development can accelerate. Group work and shared classroom experiences can be possible only if we first manage to find a way of developing shared attention with the individual. If we can begin to engage in activity with the child, the deliberations between the learner and teacher require what the late Dr Geoffrey Waldon described as a 'tolerance and constraint' (Waldon 1984).

While the process of shared attention is developing, young children are also learning about themselves, as a body in a space – with gravity, an ability to extend physically, contact and focus interest on an interesting object outside themselves. This discovery soon needs to be shared with another. The process of sharing becomes a strategic part of the child's capacity to learn from another. The learner–teacher dyad can begin to evolve.

If I have managed to share attention directly with a pupil, a lap play, peek-a-boo, or if together we have begun to look at an object of interest – a book, a computer, a toy – how can I begin to develop a potential for new learning to happen? As a teacher I might want to introduce an idea to my pupil. How do I go about it? What clues, ideas, guidelines and triggers can I give to coerce, lure and interest our anxious and avoidant learner? What, where and how do boundaries or constraints influence the learner? Can the child cope with a small change I have introduced? Is it avoided, ignored, swept, away, spat at? It is in the area of tolerance and constraint that most problems arise. We can introduce change too quickly. We unwittingly miss out simple steps, we don't prepare in advance of change, 'sit down, stand up, finish now, book away'. We need the strength of the contact, the trust, the relationship between the learner and the teacher to help the child to tolerate a change, to look from another's point of view.

Dr Waldon described the interplay between tolerance and constraint as one of the most powerful tools for learning. Many of the skills we teach assume an underlying gathering of this general experience. For children with autism this is rarely well established. To struggle with the solution to a small problem, the shape doesn't fit or the button which won't do up requires that the learner persists in the reworking and revisiting the problem. The teacher can step in too soon – or leave the child struggling too long. For each child the timing will be different. Meanwhile, the real learning takes place within the experience of the activity as it occurs. As for all teaching we can only shape up and mould the understanding and experience already in place. We cannot create it.

And so an effective teacher begins to think about ingredients of the learning experience for the child with autism. We have to attend to each other. We have to attend to and share the interest of the other participant in subject of the lesson. We have to work with tolerance and constraint. We then have to extract relevant meaning, and finally what we learn is bound into the experience shared between us.

References

Alvarez, A. (1992) *Live Company: Psychoanalytic Psychotherapy with Autistic, Borderline, Deprived and Abused Children.* London: Tavistock/Routledge.

Newson, E. (2001) 'The pragmatics of language: remediating the central deficit for autistic 2–3 year olds.' (This volume.)

Trevarthen, C., Aitken, K., Papoudi, D. and Robarts, J. (1996) *Children with Autism.* London: Jessica Kingsley Publishers.

Waldon, G. (1984) 'Meaning from movement: the creation of novel experience.' Unpublished manuscript.

CHAPTER 14

The Young Autistic Child

Reclaiming Non-Autistic Potential through Interactive Games

Sibylle Janert

Abstract

This chapter illustrates a number of 'games of pure interaction' which adults all over the world intuitively play with babies, with no other purpose than to have fun together:'looming games', 'I'm gonna getcha!' games, 'I can still see you!' games and 'mouth and face games'. Using an emotionally engaged approach, these purely social games lay the essential foundation for all further social, emotional, cognitive, and language development as they play with and promote 'joint attention', one of the main factors of concern in the child on the autistic spectrum. The principles behind these games are described as ideally suited to claim or reclaim non-autistic potential in the young autistic child. A description by Stern (1991) of such an interaction game between a 4.5-month-old baby and his mother is given as a model, which also illustrates how some avoidant behaviours may have their roots in early infancy coping strategies. Based on a triad of approaches – (1) infant developmental research, (2) emotionally informed infant observation, (3) the attentive study of the nature of the child's mental state, internal world, and its interrelatedness with that of the adult (i.e. modern British psychoanalytic object relations theory) – this chapter takes a view of human nature that assumes that there are always traces of healthy developmental potential in everyone, even the most disabled or autistic person. Giving examples of how to play these games with four very different young autistic children, two guiding principles are explained as 'walking the tightrope between fear and delight' and 'make it bigger!' The reasons why these games are able to attract the young autistic child's attention into social interaction are explained, as is the importance of the necessary quality of adult behaviours.

Introduction

Certain games are ideally suited to attract most young developmentally delayed autistic children into human social communication. Their aim is to draw autistic children into social interaction, and to find it so much fun that they want more of this typically human social 'stuff' called communication and play. They encourage an emotive feelingful approach from the adult in order to develop and 'reclaim' dormant healthy developmental potential, and are based on the view that all human beings are born to be social creatures, 'designed' to have complex feelings, ideas and internal worlds. This implies that there are non-autistic aspects in even the most avoidant, delayed, disabled or autistic child. It is these we want to find, reach, awaken, alert the child to, and ultimately 'reclaim' (Alvarez 1992). With autistic children this involves the adult in knowing where we may expect to find them, how to reach them, what to do to wake them up, and how to alert them to our presence, to their own cut-off-ness and the social communicative delights that would ease their isolation.

Such knowledge can be gained from a triad of approaches:

1. research of infant development

2. emotionally informed infant observation

3. and the attentive study of the nature of the child's mental state, internal world, and its interrelatedness with that of the adult (i.e. modern British psychoanalytic object relations theory).

All of these share the idea that the crucial foundations for all physical, social, cognitive, emotional and language development are laid in the baby's earliest social play: first a child or baby needs to have discovered the joys of 'joint attention' which is the beginnings of meaning. This leads to 'social referencing', without which there can be no meaningful communication, no symbolic or speech development.

The mental, communicative and socio-emotional development of the autistic child is often delayed around the level of a 4–9 month old. As all development is a process of growth, with new achievements relying on previous ones, we must pitch our efforts to engage the child at these early developmental levels. Understanding how babies communicate and play gives us a mental model for 'reclaiming' the young autistic child into human social interaction.

The games

The earliest *'games of pure interaction'*, intuitively played by adults and babies all over the world, usually last only a few minutes involving nothing other than face-to-face contact, vocal sounds and touch. They are non-symbolic and are played without the help of toys or other objects, using whatever traces of instinctive interest and responses. In the following example of 4.5-month-old Joey and his mother, Daniel Stern illustrates beautifully the nature and process of these early communicative games, how the 'players' respond when the child's 'optimal range of frustration' is overstepped, and how they negotiate a return to each other's emotional company:

> Joey is sitting on his mother's lap, facing her. She looks at him intently but with no expression on her face, as if she were preoccupied and absorbed in thought elsewhere. At first, he glances at the different parts of her face but finally looks into her eyes. He and she remain locked in a silent mutual gaze for a long moment. She finally breaks it by easing into a slight smile. Joey quickly leans forward and returns her smile. They smile together; or rather they trade smiles back and forth several times. Then Joey's mother moves into a gamelike sequence. She opens her face into an expression of exaggerated surprise, leans all the way forward, and touches her nose to his, smiling and making bubbling sounds all the while. Joey explodes with delight but closes his eyes when their noses touch. She then reels back, pauses to increase the suspense, and sweeps forward again to touch noses. Her face and voice are even more full of delight and 'pretend' menace. This time Joey is both more tense and excited. His smile freezes. His expression moves back and forth between pleasure and fear. Joey's mother seems not to have noticed the change in him. After another suspenseful pause, she makes a third nose-to-nose approach at an even higher level of hilarity, and lets out a rousing 'oooOH!' Joey's face tightens. He closes his eyes and turns his head to the side. His mother realises that she has gone

too far, and stops her end of the interaction, too. At least for a moment, she does nothing. Then she whispers to him and breaks into a warm smile. He becomes re-engaged. (Stern 1991)

Joey seems to be looking not only at but also *for* his mum in the sense of wanting to make emotional contact with her. With his long silent look into her eyes he eventually gets her to 'hear' his unspoken question, and without words they play a question-and-answer game, have an argument, fall out, apologise, and make up again. When his mother oversteps his level of tolerance, Joey has no alternative than to shut off, displaying avoidant behaviours to help him cope, and to preserve his emotional balance (an older child may have run away). When he has regained it, he returns emotionally to their interactive contact. Confirmed by recent research (e.g. Alvarez 1992; Alvarez and Reid 1999; Trevarthen *et al.* 1996,), this suggests that some autistic cutting-off manoeuvres may have started on a much smaller scale as a baby's meaningful coping strategies which have subsequently become entrenched and habitual. In this example simply waiting in silence, attention tightly focused on the other, letting some suspense build up as a natural motivator, is used first by Joey to alert his mother, and later by her to allow him to settle again.

These early *'looming games'* (Bruner *et al.* 1976), in which the adult suddenly and playfully sweeps forward and into the child's field of vision, saying something like a high-pitched 'hello hello helloooo!' before reeling back again, play on some instinctual communicative potential that is usually unimpaired and reachable, even in the passive or avoidant autistic child.

> Tim (age 3) was an expert in avoidance. Passively lying in a corner as usual, his immediate response to a 'looming game' would be to simply shut his eyes or turn his head. But by first moving my face *back* a little together with a noisy warning-gasp, I could catch his attention so that we would be looking into each other's eyes, at least for a split second! If I burst out immediately into an exaggerated smiling 'greeting face' accompanied by a high-pitched welcoming 'Hellooo?! Hello TIM!!?!', and followed by more surprising and unexpected mouth shapes and noises, like blowing raspberries, 'plopping' my lips, wiggling my tongue quickly and noisily from side to side, always a little different, I could hold his focused interest for perhaps a few more seconds, or even minutes.

Compared with the fleeting split seconds he has become used to, minutes are a long time for Tim, who normally seems incapable of such human connectedness and contact. Here were islands of unexpected possibilities to promote this non-autistic human potential.

Autistic children need an adult, who is sensitive to their individual levels of tolerance, to pull them out of their reduced world of cut-off-ness or auto-stimulation into a more alive animated human relationship, by always tugging lightly (or perhaps vigorously) at their mental capacities to respond to such playful human company. Through observing closely, always with the question 'What can I do with that?' in mind, opportunities can usually be found where a glance, a vocalisation, a hand or foot movement can be echoed and turned into a little interactive game by adding a little thrill of surprise, an edge of anticipation. Running away can be made into an interactive '*I'm gonna getcha!*' game, or a less pushy '*I can still see you!*' game for those children who get too scared by being followed, caught and tickled.

The '*mouth and face games*' I play with young autistic children are also simply a larger-than-life version of these baby games of 'pure interaction'. The human face is better equipped for this than anything in the world: with eyes and a responsive voice, guided by a thoughtful and feelingful mind, an interest in careful observation, sensitive awareness of our own preverbal communicative potential, a willingness to wait, watch and respond rather than to teach and demand, and to keep our concentration tightly focused on the child's face and subtle communications, it is really the most amazing cause-and-effect toy ever invented. Patrick (age 4.5) adopted 'mouth-and-face-games' as if he had been craving for something like this:

> Always active, it took some time to get Patrick to sit down. To catch his attention I made the most peculiar noise-sequence I could think of with my mouth. He looked up with sudden interest, or suspicion. I did it again, my mind expectantly focussed on him, but paused mid-way waiting for him to complete the sound-sequence. When he did not, I completed it myself more quietly rather than let our hard-won 'joint attention' go. But then he seemed to try, blowing and pressing his lips together, and I echoed him. He did it again, more confidently, and we traded 'raspberries' a few times. I added a tongue-click, and waited for him to try. He did. We now had a

'dialogue-game': 'raspberries – tongue-click – your turn!' I added a tongue-wiggle, which he copied… And then it was my turn to be surprised. Patrick's response was: '"raspberries" – tongue-click – tongue-wiggle – *punch air and shout!*"' He grinned at me, and I beamed back in amazement, before copying his expanded version. Ten minutes later he still did not want to stop, and kept asking for the game daily.

To make these communication games successful, the adult needs to create a sense of anticipation and suspense, often achieved by doing nothing: just waiting, our attention expectantly focused on the child, like stretching and stretching an imaginary elastic (usually about ten times longer than one thinks possible), increases suspense naturally. An expectant atmosphere in which nothing is happening can be made to produce a grating sense that 'something must be up!': the child will have to look at our face to find out!

There are two guiding 'principles' that are useful always to keep in mind. One I call *'walking the tightrope between fear and delight'*. For both Tim and Patrick it had to have a certain tension, enough to keep their attention on tenterhooks and careful not to let them slip off into a more flaccid state of mind – more tight, active and almost pushy for Patrick than for Tim, who had much less 'mental grip' and needed a different quality of tightness, one that was always prepared to slacken in such a way that would 'reclaim' his attention rather than lose it. With Joey we saw how 'it' fell off the tightrope, and he needed time to get back up again. The other basic principle is *'make it bigger'*: the more unresponsive the autistic child, the more the adult feels hopeless and helpless at being able to engage the child socially, and the 'bigger' we need to make whatever it is, i.e. being more dramatic, more emotionally engaging, using more expansive movements, more 'stretch' in our suspense, exaggerating how we speak, its speed, its pitch, its tones. Sometimes this means moving exaggeratedly more slowly, or stopping suddenly, or whispering. We need to make our presence unavoidable for the children, but in such fun ways as not to put them off, should they risk coming out of their shell.

However, 'making it bigger' does not simply mean more, harder, louder, faster, but tuning in sensitively to the child's feeling-state and making it into a shared experience: it's about sharing a joke with each other.

Mandy used to approach Kofi (age 3) by talking loudly to him in a shrill voice. The more he withdrew, the louder and more persistent she got, the closer she would sit, holding his hand harder whenever he wanted to run away.

Although she was using the idea 'make it bigger', Mandy's approach lacked sensitivity, playfulness and suspense. Unaware of the effects of her behaviour on him, she failed to take into consideration Kofi's likes and dislikes (he hated loud, and especially shrill, noises). Adults who approached him more slowly and quietly, were much more successful with Kofi, and also felt less hopeless about him.

The success of these games hinges on the adult's understanding that they are not educational in a functional sense, but about playing with intentions and feelings, about building up expectations, arousing curiosity, and then stretching, breaking, remaking and mucking about with them, with no other aim than to have fun – always 'walking the tightrope between fear and delight'. Perhaps the child does indeed feel somehow threatened, but there is something odd about this so-called 'threat': it is coming at the child and disappearing, or changing, too fast for what would instinctively qualify as a serious threat. The moment the child is ready to retreat or run away, the 'threat' itself has retreated. What is going on here? The child cannot withdraw safely, because that 'threat' is still hanging around somewhere. Where has it gone? So the child has got to look. The repeated sudden disappearance of the 'threat' that was coming draws the child's attention to it, curiosity is engaged, the mind alerted, the senses drawn together into one focus, so unusual for autistic children – and so good for them.

Running to and fro as usual, Fred's (age 4) keyworker Linda would slowly creep up on him, and he never knew whether she would suddenly pounce and tickle him, or stop dead – or in fact what on earth she might do! Occasionally Linda asked him to put on his shoes, but then put them on the 'wrong' child, or pretended to put them on herself. This made Fred, usually not prone to co-operating, come running to rescue his shoes. At dinnertime she might offer him a spoonful of food, holding it in mid-air for a long time without moving, and then, just when he thought she was going to force-feed him, put it back on the plate or eat it herself.

If the adult manages to create a situation that is ambiguous enough to arouse the need for curiosity, carefully scaffolded in an atmosphere of friendly affection, then the young autistic child is usually drawn to engage and interact socially in similarly unexpected ways. Some responsive non-autistic capacities may have been hibernating, waiting to be claimed, or reclaimed, through moments of playful communicative contact that can thrill and enliven the passive or avoidant child, and the desparing or worn out adult too.

References

Alvarez, A. (1992) *Live Company*. London: Routledge.

Alvarez, A. and Reid, S. (1999) *Autism and Personality*. London: Routledge.

Bruner, J. and Sherwood, V. (1976) 'Peekaboo and the learning of rule structures.' In J.S. Brunner, A. Holly and K. Sylva (eds) *Play: Its Role in Development and Evolution.*. New York: Basic Books.

Stern, D. (1991) *Diary of a Baby*. New York: Basic Books.

Trevarthen, C., Aitken, K., Papoudi, D. and Robarts, J. (1996) *Children with Autism*. London: Jessica Kingsley.

Further reading

Frith, U. (1989) *Autism: Explaining the Enigma*. Oxford: Blackwell.

Hobson, P.R. (1993) *Autism and the Development of Mind*. Hove: Erlbaum.

Hocking, B. (1990) *Little Boy Lost*. London: Bloomsbury.

Janert, S. (1995) 'Play in the first 6 months.' *Nursery World*, February.

Janert, S. (2000) *Reaching the Young Autistic Child*. London: Free Association.

Stern, D. (1977) *The First Relationship: Infant and Mother*. Cambridge, MA: Harvard University Press.

Stern, D. (1985) *The Interpersonal World of the Infant*. New York: Basic Books.

CHAPTER 15

Play, Performance, Symbols and Affect

Dave Sherratt

Abstract

This chapter outlines the importance of play for children with autism. The relationship between symbolic competence and performance skills in the pretend play of children with autism is explored. Finally key points are given which suggest that affective techniques can contribute to the development of play in children with autism.

'Ladies and Gentlemen, please put your hands together'...the street artist jumps on to his roadside stage...he emerges from a swirling black cape to stand motionless...his every muscle posturing in pensive anticipation...the gathering crowd hang on his quizzical raised left eyebrow and his shallow cheeks. What will he do next? In soundless expression he talks to the crowd through an imaginary window that he has just cleaned with imaginary soapy water. Leaning on the window catch, he falls forward screaming, the crowd jump back as the silence is shattered and the imaginary water showers the people nearby.

As this show unfolded the performer engaged his audience within a shared understanding of a story that evolved through their interaction. The show involved the skilled performance of creative and spontaneous pretence and communicated highly emotive meanings that were shared between the performer and the audience. This chapter examines the skills that many children with autism have in symbolic modification within pretence. It also explores the difficulties that children with autism have in the performance of symbols, whether these represent a thought or a feeling, in a word or a raised eyebrow. Finally these two aspects are considered in light of practical strategies for promoting spontaneous play in children with autism.

Children with autism do not have or use the same levels of social understanding, communicative competence or flexibility of thought as those seen in the skilled performance of the street artist above. The very skills that were seen in the performance and that absorbed the passing pedestrians are impaired in autism. For most normally developing children, play offers frequent opportunities to explore and practise these skills. Children with autism do not usually use opportunities to play in the same way. In particular these children are often impaired in symbolic pretend play (Cicchetti, Beeghly and Weiss-Perry 1994). Symbolic pretence is the ability to modify an idea in the same way as the street artist made a bucket of hot soapy water and a window to wash. These clearly did not exist, even though he was able to communicate to other people that these things were in his mind as if they were real.

In their first year of normal development, children engage within play that is limited to the properties of the world around them. During this period, early reflexes lead into voluntary social responses and imitative play or object related sensori-motor play. From about one year, most children become able to use symbols within their play. In this way, a model horse is used in the child's mind as a symbol for a real horse. By the end of the second year, most children are starting to discover an ability to modify thoughts, so that they change the physical properties of people and objects in their mind. Now a cardboard box can be thought of as a horse and when it collapses under the child's weight, it can be thought of as a dead horse. As the child grows, play generally becomes more symbolically complex, sequenced, spontaneous and social.

Although children with autism do not usually develop such spontaneous symbolic play, evidence shows that many children with autism are able to modify and manipulate symbols at much higher levels than is evident in spontaneous performance (Charman and Baron-Cohen 1997). Thus children with autism are able to use important thinking skills, providing these are evoked within a structured setting. This can be explained by difficulties that children with autism may have in initiating creative and novel acts within their play (Jarrold, Boucher and Smith

1993). Other authors explain this in terms of a delay in the capacity to use pretend play (Baron-Cohen 1989). Whatever the nature of the impairment, research in this area has demonstrated the potential that many children with autism possess to create an act of pretence. Being able to construct complex, symbolic sequences is an important skill within play. However when we look at skilled and competent players either in the streets of York or in a nursery classroom, we see that play results in observable behaviour and this is often shared with others.

The foundations of normal social play can be seen in early mother–baby interaction in which patterns of turn-taking are developed. By the end of the first year, children can engage another person by jointly focusing on an interesting object. In the second year, the child starts to represent affective experience within their play (Greenspan and Lieberman 1994). Elements of pleasure, fear, disgust, affection and disappointment are used to elaborate the child's play. Increasingly, linguistic symbols are used instrumentally to facilitate greater interactivity in the child's play. In this the child may engage an adult or alternatively talk to (and on behalf of) a doll. In the child's third and fourth years, play has typically become rich and diverse, symbolically complex, fluid and flexible, highly interactive and often socially oriented. It frequently uses speech to describe, to signal social rules and to communicate. Play can often contain sequences that are drawn from memory or planned in advance of the child's actions. The child's social competence in forming relationships with peers has been linked to their social pretend play abilities (Howes 1992). Play then offers an important panacea in developing thought flexibility, emotional understanding and stability, social understanding and linguistic competence. Play can offer this because it is inherently pleasurable. The child is frequently motivated to use the ubiquitous possibilities to play and consequently develops skills and understanding through repeated practice. However most children with autism do not benefit in the same way from the play experience.

Why should children with autism who have sufficient symbolic ability not benefit in the same way as most other children? This chapter suggests that the difficulty that children with autism experience in pretend play is primarily concerned with the generation of pretence combined with a specific developmental delay in play. However, children with autism are also impaired in social understanding and in social communication (Mundy and Crowson 1997). Children with autism also have difficulties in understanding emotions and often struggle with the use of personal pronouns (Jordan and Powell 1995). These abilities are also important in children's play. Yet the profile of play skills that is frequently seen in children with autism is not solitary symbolic play appropriate to the abilities of the child but an absence of flexible and spontaneous play. Children with autism are restricted in their representation of emotion in self-generated play. This may be due to difficulties in accessing event–affect representations or relating these to a novel play situation. However, the play of children with autism is frequently devoid or restricted in the use of affective markers. As pleasure is a necessary attribute of play, the difficulty experienced by children with autism in using emotional representations in their play may result in the play process lacking meaning and relevance for the child. From this analysis, clear implications for the development of play in children with autism can be drawn.

Play offers opportunities for children to develop a range of socio-cognitive abilities and many of these are impaired in children with autism. Children with autism may have symbolic abilities that are in advance of their spontaneous performance in play. These abilities are largely unused in play, unless they are elicited within a structured setting (Jarrold *et al.* 1993). There are other performance criteria that are important in self-generated play. The play should have a communicative or reflective intention. The child should communicate meaning to others or to self. This meaningfulness should normally have an affective intention and subsequently a personal relevance to the child. When the child's play has a personal relevance, it may also have a communicative relevance. A child with autism, who has been trained how to feed a doll with a spoon and bowl, is unlikely to endow this behaviour with an affective intention. This is due to a difficulty in accessing personal information associated with feeding and linking these with a trained behaviour. However, when real or imaginary events trigger highly charged emotion effects, there is a significant effect on the child's ability to access this information and to distinguish between reality and pretence (Lillard 1994). Affect has been effectively used to promote pretend play in a group of young children with autism and learning difficulties (Sherratt 1999a). Melodrama was used to accentuate the affective significance of modelled imaginary situations. This was found to have a motivating effect on the children. The obsessive interests of children with autism can in some circumstances provide a very powerful personal relevance and promote play. Sherratt (1999b) describes the key conditions of structure, interests and affect and how these can be used to facilitate the development of symbolic play in children with autism.

Children with autism will be encouraged to extend their understanding of the world and themselves through play if settings are established that identify levels of linguistic competence, identify suitable interest areas or recent experiences, make the affective relevance explicit and are resourced with interesting, exciting and appropriate items. Furthermore the social preferences of each individual should be taken into consideration during the design of play interventions. Children at the earliest stages of play should be introduced to a wide range of shape, colour, size, texture, and category modifications. This should aim at broadening the child's experience and interests. Where possible this sensori-motor play should provide a shared focus of interest. The teacher may be allowed to show an interest in the focus of the child's play and at a later stage comment on it enthusiastically. A group of children may possibly be allowed to join in with this. An additional method of encouraging such a shared focus uses mirroring of the child's actions by a competent player with an identical set of objects (Beyer and Gammeltoft 2000; Donald 1999).

As children with autism start to use words and develop early symbolic play, opportunities should be sought to extend simple car, tea-set and house play. Children should be encouraged to build two or three action sequences and again where possible these should have an interactive or communicative function. As the child becomes able to use short phrases and novel linguistic constructions, the potential for symbolic modifications starts to emerge. These modifications change the properties of subjects or objects (Sherratt 1999b). These can be encouraged by using non-representational materials in place of real objects or toys; creating, transforming and modifying the existing properties of these objects and subjects. There is also a need to show children how to play if they have not learnt this through imitation of peers (Fein and Kinney 1994). If this demonstration is performed by the teacher, it is important to emphasise a personal relevance by giving it an affective resonance. It must resound with excitability, fun, shock, despair, or mock horror so loudly that the child starts to 'resonate' but is not over-faced by the display. When working with a group of children, the teacher should work the audience in a style that shares similarities with the work of the street artist. The teacher must maintain a sensitive balance in this, managing the tensions and the dynamics on behalf of the children (Peter 1994). When children become competent at a simple symbolic level, they should be encouraged to build sequences, which contain symbolic content and to work towards a rough planned 'script'. Sherratt (1999b) gives practical ideas to start developing this type of symbolic sequencing.

Play in itself is often considered less useful than the development of language. Consequently the emphasis given to play is frequently minimal. Some teachers may also believe that language offers children with autism a key to unlocking the child's difficulties. However, we know that many children with autism have abilities in symbolic play that they are not using. Play is a powerful tool for learning that should not exclude children with autism because they experience difficulties with its performance any more than they should be excluded from language because they experience difficulties in communication. Children with autism need to be explicitly taught how to play and think flexibly. To do this teachers should structure access to the child's representational system using affective techniques and encourage the development of performance and symbolic skills.

Acknowledgements and notes

I would like to thank the pupils, parents, staff and governors of Mowbray School for their support in this work and my family for their encouragement and tolerance in writing it up. The term 'teacher' is used to denote an adult who intends to teach and includes parents, therapists and other educators. The term 'performance' is used to refer to any communicative behaviours used in acts of pretence.

References

Baron-Cohen, S. (1989) 'The theory of mind hypothesis of autism: A reply to Boucher.' *British Journal of Disorders of Communication, 24,* 199–200.

Beyer, J. and Gammeltoft, L. (2000) *Autism and Play.* London: Jessica Kingsley Publishers.

Charman, T. and Baron-Cohen, S. (1997) 'Brief report: prompted pretend play in autism.' *Journal of Autism and Developmental Disorders 27,* 3, 325–332.

Cicchetti, D., Beeghly, M. and Weiss-Perry, B. (1994) 'Symbolic development in children with Down Syndrome and in children with autism: an organizational, developmental psychopathology perspective.' In A. Slade and D. Palmer Wolf (eds) *Children at Play: Clinical Approaches to Meaning and Representation.* New York: Oxford University Press.

Donald, G. (1999) 'Mirroring: a social reciprocity approach for children with autism.' Personal correspondence, 21 November.

Fein, G.G. and Kinney, P. (1994) 'He's a nice alligator: observations on the affective organization of pretence.' In A. Slade and D. Palmer Wolf (eds) *Children at Play: Clinical Approaches to Meaning and Representation.* New York: Oxford University Press.

Greenspan, S.I. and Lieberman, A.F. (1994) 'Representational elaboration and differentiation: a clinical-quantitive approach to the clinical assessment of 2 to 4 year olds.' In A. Slade and D. Palmer Wolf (eds) *Children at Play: Clinical Approaches to Meaning and Representation.* New York: Oxford University Press.

Howes, C. (1992) *The Collaborative Construction of Pretend: Social Pretend Play Functions.* Albany, NY: State University of New York Press.

Jarrold, C., Boucher, J. and Smith, P. (1993) 'Symbolic play in autism: a review.' *Journal of Autism and Developmental Disorders 23,* 2, 281–307.

Jordan, R. and Powell, S. (1995) *Understanding and Teaching Children with Autism.* Chichester: Wiley.

Lillard, A. (1994) 'Making sense of pretence.' In C. Lewis and P. Mitchell (eds) *Children's Early Understanding of Mind.* Hove: Erlbaum.

Mundy, P. and Crowson, M. (1997) 'Joint attention and early social communication: implications for research on intervention with autism.' *Journal of Autism and Developmental Disorders 27 (6),* 653–675.

Peter, M. (1994) *Drama for All.* London: David Fulton.

Sherratt, D. (1999a) *The Development of Pretend Play in Children with Autism.* London: Teacher Training Agency.

Sherratt, D. (1999b) 'The importance of play.' *Good Autism Practice 1,* 2, 23–31.

CHAPTER 16

Facilitated Communication at the Chinnor Resource Unit

A Journey

Lydia Otter and Emma Masefield

Introduction

It was the last week of the summer term, and a glorious day. We took twelve students for a walk to the river. Not unusual; except that, this time, the planning for the whole occasion had been given to the students. They had been encouraged to participate in choosing every last detail: the venue, the time of day, the event, right down to the Marmite sandwiches in the picnic. The swapping of ideas had been carried out through letters written back and forth to each other across the bases of our Unit, and in typed conversations held in school Facilitated Communication (FC) sessions. These twelve were the older students on our FC programme.

When we arrived at a circle of seats in the park, the students sat down in pairs and small groups. They were invited to use their letter-boards with their staff facilitators, if they wished. After some help with working out who was who, several of them began to type continued aspects of the conversations they had begun in their letters. Two boys had a shared interest in music. Their conversation started like this:

'Do you like musicals?' typed Philip.

'Yes,' replied Simon, 'Marriage of Figaro.'

'Shame,' responded Philip, his great love being for Lloyd Webber musicals!

Five years ago this would have been unthinkable. Then, we had felt so uncertain about Facilitated Communication as a strategy for augmenting communication, and we were so apprehensive about the controversy surrounding it that, although we had originally responded enthusiastically to it, for a while we had quickly dampened our approach to it. Only now do we feel ready to tell our story.

The journey begins...

In the interests of finding better ways of enabling the students in our care to communicate, we embarked upon a journey. We were unsure in which directions we would be taken or where we would end up. There have been times when we may have thought about abandoning it, and the risks and the worry about what may or may not be the end destination have been high. Despite the frustrations and uncertainty of travelling without a 'map' or 'guidebook', we have persisted. As we hope this chapter will demonstrate, our energy has been fuelled by the fact that we knew something good was happening for those students we took along with us; exactly what, we are still sometimes unsure, but definitely something good.

This chapter charts the ups and downs of our journey in employing Facilitated Communication as a strategy for augmenting communication with young people with autism. It also puts forward possible reasons as to why FC users with autism have previously failed in experimental validation studies (Hudson, Melita and Arnold 1993; Szempruch and Jacobson 1993; Wheeler *et al.* 1993).

The strategy

We are assuming that readers of this chapter have some knowledge of Facilitated Communication. The following, therefore, is only a brief description:

What is FC?

A strategy that may enable some people with a severe communication difficulty to point to objects, pictures, words or letters for communication purposes (Queensland Report 1993).

How does it work?

By providing physical and/or emotional support for the person using it (the user). This usually takes the form of a person (the facilitator) supporting the user's hand or arm in order to enable them to point successfully. The role of the facilitator, physically, is to provide backward pressure in order to provide stability to the muscles in the arm of the user and to provide the sensory feedback that the user may not be able to feel otherwise (Queensland Report 1993).

Why is it controversial?

Because of the real possibility of the user being influenced by the facilitator (Biklen 1990; Schubert and Biklen 1993).

Good practice: the essential list

When we began, FC was not being practised in any other school in the UK. During the development of our programme, we have discovered factors that we now see as being essential to setting up a successful FC programme, to safeguard and enlighten participants. This section provides a brief run through of this list of factors and, in the rest of the chapter, we illustrate how we decided upon these criteria.

FC policy document

An FC policy document is essential for safe and competent implementation of the strategy. It should detail the managerial structure, the training requirements and provide strict guidelines on how to deal with the expression of potentially life changing or controversial information.

Training of facilitators

It is vital to have enough trained facilitators for users to have access to FC across as many environments as possible; FC is a communication strategy and the young person needs to be able to communicate wherever he or she is.

Specific training provided by accredited trainers is essential to ensure good practice is maintained. Untrained persons should not embark upon FC unless supervised by a trained individual.

Set-work file of graded material

A set-work file of graded material is a collection of worksheets that are graded to develop specific pointing and communication skills. This will be described in more detail later. It is particularly useful for getting people started, users and facilitators, and for modelling ways of presenting and adapting material.

Multidisciplinary team involvement

All aspects of a student's development and welfare need to be taken into account in order that they have the greatest chance of success, i.e. emotional, physical, social, and educational development and welfare. Therefore, all persons involved in these different aspects of the student's life need to be involved.

Equipment – low and high tech

At the Chinnor Unit we have experimented with many tools. The success of equipment is individual to people and circumstances. We now use a combination of letter-boards, Canon communicators, word processors and computers.

Training of FC users

FC is not an innate skill. Potential users need to be taught the skills, physical, communication, and the transfer between different media and facilitators. They also need ongoing support and training to ensure development in these skills.

Parental liaison and involvement

The parents' knowledge of a student is vital. They are the most important and probably the most consistent people in the student's life. We, at the Unit, encourage them to participate in FC training whenever they wish.

Training for fading to independence

FC is about training for *independence* in communication, not *dependence*: physical, emotional and social independence. We realise that this will not be easy for a person with autism. It may not be possible for individuals to achieve total independence, but an FC programme needs to provide training and support to enable the individual to become as independent as is possible for them.

Training in validation

Validation refers to the communication of information previously unknown by the facilitator. It is a very difficult yet vital skill. We have found that practising the necessary skills can make it possible. In our programme, we now give specific training in validation skills to users and facilitators.

FC is one part of a whole communication skills package

Communication comes in many forms. FC should be one part of many communication strategies offered to students. The students who form our FC programme continue to have support in speech therapy, signing, picture communication systems, social skills training., whatever is appropriate for the individual students.

Record keeping

Record keeping is essential to maintain progress through evaluation. It is difficult due to the amount of information produced, the number of personnel involved, the variety of settings and the limitations on time, but we try to work at it.

How did it all begin?

In October 1992, the managerial staff of the Chinnor Resource Unit invited representatives from the Geneva Centre in Canada to present a two-day conference on Facilitated Communication and their use of it. This was provided for staff at the Unit as in-service training and was open to colleagues in Oxfordshire's Service for Autism. The presenters then spent three weeks touring the different bases of the Unit, giving hands-on training to staff, students and parents.

The conference told us what FC was. The videos were particularly helpful as they demonstrated the physical technique, the 'what to do' and 'how to do it' and they demonstrated the set-work sequence (explained in detail later in the chapter). The speakers confirmed for us the sense that there might be more to our students than initially meets the eye, effecting a shift in belief for many staff about the people in our care. Their input also raised the question of whether there was a previously undiscovered key to communicating with people with autism and this created great excitement among the staff of the Unit. FC introduced a new way of approaching our students and raised their status by possibly giving them a chance to express their knowledge and opinions.

> One of the most striking images of this time was of a young boy of 9 who could not sit still for more than 40 seconds. He had a compulsion to sprinkle coffee, sugar, paint, and anything upon which he could lay his hands. He was highly volatile and had many anti-social behaviours. However, when his key-workers sat next to him and took his hand and worked with him using FC, he was able to remain seated for up to 40 minutes. The sprinkling reduced, the volatility diminished and there were periods of stillness in his life.

These beginnings raised many issues for us as a staff team. All interested parties, teachers and learning support assistants were 'having a go', with no one to monitor. There was no regulation of practice and no guidelines to follow. The only direction we had was the set-work sequence, which gave us the progression of pointing to pictures, through to the spelling of words. Consequently, a loss of structure was brought about, with key-workers and students making decisions about curriculum implementation. One member of staff later described his sense of bewilderment and anxiety as he watched students and staff in the base. What the students were saying, via FC, became a pressing issue. Students were reported to be expressing their anguish and their despair at being imprisoned by the condition of autism, expressing ambitions for their futures, and parents and staff were requesting curriculum changes in order to support these wishes. In addition, there seemed to be a need for unquestioning belief by the facilitator in order for FC to work. Staff, who had doubts about the veracity of the strategy, had their doubts confirmed by their failure to reproduce communications with students reported as using FC by other staff. Division among staff and anxiety levels ran high about the discrepancy between the level of knowledge communicated independently by students and that which they communicated through FC. Moreover, the reported literacy levels of the students using FC did not fit with teachers' training about the development of literacy skills. There was also a great need for emotional support for parents and carers who felt guilty about their previously low expectations of students' capabilities.

In spite of all this, we could still see positive aspects, such as the story of the young boy cited above. However, FC could not continue in this unstructured and divisive manner and so we had to consider how we could make it safe.

In September 1993, our headteacher and Lydia Otter placed an embargo on all the types of open conversation described above in order to attend to this increasing distress and division among the staff. At the same time, however, one boy had been able to settle to pointing with FC for topic work so effectively and unusually that Lydia was asked to develop the set-work given to us by the Geneva Centre. For the Unit's purposes, worksheets were found or made for each level of the skill at all ages. These were reproduced as a file of material for each base. Graded set-work was then made available to all the bases of the Unit.

The set-work sequence

The set-work sequence was based on the need to develop certain pointing and communication skills. The levels within the sequence are as follows:

Pointing to:

Level 1.   *Objects* – students are asked initially to make a choice out of three or four

Level 2.   *Pictures* – again, initially out of a choice of three or four

Level 3.   *Letters / Numbers* – e.g. show me the letter P on a letter-board, computer

Level 4.   *YES / NO* – using yes or no to answer questions

Level 5.   *Multiple Choice Words* – make a choice out of four words (spelling)

Level 6.   *Single Words* (cloze) – spell a single word that is known to the facilitator

Level 7.   *Words, Phrases, Sentences* (cloze) – spell several known words

Level 8.   *Open Conversation* – spell a word or words unknown to the facilitator

As our 'Good Practice – The Essential List' indicates, this remains a highly useful training tool for our programme. Both user and facilitator are trained through the different levels. A user, in the training of a new facilitator, may have to work at a lower level than is usual for them for the purposes of the training. It is critical that this is explained to the user and that the material used continues to be interesting and appropriate to his or her age. In this way, each facilitator and each user has their own 'level' at which they can expect to work successfully. Training and support works by *success leading to success* and by never risking communication failures that might jeopardise the relationship with that student.

How did set-work help our situation?

The combination of the embargo and the set-work provided a welcome period of calm at this stage because nothing controversial was being spoken. The facilitators and users were being given space to gain skills in pointing and communication. The set-work provided a resource and a structure for sessions, where progress through the set-work levels could be achieved for students and staff.

> A young girl of 11, who felt so threatened by any academic or topic work that she would sabotage a session to prevent the chance of failure, was able to sit and work through the carefully graded material for up to 20 minutes. Her commitment was fuelled by her success at each stage. This was the first time her key-worker had been able to work with her on any new material. Previously she could only be engaged by using books and resources with which she had already worked time and time again.

However, because of the previous upset, FC was happening only behind closed doors between a member of staff and a student. The set-work file was regarded only as providing a resource for individual sessions and was used to support individual staff. It did not help to bring FC into the wider community. In fact, it had the unfortunate effect of isolating FC users and facilitators further, with set-work being seen as 'special' material. In order to do FC, it seemed that specially designed resources were required, rather than the set-work file being used as a template from which staff could create or adapt their own work. Also, staff relied on the file and students became bored with doing the same worksheets with new facilitators.

What more did we need to know?

We felt that we needed more input from experienced facilitators and so, in January 1994, Rosemary Crossley (Director of the DEAL Communication Centre) was invited to provide further training through one day workshops. This input offered lots of practical advice, such as using flip albums with word choice for easier access and portability, and multiple choice boards with phrases such as 'I am feeling hungry' or 'I need a break', to cut down the effort exerted by the user. FC is extremely laborious and tiring; imagine having to type every single letter of every word you wish to utter! Crossley's ideas cut down the amount of strain, and also provided easier access to expressions of need and want, which previously we may have tried to anticipate or guess at, depending on the student's behaviour and our knowledge of them.

Furthermore, Rosemary Crossley had first started using FC with a young woman with cerebral palsy (Crossley and MacDonald 1980) and was very discerning in recognising imprisonment within a body and at empathising with people with physical problems. She helped us to focus on the movement difficulties being experienced by our students. For example, she discussed how problems in proprioception results in the individual not receiving the feedback necessary to determine where the body is in space. An individual not lacking in this sense does not need to look at the elbow to tell it is bent, but people who have problems in this area find the process of pointing much harder. The use of touch and backward pressure in FC enhances feedback and aids pointing.

Rosemary Crossley also insisted that students should look at their letter-boards and materials. She did not support the idea that individuals could accurately type without looking at the letter-board. She believes that, unlike touch typists whose fingers hover over home keys, giving them a point of reference, individuals, pointing with one finger, do not have points of reference and, thus, cannot accurately select the keys they need without looking. To help individuals achieve looking at the letter-board, she encouraged us to offer as much practical support as possible, by inclining the work on a leaning board, rather than having it flat on the table. She also suggested exercises to encourage independent index finger isolation, she recommended materials to prevent worksheets (and students) from slipping off the table (or chair) and she insisted upon realistic interpretation of communications. If a student produced a row of nonsensical letters, they should be made aware that their communications did not make sense and they should try again. Facilitators should not try to read, into a series of letters, words that may not be there. This, she explained, could cause further distress to students as the possibility of mis-interpretation would be high. She also encouraged us to check the students' understanding of words and to question whether the student had communicated all that they wanted to say.

All this helped the children to perform better. The practical skills gave us welcome new strategies. However, this still did not serve to bridge the gap between those staff who were having success and those who were not. Those people, for whom FC was not working, felt criticised and these very practical suggestions perpetuated this feeling. Rosemary Crossley's advice unwittingly seemed, to them, to be saying that the problem was with the staff rather than with the students, and that if one 'got it right' physically, emotionally and environmentally, then it would work. Indeed, this was not the case for some staff and morale continued to be low. Furthermore, the questions raised by the staff that were sceptical of the validity of the strategy had not yet been addressed. We were still experiencing validation difficulties, namely that students did not seem able to communicate information unless it was already known to the facilitator.

How do we protect good practice?

Further training was required, and so, in September 1994, Lydia Otter participated in an intensive three-day training course, along with a small group of speech therapists, parents and teachers also interested in, and using, FC. The course was taught by Jane Remington-Gurney, a speech and language pathologist from Queensland, Australia, who had begun using FC with Crossley. From her work with Crossley, she became increasingly involved with issues of validation, the need for it and how to achieve it. She was also closely involved with the Queensland government's insistence on regulating FC through thorough research and training. Jane helped to develop an accredited training programme and the participants of the course stated above, were the first trainees outside Australia.

On completion of the training, Jane suggested that the group of participants should form themselves into a UK Steering Group to promote and develop good practice in the UK. This group has continued to meet annually, and are currently running a closely monitored FC Project. The peer group evaluation gained has been vital, especially in the absence of text books or accessible tutors.

Jane Remington-Gurney also visited the Chinnor Unit as part of Lydia's need for hands-on assessment to complete the training. She met with a small group of senior staff and suggested that we needed to establish a pilot study to evaluate the place of FC in the Unit.

Jane Remington-Gurney's vital contribution to the development of FC at the Chinnor Unit was threefold:

1. to form the FC Steering Group UK, which has now increased its membership to include all those individuals trained to 'Advanced' level of the Queensland training scheme and offers support to facilitators and users of FC, nationwide

2. to establish a pilot study at the Unit

3. to focus on the absolute need for validation.

We began to develop materials to address this critical issue of getting the students to tell us information we did not already know. We enlisted the support of parents in this part of the programme, inviting them to come into school and work with us and their children. Despite our efforts, however, naturalistic validation continued to present us with problems. Parents knew that their children knew the answers to questions about the colour of their bedspread, what was their favourite video and so on, but the students just did not seem able to tell us reliably. They became resentful of the constant pressure of being 'tested' for validation and the boost in self-esteem, which they had experienced from using FC, was being undermined.

The inability of the students to validate also affected staff morale, and staff, who had originally been enthusiastic about FC, began to doubt what they had been experiencing.

How do we offer support, training and therefore maintain control?

The effects, evident in many of our students using FC, of increased concentration, of reduction in anti-social and 'avoidance' behaviours, of an increase in independent skills (including word processing skills) and of an increase in verbal skills, demonstrated to us that something good was happening for them. However, the need for support for staff was great, at this time. Without validation, people felt uneasy about the authorship of communications and the claims being made for some students and their academic ability. So, Lydia Otter was asked, by our headteacher, to develop a training programme which involved visiting all the students that were using FC and working with them and their facilitators in order to try to ascertain what was happening in these partnerships.

We were still trying to use naturalistic validation (i.e. the communication of events happening naturally within the context of the student's life). In a school setting, it might be easier to start with semi-formal validation exercises. These took the form of games. The students would choose an object and hide it in a little box. The absent facilitator would be invited to come back and ask 'What's in the box?' The student would then point with facilitation to either a matching object or a picture of the object. Many sessions could precede any success at choosing the object actually hidden, even though there was no difficulty in matching the objects when one was not hidden. We persisted with these types of exercises, believing that if the students could be taught how to 'play the game', then they would be successful. Success did come gradually, such sessions became 'training' sessions for all students and staff in the programme. Detailed records were kept of these sessions and, over time, an increase in the success rate of most students could be seen. These findings support Biklen's studies (Biklen and Cardinal 1997), showing that practice at validation exercises can improve success in FC users in communicating information that is not known by the facilitator. They also support the idea that FC users need to be taught the rules of how to communicate unknown information.

Through the tiny validation successes we were having, we began to know that the students could tell us information we did not know.

How is movement disturbance involved?

In spite of these successes, however, some students suffered under the pressure of the need for validation and dropped out, refusing to communicate any more using FC. They seemed to be disillusioned about what FC could actually offer them. We felt there was much more we needed to know. We turned our attentions towards the movement difficulties of our students to see if knowledge in this area could inform our practice.

In June 1996, a conference was held in London on Movement Disturbance. The presenters, Martha Leary, a speech pathologist and communication consultant from Toronto, and Dr Anne Donnellan, a professor at the School of Education, at the University of Wisconsin, Madison, USA, spoke about how the symptoms of autism linked with those of movement disturbances and further developed, for us, the idea of new explanations for some of the students' behaviours.

In relation to the ideas about movement difficulties, we, at the Unit, decided to seek consultation with a physiotherapist, Jill Mead, who has had a long involvement with the Unit and its pupils, especially in the use of the Waldon method (Waldon 1978). She assessed all the students on the FC training programme and also tried FC with them. Her standard tests revealed which students had difficulty in initiating or controlling their movements. These students' difficulties were also apparent to her when she did FC with them. Other students, she recognised, as we had, showed no specific movement weaknesses but needed our emotional support through a gentle touch. The idea that we are asking these people with autism to do a difficult job in pointing was supported and offering physical support can be seen as an appropriate response to a real difficulty.

Also during this term, a young woman, called Lucy Blackman, came with her mother from Australia to give a 'talk' for parents, staff and students on FC and her development in it. Lucy has achieved physical independence in her spelling for communication through FC training. She and her mother conducted a joint presentation, with Lucy spelling on her Canon Communicator and her mother talking. Lucy's mother also provided the emotional support Lucy needed to remain on task and to inhibit compulsive behaviours which detracted from her spelt communications.

Lucy's visit brought alive for us the possibility of independence for our students through FC training and impressed upon us that independence takes time; it took Lucy nine years to achieve this level of physical independence. It also demonstrated clearly that, even when physically independent, emotional support may still be necessary and that the problems of autism may still be there. In response to a discussion about independent typing, Lucy took the Canon Communicator and typed 'only problem with not touching is that there and here I must emphasize only my opinion the sensory integration factor is lost'. She herself at that time needed a touch to the elbow, when working with facilitators other than her mother.

Further support for our use of FC was provided at this time by Daphne Briggs, a child psychotherapist, who was consulted for general advice about the possible advantages or disadvantages in offering FC to children with autism. She and Lydia Otter discussed the relationship between the facilitator and the student. They talked particularly about the dependency indicated by the use of facilitation and whether or not this is constructive.

Daphne Briggs made a number of useful points:

1. Dependency is useful when part of the progress towards independence.

2. There are two forms of dependency:

   'I need you to help me do this.'

   'I can't do this, you do it for me.'

   The first is to be encouraged, the second not.

3. Students may rebel at taking an initiative and would need support to do so.

4. Support should not be withdrawn too early out of concern about inappropriate dependency.

5. Appropriate dependency should be encouraged before independence is achieved.

All this confirmed for us that our students' need for support was a genuine need, both physically and emotionally. It also supported our view that FC provides an appropriate environment, in its approach, to foster success for people with autism.

Jill Mead's physiotherapy input also alerted us to the possible use of physical aids, such as a fully articulated arm support This, we hoped, could replace the need for a facilitator to provide the physical support for the user's arm and that physical accommodations and environmental accommodations could improve the success of the students, especially in working towards independence.

> One of our students, a young man, worked for over an hour with the two of us and an arm support. This young man has quite severe movement problems and requires a lot of physical support to enable pointing. He was very interested in his arm support and the possibility of it providing him with the support he needs. He usually tires quickly of pointing, his arm becomes rigid with his effort to compensate for his low muscle tone and it becomes almost impossible to facilitate the movement for him. However, on this occasion, with his arm resting in the arm support, he was keen to work for a considerable period of time, patiently trying out the adjustments we made, in our attempts to make it as comfortable as possible. This young man's interest and effort with the arm support

was particularly striking, as he had previously refused to co-operate with staff in using FC.

At this time, we were beginning to understand better the role FC could play in alleviating the difficulties for people with autism and how we could work towards independence with the students on our programme. Emma Masefield began to develop training sessions specifically on independence skills, with the students in her care. She found, in particular, two strategies that were useful in teaching and enabling FC users to become more independent.

First, copy typing. Copy typing, in itself, is a useful skill and has vocational implications. In addition to this, it enables FC students to have the experience of typing on their own, without the added strain of having to generate the material. Training sessions in this skill have enabled some students, who previously could not attend to a task without the support of a key-worker, to progress from typing one, short phrase physically independent of their facilitator (but with their facilitator sitting next to them providing emotional support). They have become able to collect a piece of work from their drawer, set up the word processor and type for 20 minutes, independent of physical support and with only distant supervision from a facilitator or key-worker. The students have found this extremely liberating and enjoy the kudos of being able to complete a piece of work independently.

The second strategy is that of 'the two handed approach'. When trying to encourage physical independence in an FC user, the facilitator fades the support. If the user is being supported at the wrist, when working on less taxing material, the facilitator could try to support the user at the lower arm. In this way, the facilitator can gradually move up the user's arm until they reach the shoulder and then take the leap of removing the hand completely. In theory, and indeed in practice with some students, this works very well, but we have found that very sensitive individuals feel the reduction in support too unnerving and they lose their confidence. So, Emma Masefield worked on the idea of providing dual support, where the hand used to support the student is placed at the position to where the facilitator wishes to fade, and the other hand is placed at the position where support is currently being provided. As in the example above, then, one hand would be supporting at the lower arm, and the other at the wrist. Once the user was settled in to the piece of work or the communication, the facilitator experiments with removing the hand which is supporting at the wrist, until the user becomes familiar with feel of being supported at the lower arm. Support to the wrist is then added in whenever the user feels unnerved, until it can be removed completely to allow facilitation only at the lower arm. In this way, the facilitator can move up the user's arm in a steady progression. In her work with students and in training facilitators in fading, Emma Masefield has found this to be a particularly effective strategy.

The knowledge of and the work we did with the movement difficulties and the issues of dependence versus independence moved our programme on a long way and provided new material with which to train both facilitators and users. However, as always in education, lack of funding for sustained advice and recommended equipment restricted our efforts. Furthermore, another issue for staff was that the advice we had been given highlighted the continuing need for the broadening of attitudes to autism.

Why does FC work for students with one person and not others?

Facilitator transfer

A very special issue linked to movement difficulties and accommodations appeared at this time, in the form of a 14-year-old boy called Richard. He had been reported by his family as using FC to access age appropriate National Curriculum work since the mid-1990s. However, in the Unit, he even had difficulty in demonstrating letter-to-letter matching. Video sent in from home of him, working with his first facilitator, persuaded us that we must take his skills seriously. This started a steep learning curve for us.

The person he had first facilitated with was his school teacher, during integration into a mainstream primary school. She had developed certain approaches and accommodations that enabled him to demonstrate his inner skills. She had worked on fading physical support and could facilitate him by just touching the top of his head for much of the work. In addition to this, she removed all distractions from the room, because if they were present he would have to talk about them. She gave him her strength by using phrases such as 'You'll be fine' and 'We can manage this together.' Furthermore, she harnessed his love of competition and winning by saying a loud 'Yeah!' when he succeeded and she rewarded him with stickers. We observed carefully and then began sessions of transferring her skills to us and Richard's key-worker. We used the hand-over-hand method of transferring, whereby the original facilitator supports the hand of the new facilitator as they support the user. We also took on aspects of his teacher's style and made the same accommodations for Richard. Gradually, he allowed his teacher to withdraw her physical support and then, after two terms, she was able to remove all her support and no longer needed to be present.

The lesson was learnt: do not impose tests on these children, but instead, support and learn from them. We now allocate time specifically for facilitator transfer in our training programme.

We continued to learn from Richard. He consistently sabotaged and failed validation exercises with us, saying, 'I've got a headache' and 'I don't feel well' and sometimes dissolving into tears. Then, one day, as part of our assessment on video, we asked Richard if he would help us. He was thrilled and excited about being on camera and about helping us in our tasks. We used the semi-formal validation exercises with him and he consistently succeeded at telling us pictures and words that we, as facilitators, did not know. When we had finished, he pointed to the camera and said, 'They've done it!'

Helping us to win was OK; having his abilities tested was not. This was his very clear message to us.

Thus, we have learnt that documenting precisely what conditions are necessary for FC to be successful for individual students enables a smoother transfer of skills between facilitators. Conditions might include factors such as handedness, favoured equipment, level of support, set-work level, interests, accommodations etc. These factors should be documented and regularly updated and referred to. They should move with the student. We also learnt that the strength of the FC relationship is such that the trust that has been established between first facilitator and user can be drawn upon to establish a second relationship. Successful strategies are essential for the student in order to continue and it is the student's style that is important. Changes in our approaches are crucial in order to foster success, rather than expecting the student always to comply with our ways. Unfortunately, facilitator transfer creates a short-term problem of resources. FC is labour intensive, as it requires one-to-one support for students. Transfer requires two to one. However, it is vital, and we have found that experienced facilitators are able to 'take over' facilitation more quickly with a student, than someone who has not used FC before. It is essential, then, that a number of staff in a team be trained in FC and that each user has a number of facilitators.

Concurrently with these developments, we were putting together guidelines about what to do if life-changing or controversial information is communicated by students during FC sessions. The guidelines had first been adopted as policy by the FC Steering Group UK; we just made ours more specific to our Unit's needs. We insisted on a strict, named staff hierarchy to be consulted in such a case, always leaving one of us free of knowledge of the case, so we could act as a 'clean' facilitator if needed. We also insisted that unless the detail of the information was exactly reproduced to the 'clean' facilitator, the information would go no further.

Monitoring of staff

Although we had set up a training programme and the controversial information guidelines had been communicated to all staff involved, we were concerned about the competent implementation of FC and the need to monitor staff. Many staff on our programme had come from very different backgrounds in FC and, thus, had received different types and amounts of information. We felt that we needed to bring all staff into agreement and to provide them with more thorough training, as described to us by Jane Remington-Gurney. Lydia Otter was awarded a grant from St Matthias's College, and along with the other members of the FC Steering Group UK, organised for two trainers to provide training at three levels of accreditation. It resulted in two gaining the qualification of Instructor and four other Unit staff the qualification of Advanced Level. In addition, fifteen Unit staff became Basic trainees.

The training provided a welcome commonality of approach among the staff of the Chinnor Unit. We had the same understanding, used the same language and shared the same expectations at last. It provided a structure for the continued training of staff and introduced us to Discourse Analysis, which is another potential tool to measure validity of authorship, but, in our opinion, is better handled by speech therapists because of its complexity!

Autism or FC

By now, we had practices in place for developing and evaluating skills, monitoring progress, supporting training, but we were still not getting reliable naturalistic validation. Some students had begun to integrate into mainstream school for GCSE (General Certificate of Secondary Education) courses, having attended classes with their peer group through preceding years. We felt we needed to get validation towards the level at which the students were operating in classes. This would then enable us to present a sound case to the GCSE examination boards to get FC users access to accredited examinations. We also felt that the students' futures could be greatly enhanced if it could be shown that their use of FC had been validated.

We decided that we should loosen the reins a little and give the students more freedom to respond, though still within a known context. We decided we would use the FC group sessions we had been running, to teach validation at an open conversation level. Group sessions were happening for certain curricula areas such as humanities and science. Validation training had been happening on an individual basis because of our concern for the students' confidence and for the need for them never to feel that they were failing. FC group sessions were still, at this time, about the teaching of set-work, transfer and fading skills. It became so necessary to obtain naturalistic validation, that we lifted the embargo on open conversation within these sessions. Within a strictly controlled context, the students were invited to tell us information that only they knew. We knew by then that they must be allowed to talk about things that were relevant and personally meaningful, in order to motivate them.

We introduced a new 'game' of, first us, then them, bringing in valued items from home to describe to the group. The owner of the item obviously knew everything about it, another member of the group was allowed to feel it in a bag but not look, and another student knew nothing about it at all. Then we asked for details about it. To our amazement, all the students tried to volunteer information about the object, in response to questions about its colour, feel, use etc. These exercises told us so much about other failed validation, where students had given us false information. They were making up answers, perhaps because they did not know how to say, 'I only know this much.' They seemed to think that the very fact that we were asking them the question meant that we thought they must know the answer, otherwise what is the point of asking them the question! We are finding that it is not that students cannot validate, rather that they did not previously understand the need or purpose of giving the 'correct' information in response to questions asked.

Emma Masefield began to make comparisons with the more fluently speaking students in her team and found similarities between the two groups. For example, it seemed that some students had difficulty with the idea of giving a consistent answer, if required to provide the information more than once:

> A very clear example of this was provided by a young man of 16, who was asked the question, 'What can you tell me about yourself?'
>
> He answered by giving details of his height, the colour of his hair, which he said was blond, the lessons he attended etc.
>
> When he was then asked, 'What colour is your hair?' he looked puzzled and, in an uncertain voice, replied, 'Black.'
>
> Emma then said, 'Is it really? Previously you had said it was blond.'
>
> To which he said, 'Why did you ask me that question when I had already told you?'

We, as effective communicators, may have found the need for repeating ourselves a little irritating, but we would have been able to remain consistent in our response, certain in our knowledge. This young man seemed to think that he was being asked a second time because he must have got it wrong the first time. She was given clues about his confusion by the expression on his face and the tone of his voice.

This could indeed be what is happening for our students using FC. The fact that changes in facial expression (changes that concur with the emotion behind the message) are not often apparent in an FC user can make it more difficult for us to understand the problems in the communication. Also, the absence of a modulated tone of voice may exacerbate the problem. We often have little idea about the emotion behind the communications of FC users, unless their vocabulary is especially accurate. Think how much more difficult it is to write a funny anecdote than to tell one verbally!

Also, it would seem that people with communication difficulties may have difficulty in being assertive in their communication, especially in the face of questioning adults. Just the very fact that we ask them to repeat themselves may make them question what they know, such that they produce a different answer each time to the same question. Think back to our earlier problems with naturalistic validation, where parents were coming in and asking the students to tell us the colour of their bedspread. The students may have thought that, if mum is asking them again, despite them having told her the answer at home that morning, then maybe they should try a different colour, because the first one had not succeeded. The rules of the game of 'telling someone something that you know but they do not' had not been understood.

Also, perhaps a syndrome of 'teachers know all' is at play here. Pupils, especially younger pupils, seem often to find it difficult to come to terms with the idea that their teacher does not know all there is to know about a given topic. Maybe some students with autism apply this same misunderstanding to all information, including personal information about themselves. This would fit in with the apparent difficulty most autistic people have in seeing another's viewpoint when doing theory of mind tasks (Frith 1989). It may be that some autistic children have difficulty seeing or accepting the real ignorance of another, they egocentrically feel that what they know others know and so a question to them is a challenge and implies they must be wrong. Since the FC relationship is built around trust and the empowering through the facilitator's non-verbally communicated confidence in the user, a challenging question threatens that relationship.

Some people with autism seem to be highly sensitive to non-verbal signals of mood and intention, even though they may not always know how to replicate these behaviours, or how to respond appropriately to them. Our FC users may be able to sense our uncertainty about what they are about to spell out, when they are asked for information to which we are not party. This uncertainty in us may be communicated via many channels to do with the physical and emotional support we are trying to provide; one can not be so certain, and therefore so confident, when one does not know what is coming. The user, sensing this lack of confidence in them, may then feel unsure about what they were going to type and try a different response in order to gain back the 'vibes of confidence' from their facilitator.

Finally, we feel we are tackling the right issues. Before, we felt it was the approach of FC itself that was causing the problems that we experienced and that we had not got it quite right. We still believe this has some truth in it and we continue to strive to make it work, but we are able now to see that some issues are to do with our students' autism. Identifying how to tackle these issues and succeeding here will clarify the value of FC and promote success.

Validation is happening now, both at multiple choice and spelt levels, and we have found that it is not that our students could not validate, rather that they did not understand the need or purpose. Indeed, they are not yet fully effective communicators. They need support and teaching in how to be so, in the same way that young children are taught how and when to separate fact from reality and how to communicate their true meaning and share information. We should also consider that a person's verbal skills are usually well in advance of their written skills, in terms of communicating their exact message. FC users are trying to talk through the medium of writing and, when we think about it in this way, we realise that their task is a truly difficult one. If syntax and punctuation are not accurate in a piece of writing, it can easily be misinterpreted. It is highly unlikely that FC users are able to exercise all the rules of syntax without being taught.

What do we see now?

Previously, before the intervention of FC, we saw the young people, now in our programme, as being unable to share attention, unable to attend to a task for any length of time, unable to relate effectively to others, especially in groups and unable to participate meaningfully or complete tasks independently. Now, in the Unit, we see many of these same young people able to focus for up to an hour in sessions, including in mainstream classes. Many are able to inhibit certain anti-social or handicapped behaviours when engaged in FC, and for some this is maintained throughout the day, even when FC is not being employed, except at times of high anxiety. For those who had limited verbal skills, we see many of them more able verbally to communicate meaningfully and some have developed an increase in vocabulary, including vocabulary specific to subject matter taught. Some can independently complete tasks, including word processing tasks using copy typing; many can switch between a variety of media (e.g. video, whiteboard, worksheets, textbooks) during sessions. Some students are beginning to read out their FC communications before they are read to them by their facilitator; many initiate the use of FC; many students can now participate in group sessions and be aware of that group, listening, taking turns and responding appropriately, verbally and with FC. And they are all beginning to tell us information we did not previously know.

We feel that we, and they, have learnt and achieved a great deal.

Where next?

The benefits to the core group are convincing enough such that FC is now being included in induction training of new staff. All new students to the Unit will receive an FC baseline assessment as part of the assessment procedure to determine their needs. It is increasingly being offered to students as a way of allowing them access to curriculum subjects, via topic work using facilitation for participation through multiple choice or spelt answers. The post of Communication Coordinator has been newly established to facilitate liaison between FC, speech and language therapists and Unit staff.

Our programme continues to develop and there are still many issues to tackle; our journey is not yet ended. FC still happens a lot in isolation and is highly dependent on staff training and on the confidence of staff. Also the availability of trained staff for students who would benefit from the strategy, is difficult to ensure, as resources become more thinly spread through cuts in funding. Finally, FC is still regarded as a 'therapy' within the Unit and our task now is to bring it into general education.

As we reach the end of this, our journey past, we feel it would be useful for the reader to refer back to our Highway Code, 'Good Practice – The Essential List'. As with all interventions, competent implementation is the key, and our guide illustrates how we aim to ensure that we travel with due care and attention to the safety and well-being of all passengers.

References

Biklen, D. (1990) 'Communication unbound: autism and praxis.' *Harvard Educational Review 60*, 3, 291–314.

Biklen, D. and Cardinal, D.N. (eds) (1997) *Contested Words, Contested Science: Unraveling the Facilitated Communication Controversy.* New York: Teachers College Press.

Crossley, R. and MacDonald, A. (1980) *Annie's Coming Out.* Melbourne: Penguin Australia.

Frith, U. (1989) *Autism: Explaining the Enigma.* Oxford: Blackwell.

Hudson, A., Melita, B. and Arnold, N. (1993) 'Brief report: a case study assessing the validity of facilitated communication.' *Journal of Autism and Developmental Disorders 23*, 165–173.

Queensland Report on Facilitated Communication (1993) *A One Year Project to Investigate the Application and Implications of Using the Technique with a Group of People with Severe Intellectual Disabilities.* Prepared for the Division of Intellectual Disability Service, Department of Family Services and Aboriginal and Islander Affairs, Queensland, Australia.

Schubert, A. and Biklen, D. (1993) 'Issues of influence: some concerns and suggestions.' *Facilitated Communication Digest 1*, 3, 11–12.

Szempruch, J. and Jacobson, J.W. (1993) 'Evaluating facilitated communications of people with developmental disabilities.' *Research in Developmental Disabilities 14*, 253–264.

Waldon, G. (1978) 'Understanding understanding.' Unpublished and privately printed.

Wheeler, D.L., Jacobson, J.W., Paglieri, R.A. and Schwartz, A.A. (1993) 'An experimental assessment of facilitated communication.' *Mental Retardation 31*, 49–60.

Addresses

Chinnor Resource Unit, St Andrew's School, Chinnor, Oxfordshire, UK, OX9 4PU.

Deal Communication Centre, Inc., 538 Dandenong Road, Caulfield, Victoria, Australia, 3162.

Department of Families, Youth and Community Care, PO Box 806, Brisbane, Queensland, Australia, 4001.

Facilitated Communication Institute, Syracuse University, 370 Huntington Hall, Syracuse, New York, USA, 13244–2340.

FC Project, Ravenswood, Crowthorne, Berkshire, UK, RG45 6BQ.

FC Steering Group UK, Ravenswood, Crowthorne, Berkshire, UK, RG45 6BQ.

Geneva Centre, 111 Merton Street, Fourth Floor, Toronto, Ontario, Canada, M4S 3A7.

Waldon Association, Leeds, UK.

PART 4

Therapy

CHAPTER 17

Editorial

Therapy

John Richer and Sheila Coates

Inevitably this part is not clearly different from Meeting of Minds. The work of Reid and Alvarez (Chapter 18) is within a psychoanalytic and developmental framework. Transference and counter-transference, the perceived effect of therapist on the child's state of mind and the therapist's perception of the child's effect on her own feelings and thoughts, are central to this therapy, and, especially when this is uncluttered by jargon and theory, there can be meetings of minds. Other factors are important too and include regularity and consistency, acknowledging the effects on the whole family, using the results of scientific developmental research involving the analysis of infant behaviour, diary keeping, separation of treatment subgroups and evaluation of treatment.

Lalli Howell (Chapter 19) describes her immensely sensitive work bringing together autistic and mainstream children for activities and play. Peer interaction is the most difficult social area for autistic children; it is usually the least structured and predictable, and potentially the most competitive. Lalli Howell's message to the mainstream children was to forget the fact that the children had autism, and to relate in whatever way worked. The autistic children benefited in their ability to play and interact with peers, but as importantly the mainstream children matured and became more empathetic. We are reminded of what Geoffrey Manser, Headmaster of St Andrew's School in Chinnor, said many years ago when reflecting on the programme which integrated the first autistic children back into his school. He said, 'I hope we have helped these [autistic] children, they have certainly helped us'.

The next three chapters involve music, a communication medium which transcends cultural boundaries and qualifies, along with English perhaps, as being a world language. Its use with these dyscultural children raises many interesting possibilities. Auriel Warwick's Chapter 20 involves music very directly in that it describes music therapy. Elizabeth Newson's Chapter 21 involves it less centrally, but nevertheless importantly, since therapy using music is one part of her approach. Ryuji Kobayashi's Chapter 22 uses the concept of the 'vitality affect' of speech: the rhythm, intonation, modulation, rather than the meaning of the words *per se*. Vitality affect is described in dynamic kinetic terms such as 'surging', 'explosive' and 'fading away'. It is intersubjective. Developmentally, as Stern (1985) argues, it precedes speech with meaning. Trevarthen describes the early interaction between mother and child in musical terms and indeed advocates music therapy for autistic children (Trevarthen *et al.* 1996). Given, as Kobayashi argues, that an autistic child is best reached through the 'vitality affect' rather than the content of speech, the value of music in communicating with autistic children is given a new meaning. Perhaps like all of us, it addresses pre-speech, pre-cultural, modes of emotional communication, which autistic children can manage better. The sort of communication that they have difficulty with involves the conventions of their culture (language, symbols, manners, conventional forms of behaviour) and involves the complex second guessing of people's intentions and feelings.

The work of Keiko Notomi seems very different (Chapter 23). She works within the behavioural/learning theory structure of the TEACCH techniques, but the interventions she describes are informed by a wider set of ideas and great clinical sensitivity.

Finally in Chapter 24, Hyde, Wimpory and Nash describe a coding instrument to look at early sociability. It lies within the psychological tradition of trying to find measures of a preconceived category (rather than the ethological tradition of directly observing and generating categories out of that). Instruments like this in the end rely upon various measures of 'validity' (including face validity, i.e. seeming obviously sensible) and are vulnerable to being shown not to fit the natural phenomena well, nevertheless as stop-gap practical clinical instruments they can be extremely useful.

References

Stern, D. (1985) *The interpersonal world of the infant.* New York, NY. Basic Books.

Trevarthen, C., Aitken, K., Papoudi, D. and Robarts, J. (1996) *Children with Autism.* London: Jessica Kingsley Publishers.

CHAPTER 18

The Tavistock Autism Workshop Approach

Assessment, Treatment and Research

Susan Reid and Anne Alvarez
with Anthony Lee

Abstract

This chapter provides an outline of the approach devised by the Autism Workshop at the Tavistock Clinic in London. Techniques of assessment and psychotherapy have been developed which are informed not only by psychoanalytic theory, but also by child development research. A particular emphasis is placed on the needs of the family as well as the child with autism. The Autism Workshop approach is currently being formally assessed through a research project designed to examine change in a group of children with autism and their families.[1]

Introduction

In the autism team based in the Child and Family Department at the Tavistock Clinic, we treat not only those who are sufficiently young and responsive to be helped back on to the path of normal development, but also those at the other end of the spectrum in terms both of the severity of

---

[1]   The approach outlined in this chapter derives from the clinical practice of Susan Reid and Anne Alvarez, under the auspices of the Tavistock Autism Workshop. Dr Anthony Lee has contributed to the section on research.

their autism and of its chronicity. In the latter cases, it may be impossible to effect a major reversal of the process, but it is often possible to have a significant impact on the quality of the autistic person's life and that of their family. The ideas outlined in this chapter represent the approach adopted by the Autism Workshop. The Autism Workshop, which was founded in 1986 by Susan Reid, is a multidisciplinary workshop co-chaired with Anne Alvarez, and attended by both students in training and postgraduates. Workshop members include professionals who currently work at the Tavistock, and also those who have moved on to take up posts around Britain. The development of the approach is described in fuller detail in *Autism and Personality: Findings from the Tavistock Autism Workshop* (Alvarez and Reid, 1999).

In the Tavistock Autism Workshop, we have developed techniques of psychotherapy which attempt to take account of the developmental delay, disorder and defensive or deviant structures in our patients' functioning (Alvarez 1999a, 1999b).

There is something so striking, so mysterious and disturbing about the condition of autism, especially the reduction of personhood in the sufferer, that it seems inevitable that researchers and clinicians tended to concentrate in the early decades on the features which autistic people had in common, rather than on those which distinguish them. In our approach we emphasise that every person with autism is different and that there is a close and dense interweaving between the symptoms and the personal motivation of the children, adolescents and young people. Each has, interwoven with their autism, an intact, non-autistic part of their personality. This non-autistic part may use, misuse and exploit the autistic symptoms, or it may oppose them and make efforts to reduce their influence. We have seen our patients begin to notice and enjoy the feeling of coming out of the 'deep freeze' of autism so that they may begin to value states of greater emotional depth and even struggle to preserve and maintain them.

Our approach is both psychoanalytic and developmental. It is psychoanalytic in its emphasis on the close observation of events in their interpersonal context. The tradition of naturalistic observation and an open-minded attempt to find a way through to the patient – instead of making a patient fit the theory – is in the best psychoanalytic tradition. We try to see the world through the child's eyes and not through the lens of some beloved theory or methodology. A major and ongoing preoccupation of our workshop is the development of increasingly effective treatment methodologies which take account of these patients particular levels of developmental delay.

It is informed by three major elements in our training. All three – psychoanalysis, infant observation and infant development research – involve a study of the nature of interpersonal relations, both in the external and internal worlds. These are applied to the very close observation of the individuality of people with autism.

Psychoanalytic features of the approach

Psychoanalytic treatment involves three major features: the regularity and consistency of the setting, the use of the transference, and the use of the counter-transference.

The regularity of the appointments, together with the consistency of the location of the sessions, is important for the recovery of all patients in psychoanalytic forms of treatment but we have found this to be especially important for autistic patients where a safe predictable setting is often the first thing which impinges on and attracts them.

Therapists use the transference – the patient's attitude in relation to the therapist – as the lens through which to view the patient's world of relationships to others. It is our experience that it is the emotionality in the contact with the therapist which promotes change in social relatedness, communication and thoughtfulness, and the development of an imagination. The counter-transference is understood as the response evoked in the psychoanalytic therapist by the patient's feelings. With our patients we are interested not only in behaviours, therefore, but also in monitoring the states of mind which accompany them and which they evoke in others. The use of the counter-transference enables therapists to observe how minute changes in their response may trigger changes in the patient, which then can be built upon, amplified and used to actively engage the patient.

Infant observation

The second major strand which informs our work is the naturalistic observation of infants. It is especially important for the study of people with autism, who are impaired in language and communication and whose signals may be faint or non-existent. The training in *emotionally* informed observation of the earliest forms of human interaction – in infants from birth – sensitises therapists to the subtlest, earliest forms of pre-verbal communication. Observation is used together with the use of the counter-transference to inform our choice of intervention.

Infant development research

This third strand is the work of the infant developmentalists. Their studies of the ways in which caregivers amplify and develop their infant's capacity for reciprocity and for entering into the world of human intercourse, informs our technique and sensitises us to the precise developmental level at which our patients are functioning at any given moment. Such work is important in our understanding of how normal development can go awry. Gaze avoidance, for example, is a normal coping mechanism in early infancy as revealed particularly by Stern's work, but it may, in the autistic person, have become dangerously habitual (Stern 1985). Such evidence may alert us to the fact that even when gaze avoidance is habitual, it may nevertheless continue to be fuelled by some degree of normal motivation.

Families

Fundamental to our approach is the degree of work pursued with the children's parents and other family members. The suffering of children with autism is, we have found, often underestimated, as particularly is the stress on their families and the tragic limitations on normal family life for everyone. The debate continues as to whether autism is emotional, cognitive or, as we suggest, an emotional/cognitive disorder. What is clear, however, is that an impairment in the capacity for social communication, whatever its cause, can be enormously distressing emotionally, both for impaired people and for those who live with them.

Children with autism are inflexible and unreasonable so their families seem to end up fitting in with them and not vice versa. The family, imprisoned to some degree by the child's condition, is now a very familiar story. It seems to be a reflection of the imprisonment of the child within the autistic condition. Families frequently become cut off from ordinary society, and the everyday features of family life may become a source of persecution and not a pleasure. A visit to the park or shops can become a nightmare because of the child's tantrums and anti-social behaviour. Without regular daily contact with other families and children, it becomes only too easy to lose any sense of what is 'normal' or 'ordinary', and so the children's behaviour can become the norm for their families.

We recognise that living with a person with autism can have a devastating impact on all other family members. Our own focus therefore is not primarily on diagnosis, but rather on attempts to discover the nature and location of the distress in the family. We also explore those therapeutic interventions which might prove helpful. Although a psychiatric diagnostic checklist for autism may confirm the presence and degree of severity of autism, it cannot convey what it is like to be autistic, and it cannot tell us what it is like to live with a child with autism. Diagnosis is only a small part of our assessment process.

Extended therapeutic assessments

Listening to many families' accounts of life with children with autism over many years has alerted us to the need for a change in our approach to assessment (Reid 1999a).

Families with an autistic child share the experience of living with a child who lives a world of their own: mysterious, separate. For parents to feel that they are not really interesting to their children, and that they have no real impact upon them or influence upon their behaviour, is to feel real despair. No matter how life started out for each of these children and their families, by the time of referral it is usually the parents who are feeling traumatised, desperate, often with little hope and with a damaged sense of personal worth. Parents' capacity to parent can easily be disturbed or disrupted by the traumatic impact of living with a child with autism and/or of receiving a diagnosis of autism. Much of our work in the early stages begins with practical help, around the areas of eating and sleeping in particular.

We also try to attend to the particular needs of any sibling as, having an autistic child in the family might be likened to having a cuckoo in the nest: the autistic child inevitably takes more and more of the family resources, but is unable to give anything much back. Equally inevitably then, other siblings get kicked out of the 'nest' of parental mindfulness and, perhaps recognising that their parents are already overtaxed, frequently become pseudo-good assistant parents. Other siblings, feeling that in order to get attention they need to behave like their autistic sibling, may indeed begin to imitate their behaviours and thus cause their overtaxed parents even more distress. Each family, to some degree, is suffering from post-traumatic stress. It is therefore important to go slowly, and because of this the usual assessment of a child in his or her family may now span several months.

Our assessments are also intended as therapeutic interventions in their own right. It has become apparent that what emerges over the course of these long assessments is a microcosm of the therapeutic process for those children subsequently offered psychoanalytic psychotherapy. The emphasis in this model of work is on the recognition that each family is unique, and that while children may share a diagnosis of autism, each child has his or her own individual personality. This unique personality may at times exacerbate the autism: at others, it may work on the side of more ordinary development.

Within our long assessments, we want to see whether we can generate in particular three things in the child – playfulness, friendliness and curiosity. In order to do this, it becomes necessary to build on the shadow of an idea where one perceives it, to fan the flicker of the flame of interest, to build upon, develop and amplify the earliest attempts at play. We try to provide a structure which is firm but flexible, and sufficiently elastic to meet the child's changing needs from one moment to the next. Within one session, and from one session to the next, it then becomes possible to see whether meaning begins to grow out of meaninglessness. Do we gradually form ideas about what the child is doing and why, and does the child begin to do things as if he or she anticipates a response? Does initially seemingly random behaviour begin to take on a structure? Is it possible to discern the beginnings of intentionality in the child's play? The observations made during the first and subsequent assessment sessions are in the service of the parents' relationship with their child. We share our observations with parents in the hope that this will encourage them also to observe their child in a new way and to open up communication. We seek to demonstrate that seemingly meaningless behaviour, which has worn parents down, may have meaning when we attend closely. It may also be that, given the freedom from other distractions, we might begin to notice things that they have not noticed before. It is important that parents, who so often feel impotent with their child, merely ancillary, should be given a new set of keys. Observing together, when meaning is revealed, can empower parents and give them hope.

Subgroups

The range of children referred to us has led us to think in terms of subgroups, each of which requires subtle but essential adaptations in the therapist's technique. Some have very strong, even bullish personalities which demand a firm, not too accommodating response if they are to notice our presence. Others impress us with their delicacy, even fragility, and extreme sensitivity and caution are required if they are to begin to tolerate engagement. We have learned, however to be open to the possibility, even probability, that as our work proceeds, the bullish children may reveal vulnerability behind their thick-skinned facades. The hypersensitive children on the other hand may well reveal reserves of stubborn determination, initially masked by their delicate presentations.

Another subgroup that has been identified are those children with autism who appear to have suffered trauma in infancy, and the term 'Post-traumatic Developmental Disorder' has been proposed to classify these children (Reid 1999b).

Keeping a diary

Over the years we have discovered the importance of a diary. We now ask parents when we first meet them to keep a diary at home, noting at the end of each week any changes they see in their child, whether these are for better or worse. This serves several functions. It encourages the continuation of observation at home and may support parents in the struggle to keep their child in mind. It emphasises the partnership that is essential between therapist and parents if a child is to sustain any changes that are seen to emerge in the consulting room. In the early stages of the assessments, a common feature is that many parents seem to find it very difficult to remember their child as a baby, in any detail. Despair and exhaustion make it difficult to remember and to note current changes. The diary supports the development of memory and emphasises where there is a potential for change. The weekly diary can be discussed in the next meeting and links made between the parents' observations of their child at home and what can be seen in the current session. This also supports and enables parents to tackle the problems at home. Respecting the parents' own observations of their child supports this possibility of a real dialogue. It aids in thinking about ways in which a family may change things at home, not based on some prescriptive notion of what autistic children need, but based rather on what we have seen together, using the particular style of parenting which is unique for this particular family. Some parents find it impossible to keep a diary at all, while others remember to keep it only in a sporadic way. Some fail to keep it at the beginning of the assessment but then, as their hope for change develops so too does their capacity to keep a diary. Others seem to engage with the notion of keeping a diary from the beginning. We take the different responses to the diary-keeping as a significant reflection of the family's capacity, at this point in time, and as an indication of where further support may be needed.

Using the model outlined in our book (Reid 1999a) we try to make a realistic assessment – of both needs and resources – concerning a child's capacities for change, and support for such change in their family.

Involvement in the assessment seems to make our approach and ideas more comprehensible to many parents, so that together we can devise a treatment plan that takes cognisance of these factors.

Following our assessments, a report is prepared for the referrer and general practitioner. Because of the complexity of the work with autistic spectrum and developmental disorders, every effort is made to involve other agencies and to include a professional review meeting. With the parents' permission, contact is made with the child's school.

Treatments

At the conclusion of the assessment, a review is held with the parents to discuss what interventions may be helpful. Some children are offered individual psychotherapy which can range from one to five times weekly and usually lasts for several years. All parents, when their child is offered individual psychotherapy, are offered support for themselves. Other families continue to be seen as a family group. We also offer a parents' group and group psychotherapy for some children and adolescents when they have completed a course of individual psychotherapy. Siblings may join a therapy group for the siblings of referred children and, where appropriate, are offered individual therapy in their own right. Consultations and support for involved professionals is offered in an ongoing way.

Outcome research

We have begun to evaluate our new techniques of psychotherapy which treat both the element of disorder and the developmental delay: the techniques are appropriately tuned to the child's delayed developmental level. This, combined with our emphasis on helping parents, both individually and in parents' groups to capitalise on their child's beginning emergence from autism, has enabled us to obtain extremely rewarding outcomes. We are now engaged in evaluating our practices and there are currently five ongoing research projects. We now describe an ongoing research project, begun in 1992, which has been designed to formally evaluate the impact of the Extended Therapeutic Assessments on the child with autism and the family.

Psychotherapists from the Autism Workshop working with children with autism and their families strongly feel that the technique of psychotherapy has profound benefit for these children. Indeed clinical experience has shown that most children seemed to make advances from the psychotherapeutic assessment themselves, which are conducted prior to children entering long-term treatment. The research project was designed to investigate the degree and nature of the change during the course of the psychotherapeutic assessment.

In an attempt to account or control for other factors that may be used to explain the predicted change, we decided to recruit into our sample only those children referred with autism to the Autism Team who were male and under 5 years of age. The parents of all such referrals were sent a letter outlining the study and asking them to consider participating. For ethical reasons, it is not possible to have a 'non-treatment' phase nor to withhold treatment for periods of time. To control for the effect of general developmental factors, therefore, a group of twelve children with autism, matched for sex, age, severity of autism and developmental level will be recruited. These children will be drawn from a population outside of London for whom psychotherapy is not currently available. We predict that the nature of and degree of development in the treatment group will be significantly different from that in the non-treatment control group.

There are three phases: pre-psychotherapeutic assessment, psychotherapeutic assessment and post-psychotherapeutic assessment. During the first phase, the research psychologist (Dr Tony Lee) makes a series of home visits. In the first of these visits a play-based session is videotaped capturing what the child typically does at home, the child's capacity to explore a set of standard toys and to engage in joint play with a parent. This is followed by a separation and reunion event. Subsequent home visits during the pre-treatment phase are conducted with the parent(s) alone, and are used to complete the Autism Diagnostic Interview (ADI-R: Lord, Rutter and LeCouteur 1994) and the Vineland Adaptive Behaviour Scales (VABS: Sparrow, Balla and Cicchetti 1984). The former measure aims to provide a lifetime assessment of the range of behaviours relevant to the differential diagnosis of pervasive developmental disorders in individuals. The latter measure provides an index of current functioning in the domains of Daily Living Skills, Communication, Socialisation, and Motor Skills.

In addition the Childhood Autism Rating Scale (CARS: Schopler, Reichler and Renner; 1986) was completed by the psychologist after observing the child over this phase to provide an index of severity of presenting features.

The family is then invited to the Tavistock for the psychotherapeutic assessment. This treatment phase may last between six and twelve months. All of the sessions are videotaped, and the therapist makes detailed processed notes after each session. In addition, the parents are asked to keep a diary of their observations and thoughts throughout the treatment period.

In the final post-treatment phase the psychologist returns to the family home. The play-based session is repeated along with a reunion and separation event. Apart from their impressions of the treatment received and their personal appraisal of how their child fared, the VABS are re-administered. Finally, the CARS is completed by the psychologist after observing the child during this final phase.

The measures detailed in the pre- and post-treatment phases will be administered to the participants of the control group. In addition, a detailed assessment will be made of the educational and therapeutic attempts to work with the child during this 'non-psychotherapeutic assessment' phase.

To date we have recruited twelve families into our project. Three families withdrew from the extended assessment and were not available for a follow-up. Seven families have undergone the extended psychotherapeutic assessment. We can report that of those who have undergone the follow-up phase, six of the children have changed in a manner consistent with our predictions. Without a formal contrast with the control group, however, these findings must be treated with caution. We hope to recruit a further three families over the next year. In addition, we will begin efforts to recruit families to comprise the control group.

Conclusion

We are optimistic that the results of our research projects will allow us to share with other professionals our own conviction, based on our clinical studies, that our methods can help many of these children and their families to have more meaningful lives.

References

Alvarez, A. (1999a) 'Addressing the deficit: developmentally informed psychotherapy with passive, "undrawn" children.' In A. Alvarez and S. Reid (eds) *Autism and Personality: Findings from the Tavistock Autism Workshop.* London: Routledge.

Alvarez, A. (1999b) 'Disorder, deviance and personality: factors in the persistence and modifiability of autism.' In A. Alvarez and S. Reid (eds) *Autism and Personality: Findings from the Tavistock Autism Workshop.* London: Routledge.

Alvarez, A. and Reid, S. (eds) (1999) *Autism and Personality: Findings from the Tavistock Autism Workshop.* London: Routledge.

Lord, C., Rutter, M. and LeCouteur, A. (1994) 'Autism Diagnostic Interview – Revised: a revised version of the diagnostic interview for caregivers of individuals with possible pervasive developmental disorders.' *Journal of Autism and Developmental Disorders 24*, 659–685.

Reid, S. (1999a) 'The assessment of the child with autism: a family perspective.' In A. Alvarez and S. Reid (eds) *Autism and Personality: Findings from the Tavistock Autism Workshop.* London: Routledge.

Reid, S. (1999b) 'Autism and trauma: autistic Post-Traumatic Developmental Disorder.' In A. Alvarez and S. Reid (eds) *Autism and Personality: Findings from the Tavistock Autism Workshop.* London: Routledge.

Schopler, E., Reichler, R.J. and Renner, B.R. (1986) *The Childhood Autism Rating Scale (CARS) for Diagnostic Screening and Classification of Autism.* New York: Irvington.

Sparrow, S., Balla, D. and Cicchetti, D. (1984) *Vineland Adaptive Behaviour Scales (Survey Form).* Circle Pines, MN: American Guidance Service.

Stern, D. (1985) *The Interpersonal World of the Infant.* New York: Basic Books.

CHAPTER 19

Integrative Play in Children with Autism and Asperger Syndrome

Lalli Howell

I have been working with autistic children, adolescents and young adults, their parents and their siblings since 1990 both in Britain and in Italy. Over this time, we have all gone through the whole range of emotions – traumas, upheavals, success and failure – attempting to make their lives, and of those around them, better.

What had struck me more than anything else in both countries was that autistic people lacked real exposure to their peer group. People with autism often live in homes where, given the nature of their condition, the adult is the main source of interaction, even with the presence of siblings. Friendship and exposure to their peer group seemed to me a big gap in their lives. It is extremely difficult for parents of children with autism to organise other children to come to the house. Often these children go to special schools, and to respite care centres where they mix with other children with other learning difficulties, but rarely with mainstream children.

A social exchange with their own peer group becomes an impossible task. Autistic children have difficulties in playing, anyway, and it is not just a matter of inviting friends, because they won't be able to initiate any playing unless they are supervised by somebody who knows what to do, and when to intervene without appearing intrusive

I have also worked with siblings of autistic children, often enough to realise that it was very hard for them to live with a brother or sister with a condition such as autism, let alone play with them. Often they felt excluded and neglected by their parents, indeed so much energy goes into the upbringing of a child with autism. Other siblings have expressed embarrassment having to bring friends home. All this leads to further isolation and leaves the child with autism in a further autistic state, where the outside world feels even more hostile and unreachable. Playing activities between the child with autism and the siblings seemed to be again an impossible task.

On the other hand I have seen siblings who have a brilliant attitude with their autistic siblings, and have taken on a lot of responsibility for the upbringing of their autistic brother or sister; in some of these cases I wondered how fair it was for these young people to have such a load so early on in their lives. I remember a 9-year-old girl who was the only help a mother had around a very difficult and challenging autistic boy of 7. I felt sorry for the girl who spent every single day after school looking after her brother, and didn't have the time or the energy to play or be with her own friends.

I have also taken autistic children in mainstream classes, as part of their educational programme. Definitely a step further, as here they could breathe some kind of normality. However, I always felt that we were guests. I began then to invite mainstream children in our sessions in our environment, in our classrooms, at the special school where I am working. It felt better. Our children were more relaxed, because they felt safer in their own environment, and the anxiety was felt more by mainstream children than autistic children. Now mainstream children were in an alien environment. Maybe, by being in a different setting and therefore experiencing anxiety, mainstream children could better understand the state of mind of these children during their integration programme and therefore build up a better sense of empathy.

I then set up meetings with those mainstream children, joining in their circle time in class; we talked about issues around integration, and the mainstream children began to develop a different attitude, they felt more involved and that involvement filtered through in activities such as the playground during break times and at lunchtime in the dinner hall. Integration felt more appropriate because it wasn't limited to an hour or two a week in a class situation, but it spread across more social activities within the school. However, in schools, integration is relatively easy to achieve, the structures are there, and it is quite easy to organise groups of mainstream children to participate in activities with autistic children.

The problem seemed to start at home after school hours. I tried to meet with mainstream children's parents to set up an after school programme, so that the autistic children could experience a normal after-school life.

Unfortunately only the more able of these children managed to get invited to parties, sleep-overs, and similar activities. The children who were more remote and presented a more challenging behaviour were very rarely included in the mainstream life of the other children, outside school hours.

Having also worked with the parents of children who are more severely affected by autism, the need for integration was also felt in an after-school situation. What could autistic children do after school? The level of after-school activities is linked to the severity of their condition. Some children and adolescents can join in activities such as sports, youth clubs, music lessons etc., but for others this is not possible, because the level of support is not available. It can also be argued that, despite the severity of their condition, these children need the time and the space for breathing the air of normality, without necessarily being structured in sports and other activities.

How was I going to make that happen? I looked at my own children, and at what they did after school. After a short period of relaxing, they sought their friends. We often have friends staying over. Their interplay does not involve a particularly rigid structure. Sometimes they just talk, play games, or mess about in the garden, other times they go out, or cook their evening meal, or bake a cake. I thought of re-creating a similar environment for autistic children and adolescents, who, for obvious reasons, could not experience a normal after-school life.

I then asked my children and some of their friends, who were all between the age of 9 and 13 then, if they were interested in organising an after-school club where the after-school home environment could be re-created, without a rigid structure or too many activities. They all liked the challenge, and we found a hall near to the schools attended by the autistic children. We started with six mainstream children and six autistic children. I wanted to keep a one-to-one ratio, initially, so that each young worker could be closely monitored and observed with the child they were working with.

I briefed the young workers, but I also told them that they had to find their own feet and their *modus operandi*. I was there for advice and support. I didn't want to burden them up with theory and strategies. I just wanted them to be children playing with other children, without creating preconceived ideas.

My constant message to the young workers was to act as normally as possible, using their common sense, and forget autism, just be, and see what they could do. I was there in case of necessity. At the end of each session, once the children went home, we had a debriefing discussion, where we brainstormed and troubleshot, and gradually my young workers became very competent with their own children. It started very well, and the autistic children responded very positively.

My aim was to train each worker so that they became interchangeable and could work with any child. There is without any doubt a value in the concept of the key-worker, but in this particular case it felt limiting.

What became immediately apparent was that the young workers were natural competent practitioners, unfazed by eccentric and bizarre behaviour, accepting, understanding, and supportive of a different way to see and experience life.

One of the young workers has a younger brother with autism, and it was interesting to see how her experience helped her in dealing with certain situations. It also led her and the others to realise that being autistic meant being an individual with a varied and complex range of difficulties.

The natural way in which these young people worked brought changes and shifts in some of the eccentric behaviour. Levels of anxiety lowered, everyone felt safe and relaxed, and I can count on the fingers of one hand difficult situations which have arisen in the two and half years we have been together.

However, it is not as easy as it seems, and the hard work has all to do with prevention. This requires a certain amount of skilful observation, and the ability to read each situation and predict what could happen next. This is the key of working successfully with children with autism. If the environment is favourable and safe, difficult situations do not arise. To be able to do that the staff–child ratio has to be very high.

There aren't two ways about it. The ability to prevent a difficult situation comes with experience and the level of knowledge of each child.

For instance, if a child cannot cope with sitting at the table with the others for our evening meal, that child will become quickly distressed as soon we start to get ready for dinner. Children, initially, have to be removed from a situation they find stressful. Not only will they have to be removed from the room where dinner takes place, but will have also to be distracted from the tidying up leading up to dinner. Autistic children are extremely sensitive to changes, and they can read what will happen next according to their ability to remember the phase prior to the high anxiety inducing situation. They are often a step ahead. The trick is to be able to be one step ahead of the step ahead. This is what I constantly tell my workers.

Children who find the evening meals stressful will be involved in games and activities with their young key-worker but leave before the tidying up session which leads to getting the room ready for dinner. If we wait for those children to leave the room while dinner is set up, the message will be that they will have to stay for dinner; they will become quickly distressed, and the effort to calm them down and reduce their anxiety will be difficult to achieve. It will distress other children. Only by creating a more favourable situation for that child is a crisis avoided.

Learning to cope with social situations is very hard for children with autism. Each situation has to be carefully monitored not to cause unnecessary distress which will prevent social learning, and will corner the children more into their autistic state. All this requires patience and a very positive frame of mind. People who are exposed to these children have to feel strong, and persevere in what at times may seem a losing battle.

This is one of the main reasons why I have chosen to work with younger individuals, who seem to have more enthusiasm and are less disturbed by apparent failure. They also seem less discouraged by repetitive negative behaviour and tend to disregard it. This in a way puzzles the autistic child who responds favourably, and at times amusing to people who are not prepared to notice certain reactions.

However, it is important to stress the importance of an adult presence who is experienced in autism, and has a good knowledge of the children. The young workers also need constant reassurance and positive reinforcement. Although operating in a more natural way, they find the work at times stressful and physically tiring.

What has also gradually surfaced from this project is the concept that not only the child with autism is benefiting from this type of intervention, but also the young workers benefit tremendously by being exposed to this kind of work.

I have seen these young workers develop and mature, I have heard their parents telling me that this experience has made them more sensitive and open to other difficulties experienced in other areas of their lives. These are youngsters in a delicate phase of their life, where confusion and lack of direction are often experienced.

This type of work has given them a focus. They still have their busy social and school life, but with something more. This will help them through difficulties in their adult life, and they will always be open and accepting of people who, for a varied number of reasons, experience difficulties in their life. It is wonderful to see a group of 14 to 18 children, mixing together, learning together, experimenting ways of behaving, trying to find a common ground although coming with such different perspectives of life.

It is extraordinary to see that such a large young group can so easily and naturally operate with just one adult supervising, and often I am in another room, with a cup of tea, reading a book or catching up with my work. It is also interesting to note that despite the fact that, normally, autistic children are considered not able to cope with change, and with not having a routine, on this occasion they accept the changes, and they do not expect a routine, because we do not have one.

This type of work is helpful both for autistic and mainstream children. The autistic ones benefit from having the opportunity of making friends, while the mainstream ones develop a better attitude towards people who have started life with a disadvantage. I hope that this exercise will widen awareness and understanding of autism in the young community.

CHAPTER 20

'I Have a Song – Let Me Sing'
Relating Part of a Journey through Music Therapy with an Autistic Boy

Auriel Warwick

Abstract

It is accepted that most autistic children respond well to music. This chapter sets out a case study of an autistic boy, describing one period during his four years of music therapy. It aims to show how music therapy can build a bridge across to the child's world, giving the opportunity for communication, interaction, a means of releasing feelings and learning how to understand them.

Introduction

Thomas arrived for his first assessment session for music therapy one day before his fifth birthday. He came to the special school which he would be attending the following September. When I met him, I sang a quiet 'Hallo' in greeting. He was prepared to take my hand, not appearing unduly anxious, and walk with me to the therapy room. I noted his beautiful dark brown eyes, eyes which looked beyond, never directly at.

Thomas was referred for music therapy by the Integrated Nursery staff because of his often bizarre autistic behaviour, his communication problems and his positive response to music. It was hoped that he might benefit from a specific approach through music to meet his particular needs. Thomas did not speak. He was concerned with his own agenda and relating to people was very difficult for him.

For the initial assessment session, a video camera was set up in one corner of the room. Thomas appeared to ignore it. He took little notice of me – but he was very aware of our music, turning towards the source of those musical sounds which were not his own. The room was set out with instruments – a digital piano and an alto xylophone, with a collection of untuned instruments of varying sizes, from a large ocean drum and cymbal on a stand to small hand-held instruments. From the beginning of the session, as I continued to sing 'Hallo' to him, Thomas was more attracted towards exploring the large instruments. He approached me at the keyboard and played the black keys before the white. When I began to play, he stopped and looked about him before moving away to choose another instrument. When I began to improvise a song, describing what he was doing, he smiled. It didn't take him long to work out that the xylophone bars could be removed, but after lifting off two, he decided that playing was more rewarding.

As the session progressed, Thomas seemed to realise that this was his agenda and that I was prepared to follow and support him through my music. He began to vocalise in short phrases and appeared to listen when I sang. He hid under the table which contained some of the instruments and retrieved the ocean drum so that he could explore it safely on his own territory. The 'Goodbye' song contained my singing and our shared beating on the ocean drum. Thomas accepted the sharing but there was no sense of turn-taking. During this session, I was encouraged by the lack of his stereotyped mannerisms, apart from one or two instances of brief rapid hand flapping.

To meet his needs, I recommended three main aims in music therapy:

1. to encourage Thomas's musical initiative-taking

2. to develop musical interaction through turn-taking and improvisation

3. to provide him with a non-verbal means of expressing himself and communicating through a medium which was meaningful, within a safe and supported environment.

Sessions would take place each week, each to be 25 to 30 minutes long, depending on how Thomas was at the time.

In those early days, I believed that music therapy could be an important part of Thomas's developmental curriculum. I had no idea then of how vital it would prove to be when his world fell apart around him – and how he gave me the means to work with the counter-transference I was to experience. Working with someone like Thomas – where there is the sense of a real intelligence but where there is confusion and disorder – has consolidated many years of learning how music can form bridges when the world lacks meaning or the senses are overwhelmed.

The therapy

The first eighteen months of therapy were centred in shared music-making and establishing a bond of trust between us. Thomas was happy to make his choices. My role was to give musical support and the time and space in which he could explore the potential of both the instruments and his voice. If I initiated, he was able to respond although he didn't always choose to. Thomas enjoyed the instruments placed in a big circle on the floor, moving in and out of the circle at will. However, as soon as he felt comfortable within the structure of the session after several weeks, he began to challenge the boundaries. Usually, this involved attempting to climb on top of furniture and cupboards, looking at me and giggling. I had to be very firm and establish with him that this was a 'no go' area, marking the contrast between my usual accepting demeanour and making it clear what was not acceptable. After five sessions, Thomas understood that I meant what I said and stopped the controlling behaviour. Musically, our relationship strengthened through vocal and instrumental turn-taking. Thomas's voice was clear and tuneful – his single sounds were often extended into short melodic phrases. He let me know that he wanted to communicate – and music made it easier for him. It was also important, without breaking confidentiality, to keep the staff aware of the developments taking place in therapy and in turn to hear how he was coping in class. At the same time he was challenging me, he was challenging in the classroom. This was noted in the statutory annual review meeting between parents and professionals.

After one particular half-term break, a dramatic change took place. I had Mark, a trainee music therapist, with me on an observation placement. With hindsight, I realise that his gender was possibly a factor in what eventuated. Mark was sitting in a corner near the door. I had given him instructions to avoid eye contact with Thomas. From the outset, Thomas gave me an indication that something was wrong. He walked into the circle of instruments and, while I was sitting on the floor singing 'Hallo', accompanying myself on the xylophone, began to pick them up, one by one, placing them on the line of chairs in front of the bookcase. Thomas came over to me and removed first the xylophone, then the beater from my hand. I experienced a very powerful transference. I felt totally bereft and powerless. I was alone with nothing, a complete loss of identity. The feeling was desperation. This was a cry for help from Thomas. He had to make me understand how he felt. I moved over to the instruments where Thomas was standing. He looked towards me and tapped with his hand on the strings of the autoharp. My response was to tap on the guitar strings. He responded on an upturned drum. I replied on a different drum. Where Thomas's face had been withdrawn and sad, there was a sudden smile in response, perhaps an acknowledgement that he understood that I was trying to meet him where he was. The session duly ended and Thomas and I returned to class. Mark's opening remark when I arrived back was, 'We have seen video of music therapy sessions during which we were very moved, but I didn't realize the real thing was quite like this.'

This experience raised the issue of how therapists protect themselves and work in the counter-transference with the client. It is important to understand where the powerful feelings belong. I was sure that what I had experienced were not my own feelings and all I could think was that something had happened at either school or home. Later, Thomas's teacher told me that there had been trauma at home. Dad was on the verge of a breakdown and had left home during the half-term to try to sort himself out. For Thomas, it must have felt as though his safe world was disintegrating. He felt helpless, losing a sense of self which was already fragile. Later, I had the opportunity to talk to Thomas's mother. He is fortunate to have a very loving and supportive family who are only too willing to share with the multidisciplinary team. The situation at home had indeed been traumatic. At this time, Thomas was coming out of an acute stage of his autism, becoming more aware of the world about him and therefore more challenging. His father felt powerless, not believing that he could do anything for his family. He had given up full-time employment to help his wife with Thomas. Perhaps Thomas couldn't bear his father's pain. Mother also had extreme bouts of depression and desperation while making supreme efforts to keep the family together.

Dad was away for ten months although during that time he regularly visited his family several times a week. When he visited, Thomas wouldn't have anything to do with him. It was a make-or-break situation. Fortunately, Thomas's parents were determined to work hard at resolving a difficult issue. In the mean time, Thomas had grown closer to his mother and when Dad did return home permanently, Thomas was jealous. When he understood that his father was really home, and experienced the renewed strength of the family, he became Dad's boy again.

Thomas's working through the trauma was quite explicit in the music therapy. Within six months of Dad's leaving, Thomas was resolving some issues for himself. From my own supervision (from a child psychotherapist) I felt supported in the view that Thomas's piling up the instruments was his trying to make sense and order from what was happening. In the acute phase, this could be as many as three cycles each session. Gradually this lessened to stacking at the beginning of the session and taking down again as soon as I began the preparation for 'Goodbye'. While the instruments were on the chairs, Thomas and I could still communicate using the instruments and our voices. Thomas's vocal phrases were usually a falling interval, describing his sorrow. I reflected this feeling back to him so that he could be aware that I was trying to understand. But it wasn't all sad. There were also flashes of impish humour in the ways he played and he seemed very aware when I acknowledged what he played.

There was another change. Because of Thomas's parents' determination to keep a sense of unity as much as they could, I felt that he was becoming less vulnerable and that I could risk being less containing. I moved away and began to support from the keyboard. Immediately, Thomas turned around and left the instruments to join me. He sat at the treble end and played a series of chord clusters on the white keys. We played together, able to share a tonality. This felt like another strong meeting point. The play of expression on Thomas's face switched between intensity and more relaxed pleasure when he leaned towards me with fleeting smiles. I found my rhythms and tonality becoming more syncopated and jazz-like as we became a partnership. Then, perhaps because the interaction was becoming too intense for him, Thomas stopped playing, leaned away from me and beat on the floor with one hand. I matched my chords with his beating. After about ten seconds, he straightened himself and returned to improvise with me.

The time for the end of the session was close. I sang that it was nearly time to go – time for the 'Goodbye' song. He left the keyboard to take down the instruments from the chairs. Thomas spontaneously returned to the keyboard for the ending of the session. After I sang a 'Goodbye' to him, he sang an accurately pitched 'Goodbye' in reply. When I followed this by singing, 'Time to go now,' Thomas surprised me by quietly intoning an approximation of what I had just sung. This happened twice with other phrases. After the months of crisis, this was a magical moment of connection with a boy who was able to meet me in our music.

Conclusion

Thomas's music therapy sessions ended during the summer term of the next academic year. He was at the point of moving up to another class and after four years of therapy, the aims set out had been achieved to a considerable degree. When therapy should end is never clear-cut when clients have Autistic Spectrum Disorder. Thomas has taken the first steps towards some understanding that a shared activity with another person can be good and positive. He discovered non-verbal communication through using instruments and his voice. He is now much more confident in his ability to communicate and he is beginning to talk. Thomas was able to let me glimpse some of his pain, confusion and sadness but was also able to communicate that life was beginning to get together again.

Thomas had used the therapeutic space with intelligence and our relationship grew in trust and mutual respect. It was time to let him go in the knowledge that he was less fearful and more communicative. I had to be strong for him at a time when he was unable. The therapeutic boundaries needed to be firm without being rigid so that he could venture, however tentatively, into the world beyond his autism and become aware of the non-autistic side of his personality.

CHAPTER 21

The Pragmatics of Language
Remediating The Central Deficit
for Autistic 2–3 Year Olds

Elizabeth Newson

When we are faced with an autistic child of 4 or 5, and have to think about how to educate him effectively, the contrast between him and the non-autistic child on entry to school is obvious and extreme. However, as we succeed in diagnosing earlier and earlier, the most striking contrast for the clinician with a developmental psychology background is between a child with autism in the second year of life and the normally developing baby of a similar or younger age. It is particularly interesting to look at normal babies *before* they develop speech, and consider their sophistication as communicators before they have the words in which to express their thoughts, emotions and wishes.

The building-blocks of communication, *until* we get to speech, are almost entirely biological and developmental: that is, they are not taught to ordinary babies as skills, but develop naturally, and simply increase in sophistication through practice. Obviously the baby needs the motivation to continue to practise them; but (provided the emerging ability is there) this will, in itself fuel the motivation so long as someone is available to communicate with. A repeated comment of parents whose first child is autistic and second child normal is how much earlier they would have worried about the autistic child – by 6 or 9 months, they often say – if they had known how actively normal babies communicate before they have words. They realise that they can have a better conversation – non-verbal 'baby chat' – with their 6-month-old normal child than they have ever had with their autistic 3 or 4 year old.

The linguistic tools that ordinary babies use before spoken language is available to them are in fact the 'pragmatics' of language: all of these are the abilities that they will eventually need in order to transform speech into *conversation or dialogue.* What is important is that the pragmatics are not added on to speech after it has developed; they develop long before speech, are increasingly practised throughout the first year, and thus make ready for the speech that normally follows. For autistic children the pragmatics are lacking or deeply disordered; in some ways this is a more serious disorder than the speech deficit because, developmentally speaking, it comes at an earlier and more significant time. Even for the verbal Asperger children, failure of pragmatics ensures that their speech, whose language may eventually be normal or even too perfect when written down, comes across as odd and stilted; intellectually gifted Asperger people may be socially handicapped all their lives by their pragmatic disorder.

Perhaps it is helpful here to list the major pragmatics, so that we can see how necessary they are to communication (see Table 21.1). In practice they include almost all the *body language* we use, and this in itself would be a serious loss; but there is another aspect that governs everything else, and so should take precedence: *social timing.* The way in which we time our communications, verbal or non-verbal, in relation to another person, is crucial to starting and maintaining a *dialogue flow:* it contributes to the meaning of what we say (consider the use of hesitation in relation to how another person interprets our meaning); it ensures that we do not abandon our listener (as autistic children – and adults – do). It governs the other pragmatics in terms of how they are used *together:* for instance, a pointing gesture will be accompanied by transfer of gaze from the object to eye contact, and will be marked by a sound of some sort: 'Da!' in the preverbal baby. It can be seen that social timing has close connections with *social empathy,* which is a term I much prefer to 'theory of mind' because it rightly embraces the *emotional* aspects of thinking, instead of taking us down a too-narrow cognitive route.

Body language can be broadly divided into *facial expression, gesture* and *posture or stance* (for simplification). Facial expression includes eye contact, and is normally marked by mobility and variety. Autistic children's expressions are rather static and lack variety: we can read whether they are happy,

Table 21.1 The major pragmatics of language – receptive
and expressive (lacking or distorted in autism:
social empathy is the foundation)

Social timing	(implicit in all pragmatics)
Body language	facial expression (including eye contact)
	gesture (especially pointing)
	posture, stance, personal space
Listening skills	turn-taking
	noticing signals of impending speech
	knowing who is being addressed (identifying with group)
	maintaining attention to body language
	showing that you're attending
Intonation	for meaning
	for emphasis
Volume	for meaning
	adaptation to distance (including attentional distance)
Understanding intention	teasing (6 months onward)
	joking, sarcasm, metaphor, irony (later)
Shared understanding	with acknowledgement:
	includes *social imitation*
Sharing intention	and acknowledging this
Sharing interest	drawing attention to
	for parents' *interest*
	bringing to show
	for parents' *interest*

sad or angry, but not much more; and they have the same difficulty with
our expressions. As one perceptive Asperger adolescent said, 'People send
each other messages with their eyes, and I can't understand those

messages'; at least he knew the messages were there, but most autistic children do not.

For all preverbal children, *gesture* is crucial, the first and most important being pointing, about which I'll say a little more later on. Waving bye-bye (with eye contact) is less important, but very noticeable if it is lacking: as are nodding, head-shaking and beckoning, whose lack causes still greater problems when the child doesn't respond to these. More serious for an autistic child is that it is usually very difficult for speech to be replaced or augmented by sign language. *Posture* is less important than these, but can cause social difficulties later, especially when children can't interpret the teacher's posture, or when they do not face the person they are trying to communicate with.

This brings us to *listening skills*, which include the use of all of the other pragmatics as well as the realisation of the need to attend to them in other people. The child with autism fails to notice that someone is about to speak, and fails to maintain attention to their body language as well as speech. Listening skills include *knowing who is being addressed* – for instance, knowing that he or she, too, is included when the teacher says 'Now children...'. In practice, lack of listening skills is probably the major practical problem for Asperger children in mainstream school.

Knowing how to get attention is as necessary as knowing how to listen, and part of normal communication is to do with *using intonation* to establish subtle aspects of meaning; in particular, the child needs to adapt both *volume and emphasis* to the attentional state of the other person. Ordinary babies do this non-verbally before they have speech. Clearly the other person may be 'distanced' by being in the next room or just watching the television, and the non-autistic baby soon has enough empathy to adapt his or her voice to overcome these obstacles.

For very young children, *understanding intention* is the forerunner of listening skills; failure to do this is linked with both lack of social empathy and lack of social timing. Ordinary 6-month-old babies are very well able to enjoy and respond to the teasing element of anticipation games (such as 'I'm...coming...to...GET you!'), and by a year they are teasing their parents themselves very consciously; autistic children have to be taught this, and with difficulty, except for the simplest of games such as 'peep-bo' and tickling. Use of eye contact is especially strong when children tease their parents, which certainly doesn't help the autistic child. Ordinary 2 year olds are good at judging their parents' mood: is Mummy serious, or can I make it into a joke? Children with autism, even those who are bright, fail lamentably at this social ability. In older and verbal children with autism, their inflexibility adds to the difficulty by making joking, sarcasm and metaphor difficult for them either to understand or to use. It is an interesting point that where the most able and verbal Asperger children have difficulty with semantics, this is almost entirely because they fail to understand *personal* meaning – not what the *words* mean, but what the *person using them* means in this context.

Closely related are *shared understanding* and *sharing either intention or interest*. The ordinary baby assumes and wants shared interest from others; for instance, the development of walking immediately leads to *bringing things to show people for their interest*, just as pointing is used for drawing parents' attention to interesting things. Autistic babies bring things for functional reasons – a cup to be filled, a book to be gone through – but not purely because it's fun to share an interest or to have a preverbal chat about things.

At this point we can remind ourselves of the communicative sophistication of ordinary preverbal children by considering a two-minute home video clip (described below) of a normal 11-month-old child, Rachel, which vividly illustrates how almost all of these pragmatics are present in the ordinary baby at the end of the first year. This clip is part of a twenty-minute episode in which Rachel, having finished her Sunday breakfast, is playing with her grandmother at the table where the rest of the family are still eating. She's pleased with herself because she's just learned to place a set of four pegs in four holes, so the toy is the shared focus for both of them. Rachel is pre-verbal, but she squeals, smiles and laughs, each time with eye contact; she gazes at an uninvolved speaker and juggles with the kinds of attention she gives to other people, especially her 4-year-old brother and including the unresponsive camera-man, so this is much more than the usual 'experimental triad' of child, adult and object. She imitates a gasp socially, with a smile and eye contact, reaches with spread fingers and finally points with stretched forefinger – just as she is supposed to at 11 months.

Rachel sits at right angles to her grandmother, with her brother further down on the other side. She has a truck with one peg already standing in its hole; they can only be fitted one way up. She fiddles with the pegs, trying them against the holes; squeals and smiles at her brother, and moves pegs around. She squeals and makes strong eye contact with her grandmother, and smiles at her under her eyelashes, looks at another (speaking) adult briefly, then fingers and fits a second peg. Looks at once to her grandmother, who gasps and says 'Oh! You did it!' and Rachel grins till her eyes are almost shut, laughs, and gasps in imitation. She partly fits a third peg and steals a glance at her brother, looks back at the pegs, smiles, turns to her grandmother, repositions the peg and turns to her again. Her grandmother says 'That's right – now you know which way up to put them'. She fits the peg properly, her grandmother gasps and Rachel turns to her and chuckles. Her grandmother says 'What about this one?' and Rachel looks at a distant peg. Her fingers are now spread but not reaching; she looks at her brother, and turns to her grandmother as she says 'Do you want this one?' She reaches her hand, fingers spread, saying 'uh'. She grasps a peg from the truck with forefinger extended, and 'points' with the peg, saying 'uh' with more force; her grandmother imitates the noise and her brother laughs and imitates too. Her grandmother says 'Do you want this one?' and Rachel reaches out her arm and makes a very clear distance-point with her forefinger. Grandmother says 'Oh! Yes! You shall have it!' and gives it to her; there is eye contact, then Rachel fits the last peg, squeals, and looks at her grandmother with a big smile and eye contact, which she holds. Her grandmother claps her: 'Well done!' Rachel looks over to her brother, makes eye contact and claps herself, smiling, as he claps her in return.

Can we teach the pragmatics of language to children with autism?

Because for many years we were carrying out research on the normal development of communication in babies, while in parallel being closely involved with a specialist school for children with autism, the contrast between the growth of pragmatics in ordinary children and in children with autism has been consciously at the forefront of our minds in our efforts to develop communicative competence in our school. If ordinary babies have been practising the pragmatics for a year, before their speech begins to appear, should not *this* be the priority for autistic children, too?

It does in fact seem common sense that, when we start with a well-researched list of diagnostic criteria, *which in fact amounts to a list of inbuilt deficits*, we will be most effective if we address those deficits very directly in the work we do. There is currently a kind of fashion, which is partly reflected in a few of the chapters in this book, for playing down the deficits of autism. However, I believe that we have to face up to a different view, given deficits that are as crucial, damaging and central as a lack of linguistic pragmatics; because if we make no attempt to remediate this loss, and as early as possible, we betray the child and fail abysmally in our responsibility towards the child.

When a child enters Sutherland House school, then – usually at about 4 or 5 – we concentrate on those pragmatics that we consider most crucial: social timing, the turn-taking which is dependent on this, shared understanding and intention, and pointing. We can address all except the last through *musical interaction therapy*, which is a specialist two-to-one therapy involving the child, the child's key-worker and the musician/therapist. We have written a great deal on this way of working (e.g. Christie *et al.* 1992; Lewis, Prevezer and Spencer 1996; Prevezer 1998), and there is no space to discuss it here, except to point out that the fact that the child's key-worker is involved means that the principles of the work are carried back into the classroom and inform every other part of the child's curriculum. However, I would like to spend a little time on the teaching of pointing, which we regard as a priority.

The point of pointing

What is so special about pointing? We can sum it up in three words: it is *intentional, intersubjective* and *symbolic*. Children, as they point, are wholly aware of what they are doing, and know themselves to be deliberately attracting the attention of another person to what will be a shared object of focus and, as such, a focus for their intersubjectivity. The distance point, in particular, is symbolic because it creates an imaginary line between the finger and the object; this imaginary line *is* the 'point of pointing'.

At whatever age our children come into school, we find they are still unable to point unless they have been expertly taught. As we've seen in ordinary babies, the active point arrives at 11 months, at the same age as the pincer grip (which also involves the separation of the forefinger, a biological 'making-ready' development, but is non-social). Children with autism develop the pincer grip but not the point.

In ordinary babies, once the point has arrived, the child's self-conscious communication undergoes an explosion, and the point itself becomes the tool for the 'What dat?' game, which rapidly increases vocabulary. Ignoring for a moment the dichotomy that has been made between the imperative (requesting: I want that) and the declarative (look at that), which we find irrelevant in actual practice (Charman 1998), pointing offers any child many different possibilities. At an early stage, before the arrival of distance pointing, it helps the child to focus on single items within an array: touch-pointing at single pictured objects, for instance, aids concentration on detail, just as a child may later run his finger along a line of writing. Distance-pointing may serve the same purpose of *focus*, reminding children what they are referring to, even before they extend this to share their focus with another person. The imperative point may have different *stages* of meaning: 'I want...so give me...now!...no, not that one, that one'. The declarative, too, has different degrees of *empathy*: 'That's interesting (don't you think?) Can't you see it?...look...no, move your head a bit...That's the one I mean (not the one you may be thinking)'. Although distance-pointing usually indicates a notional symbolic connecting line, this is not always so; it may be used to emphasise a word or to suggest another symbolic meaning which is imagined. For instance, we have a video-clip in which the non-autistic Sebastian, aged just 2, does both these things together when he 'jumps' a toy monkey, looks at his grandmother and says 'up in the air!', pointing up into a notional sky with his free hand.

Perhaps more important than any of this, the point is an exceptionally arresting gesture, whether one is pointing oneself or watching someone pointing. As such, it emphasises *intentionality* in no uncertain terms. Watching a toddler pointing, one is struck by the emphatic tautness of the tendons as the forefinger stretches up and the other fingers stretch down in opposition. This is the most uncompromising and unmistakable gesture that the 1-year-old has ever made, and it is difficult to ignore or resist, even if one wanted to. For the child, it asserts, 'Hey, I'm talking to you...and I mean it!' Thus it is likely to give a powerful message, both to the adult *and to children themselves*. Surely this must be the trigger for the explosion of purposeful communication as soon as pointing is established, and the children clearly become conscious of their power (Newson and Christie 1998).

The question is, can we manufacture a similar, even if *mini*-explosion in purposeful communication if we teach autistic children pointing as a learned skill? We know that we can, *so long as we teach with intense care for meaning*, rather than creating just another learned stereotypy. By making the pragmatics a priority, we find ourselves able to produce 'useful speech' in 65 per cent of our 6–11 year olds, rather than the usually quoted 50 per cent (if we define useful speech as having at least a variety of spontaneous two-word sentences).

The next question, of course, is whether we can reduce the age at which we can teach the pragmatics. It is not our choice that children enter school at 4–5; 2–3 would seem a much better time for the communicative deficits of autism to begin to be remediated. At the very least, if we could make these children a little more open to communication at 2, even if still preverbal, we might avoid the terrible year at 3 which so many autistic children go through as they withdraw further still into distressed inflexibility. The destructive effect of just doing nothing is one that we are both clinically and educationally aware of, and one which parents themselves fear.

Early diagnosis, early intervention

Our current research explores the close integration of diagnosis at 2 followed by immediate intervention, and is aimed to provide a package to make this viable. It adapts the work we have done in a school setting to the more naturalistic setting of the home, translating the musical interaction therapy method of school into a play-based programme that can be easily learned by parents who have no musical or other training. Similarly, we have picked apart our curriculum, teaching parents to teach their children the most urgent and necessary pragmatics, including quite complex and difficult processes such as teaching meaningful pointing. Our basic principles of working are the same as we use in the school: intervention is *adaptive*, and is based on teaching interaction, negotiation and communication tools. It is *not* based on forced imitation, coercion or control. Workshops on behavioural methods, but *within a negotiative framework*, are included.

The most important feature of our early intervention programme is to ensure that parents' full understanding of the diagnosis and its implications for the child becomes the basis for knowing *why* they need to work with their child in the various ways suggested, and what are the principles for doing so. Information on both *why* and *how*, in a number of different areas, is given through very practical *'How to do it'* booklets, which are clearly based in what the diagnostic criteria have made them aware of, and therefore give them a highly informed sense of what is needed. During the diagnosis, a pragmatics profile has been drawn up for their child as part of their diagnostic report, so that parents can see precisely how the individualised programme fits with the difficulties we are trying to remediate. Examples of the booklet titles are *Interactive Play, Teaching Pointing, The Beginnings of Structure, Understanding Language* and so on.

The 'How to do it' booklets are backed up by weekly home visits by the developmental psychologist and occasional consultation visits to the clinic to meet our musical interaction therapist, while the psychologist is herself backed up by fortnightly meetings with three specialist consultants. After the first six months, a parent workshop series is run over eight meetings, so that parents can meet each other and learn together how to deal with specific difficulties that concern them.

We have been working with 10 children over a period of 2½ years, staggered so that each family has 18 months of intervention. The children ranged from 20 months to 2: 9 on starting. The programme is evaluated in a number of ways, including independent interviews, repeated pragmatics profiles and comparison groups.

Four short videotapes are described below as 'work in progress' to illustrate the interactive play sessions with which we try to remediate the pragmatics (as a home-based alternative to musical interaction therapy). With permission, the children's names are used as they figure on the tapes. In all these illustrations, it is noticeable how enjoyable these sessions are for the children; this is true of everything we do or ask parents to do with them, including more formal tabletop sessions and teaching pointing. In this way the pleasurable heart of parenting can be kept intact, despite the much greater demands on them. It is also easy to see the principle of *negotiation* in action.

Video 1: Jayden aged 2: 5

Jayden is seen seven months into the intervention; Susie Chandler, research psychologist, works with him on this occasion while his very young mother watches as she doesn't like being on camera. Jayden had many stereotypies at 1: 10, including meaningless pointing which he had to unlearn: he then learned real pointing within two months, and immediately followed with meaningful words, though some of the content of his speech was obsessive at first.

> Jayden spontaneously jumps on the spot three times; Susie says 'jump, jump' and jumps herself; Jayden joins her jumping around, and Susie sings: 'We're jumping round the room, we're jumping round the room, Jayden is jumping, jumping round the room'. Jayden's jumps are in time with hers. They stop, and Susie starts a new verse: 'We're...walking round the room...', and continues as Jayden very deliberately starts walking around with her; as the verse ends, he crashes onto a beanbag, and Susie says 'Crash!' Jayden does it again, this time saying 'Cra-ash!' with feeling. Together they re-enact the 'Crash!' twice, then get up. Susie says 'We're... crawling!' Jayden drops to his knees and crawls with Susie as she sings this new verse. At the end of the verse, Susie sings 'We're...' and Jayden goes on crawling, and looks expectantly at Susie, who starts a second 'crawling' verse in response; this time, Jayden completes his crawl with a 'Crash!', and Susie follows suit. They re-enact the 'crash!' very dramatically, Jayden with raised arms crashing down to the floor and giggling as he says 'Crash!'

Video 2: Ollie aged 2: 10

Ollie is here three months into intervention; he is severely autistic with learning difficulties, and is especially resistant. His father has retired to be his main carer. Ollie took the whole eighteen months to learn to point, and suddenly became an active non-verbal communicator.

> Father kneels on the floor, Ollie reclines against him with bare feet stretched out towards Susie, who kneels opposite. He looks at her briefly and she says 'Are you ready for a blow?', takes a deep breath, says 'Blow!' and blows on his foot. He smiles, she says 'Again? Ready...for...(he wriggles expectantly, pushes foot forward, looks at her)...a...blow!'. He gives eye contact. Susie: 'On your foot?

Ready...(he gives stronger eye contact, settles back against his father, pulls foot back, looks expectant and smiles)...for...a...blow!' Susie blows, he laughs, says 'Aaahh!' with a rising inflection, clutches both feet, gives very strong eye contact. Susie: '*That's* a lovely look!' Olly says 'Dah' with a confirming inflection. Susie says: 'Ready...for...a...b,b,b. (no response) blow' (quietly). Ollie gets up, turns away, but then comes back and, standing, offers his other foot to Susie. Susie: 'This foot?' and blows it. Ollie jumps excitedly away.

Video 3: Edward aged 2: 4

Edward is seen two months into intervention; his mother is working with him in her bedroom on the double bed. This is because he is obsessed with videos: in the living-room he screams constantly to have a video put on. The bedroom was used until Edward was interested in interactional play for itself, when he began to be able to accept the living-room without videos.

Edward, wearing just a nappy, stands by the bed looking at a picture on the far wall, his back to his mother, who kneels at the other side of the bed with a small collection of plastic animals in front of her. She says 'Where's Edward? Edward...(he ignores)...Edward!' He turns, smiles, climbs on the bed and crawls towards her. Mother: 'What shall we do? (sings) Old MacDonald had a farm, ee i ee i oh. (Edward looks at the animals) And on that farm he had a...?' Edward selects a crocodile and gives it to her. Mother: 'Crocodile! With a snap-snap-snap here and a snap-snap-snap there' (poking the crocodile at Edward's bare tummy). She continues with the next verse; Edward gives her a horse and jumps around on the bed. She sings 'On that farm he had a horsie...with a neigh-neigh here (tickling him with the horse)'; he giggles and dances. She continues with the next verse, he falls over but comes and gets the horse again; she accepts it and continues singing and tickling. Edward dances, mainly oriented towards her, sits down, watches, listens, and chooses the crocodile again on cue. He sits in front of her, watching. He rolls around on the bed, looks at the ceiling, but as she approaches his cue again he turns back, grabs the horse in time, and makes four emphatic touch points on the horse with his other forefinger before giving it to her.

Video 4: Aaron (known as Snuggie), aged 2: 11

Aaron is three months into the intervention; his mother and Susie both work with him during this session. He has learned to point, and is doing so spontaneously and determinedly, standing under a shelf of toys while they try to see what he is pointing at.

> Mother: 'Would you like your tube? Where's the tube? Pointing – *there's* Snuggie's tube! (a coloured polythene tube, flexible and three feet long). *I'm* going to blow Snuggie's...hair!' She blows through the tube and Snuggie giggles a lot and reaches for the tube. His mother says 'I'm going to blow on Snuggie's...(he puts out his hand)...hand!' He runs to the settee, climbs on it and turns to face her; his feet are bare. Mother: 'I'm going to blow on Snuggie's...foot!' He giggles and squeals, grabs the tube and pulls it towards Susie, who says 'Are we swapping?' She plays the same game, this time singing 'Blow on Snuggie's hair; blow on Snuggie's feet', as he sits on the settee squealing and giggling, and giving her eye contact. Susie 'toots' through the tube; he grabs the end of the tube and makes it go up and down as she adjusts her tooting to his movement; the sound goes up and down in pitch as his movement goes up and down.

> Snuggie makes eye contact with Susie, and he simultaneously shakes a rattly toy in his other hand and vocalises; their play is very reciprocal. He is now adjusting his movement to her sound while vocalising in a sing-song way. He then toots himself with similar intonation to hers, while moving the tube up and down in time with the sound, showing quite complex social timing.

Conclusion

Perhaps I can sum up what we are trying to do here. We want to make it possible for children with autism to experience for themselves what other children experience naturally at an earlier age still; but they cannot do this unless we make it happen for them in very deliberate ways, intensifying and repeating the experiences until the child begins to reap the social and communicative rewards, and to be aware that these *are* rewarding. We did not know at the outset whether we could be successful with 2–3 year olds; however, all of our first batch of six have become more communicative, some have meaningful sounds and even words or sentences, all have learned to point meaningfully (even the one whose forefinger had not yet separated when we started), and none of them has entered the distressing 3-year-old withdrawal stage: that alone would have justified the intervention.

I'd like to end with some quotations from the independent evaluation interviews, so as to give parents the final voice.

> He couldn't speak or really communicate at all before, and he can speak now and point and use other gestures. Sometimes he talks too much! He can ask for things he wants; before he had lots of tantrums because I didn't know what he wanted... He plays with me now. Before, he would just run around or sit lining up pegs and bottles. He plays with his trains with me now instead of just lining them up all the time.

> Everything is explained verbally as well as in the written booklets. Pointing has been particularly helpful as you can find your place on the sheet...as to where your child is. It's the same with going through the checklist.

> What's the best thing? That it's positive...and the action you can take. You know why you're doing something...it helps you re-learn natural skills of the mother and teacher role which can be used. Everything about timing...the anticipation games...realising the need for 1 to 1.

> I now have a communicative child!

References

Charman, T. (1998) 'Joint attention impairment in autism in the pre-school years.' *Autism* 2, 1, 61–80.

Christie, P., Newson, E., Newson, J. and Prevezer, W. (1992) 'An interactive approach to language and communication for non-speaking children.' In D.A. Lane and A. Miller (eds) *Child and Adolescent Therapy: A Handbook*. Buckingham: Open University Press.

Lewis, R., Prevezer, W. and Spencer, R. (1996) *Musical Interaction: An Introduction*. Ravenshead: Early Years Diagnostic Centre.

Newson, E. and Christie, P. (1998) 'The psychobiology of pointing.' In Linfoot and P. Shattock (eds) *Psychobiology of Autism: Current Research and Practice*. Sunderland: Autism Research Unit.

Prevezer, W. (1998) *Entering into Interaction*. Ravenshead: Early Years Diagnostic Centre.

'How to do it' booklets

The 'How to do it' booklets mentioned are available from the Early Years Diagnostic Centre (Information Service), 272 Longdale Lane, Ravenshead, Nottinghamshire, and are written by Phil Christie, Elizabeth Newson and Wendy Prevezer, who are consultants to this project on which Susie Chandler is research psychologist. The project is funded by a charitable Trust which prefers to remain anonymous, but to which we are extremely grateful.

CHAPTER 22

Duality of Function of Language in Communication with People with Autism

Ryuji Kobayashi

Abstract

In our treatment of autistic children and young people, we emphasise first the promotion of a secure relationship between ourselves and our patients. Central to this process is the vitality affect of speech: the rhythm, intonation, modulation, rather than the meaning of the words *per se*. These patients often respond with excitement and joy when communication is on the affective level, and when the vitality affect of each person mutually resonates and is shared. Communication becomes less aversive and difficult.

This approach is based on the observation of developmentally primitive amodal perception in these patients especially in vitality affects and physiognomic perception. The insecure attachment of these children leads to distorted perception which is often evaluated as threatening. Speech has a dual function, it conveys emotion as well as linguistic meaning. It is believed that oversensitivity to this vitality affect carried by speech is one factor promoting communication difficulties for autistic children.

Introduction

To date, the author has undertaken clinical research focusing upon the characteristics of amodal perception seen among people with autism. Through this work, he has demonstrated that one of the foremost characteristics of their modes of perception is that the amodal form of perception is seen even in older people with autism (Kobayashi 1996, 1998, 1999). Amodal perception is perception that is not tied to any one modality, for instance a rhythm can be perceived whether it is felt or heard or seen. Amodal perception in infants has been extensively discussed (Stern 1985). Physiognomic perception (Werner 1948) is one such form of amodal perception, and is characterised by inanimate objects being perceived as if they were alive. In amodal perception, experience is affected by the psychological or physiological condition of the subject.

Not only can the amodal perceptions of infants be categorised in traditional ways such as fear, joy, anger, etc., but also, Stern (1985) argues, affect can be seen in another way. These are vitality affects and refer to the form of the experience and they arise directly from encounters with people. They are intersubjective in nature. They are described in dynamic kinetic terms such as 'surging', 'explosive', 'fading away' (Alvarez 1992). When the modes of object perception among autistic people are observed in detail in the clinical setting, it is not uncommon to see them suddenly exhibiting fear or displaying reactions of distaste towards something they are familiar with, as if they were seeing something unfamiliar. The author has conceptualised this phenomenon, calling it the 'perception metamorphosis' phenomenon (Kobayashi 1998).

In the autistic person, attachment formation with the caregiver is difficult from early infancy. For this reason, they find it difficult to establish a base of security, and they are prey to strong feelings of wariness or fear. In this frame of mind, stimuli are likely to take on persecutory or intrusive tones, making the person suddenly display fear and avoidance reactions even towards objects they are entirely familiar with. The author assumes the existence of perception metamorphosis phenomenon as background to such perceptual behaviour.

However, the type of perception characteristically seen among autistic people cannot be regarded as an abnormal phenomenon entirely removed from the perception of most people. In fact, in the healthy infant, amodal perception is carrying out an important role in enabling communication with their caregivers; communication in early infancy at the stage before acquisition of words. In other words in emotional communication, the existence of amodal perception in the form of physiognomic perception and vitality affect is indispensable (Stern 1985). Believing it should be possible to nurture emotional communication with the autistic person, attempts have been made to evaluate the type of therapeutic approach required.

Now, the dual function inherent in language in the communication with autistic persons will be discussed using two case studies.

Case 1: K

K is male, autistic with severe mental retardation, whose age at start of therapy was 22. First words were uttered at age 4½. At 6, he was diagnosed autistic. Severe panic attacks were seen from the time he was enrolled in kindergarten. He was placed in a special class for handicapped children from grade school (about 6 years), but severe panic attacks reappeared following transfer to a different school in the third year of junior high school (ninth grade). At 18, self-injury to his eyes and vandalism appeared. At 19, he even jumped out of the window of his apartment impulsively, causing injury to his spine. For these reasons, he was hospitalised in a children's ward of a psychiatric hospital for four years starting when he was 20. However, because his behaviour disorder did not improve, he was moved to a rehabilitation facility for mentally handicapped people where the author is involved as a consultant doctor.

Alongside pharmacotherapy, the author started therapy of both mother and child together. In the company of his mother, K would always stereotypically repeat the same questions. He would address his mother with words indicating his ambivalence, repeatedly saying, 'I want to do this', 'I cannot do this', 'I want to go home', or 'I cannot go home', phrased as questions. He had also come to ask his mother, 'Will you die when you turn 80?'. According to the mother, this question started after K started saying he wanted to go to New York when he turned 50. At the time, the mother replied that by that time, she would be past 80, and would no longer be alive. She indicated that this exchange must have left a deep impression on K, as he has been constantly repeating this question. The mother was seen diligently responding to the content of K's questions. However, because K would keep repeating the same questions, the mother's tone would gradually convey her impatience. How this transition in her frame of mind was elevating the psychological tension between the two was evident to the author. In addition, during the time K was questioning his mother, she would constantly be concerned with his appearance, pointing things out to him, or straightening things out for him herself.

The characteristics of communication between mother and child were as follows. The mother would be trying her best in attempting to communicate with K in words. It was as if she were speaking to someone with a full command of language. K, on the other hand, would repeat the few words he was capable of using. And the mother would be intent upon responding to his words to the best of her ability. However, because the exchange did not constitute true dialogue between the two, the mother would gradually become irritated with K's endless repetitions of the questions. In turn, K would be left with no choice but to offer further repetitions of his questions.

Case 2: M

M is male, autistic with mild mental retardation, whose age at first visit was 27. The subject had exhibited behaviour characteristics such as not meeting one's gaze, absence of babbling, lack of composure, and an obsession with turning things around and around from early infancy, and was diagnosed as autistic at 18 months. First words were uttered at 3, hyperkinesia was marked. Entering a school for handicapped children, he gradually became capable of study, and in third grade, he transferred to a special class for the handicapped. In fifth grade, due to repeated physical punishment inflicted by an overenthusiastic homeroom teacher[1] his hyperkinesia disappeared, but he became habitually anxious and fearful instead.

Following the death of his beloved uncle when he was 14, anxiety about death provoked him to repeating loudly over and over again, 'Mom, when are you going to die?' After some time, the mother, out of desperation, answered, 'I will die in 2050'. Since then, whenever M was not feeling too well, or when things were not going his way, he came to recite the question, 'What's going to happen on January 1st, 2050?' Following graduation from high school, he was enrolled in a workshop, but was victimised by a violent female. Because she came to the shop every

---

1   This is a care worker in the room which is not the classroom.

Thursday, M came to express his anxiety towards going to the workshop in the form of 'The year 2050, Thursday'. Around the same time, M was experiencing strong conflict regarding the purchase of a weekly magazine called *AERA*. Finally, he came to utter the phrase, 'AERA, 2000th anniversary, Thursday', with great apprehension.

At 27, the subject was enrolled in a rehabilitation facility where the author works as a consultant doctor. Perhaps due to anxiety towards life in the unfamiliar environment, he was constantly repeating the phrase 'AERA, 2000th anniversary, Thursday'. Having no idea what this phrase meant at first, the attending staff member asked M, 'Is the 2000th anniversary edition of AERA going to be on sale on Thursday?' To this, M fell into a panic, and screaming, 'I can't take any more' he shooed the staff member away.

However, once M became accustomed with life in the facility, he learned the names and birthdays of the staff members, and would approach them saying, 'So-and-so, born January 27th'. When staff members would respond in kind saying, 'M, born November 17th', M would respond, 'So-and-so, born January 27th', and await the same reply eagerly. The staff came to recognise that this verbal exchange was a form of play for M. They also noticed that when M spoke their names, the rhythm, intonation and tone would be different each time, which they copied in responding to him. M came to display great joy in these exchanges. And after such exchanges of names and birthdays, he came to approach the person, making a face as if he were playing a staring game, to which we responded by copying his expression. To this, M would show even greater joy, and would make all sorts of faces, waiting until the other responded in kind.

Discussion

Emotional communication and linguistic communication

Apart from being the exchange of information on the semantic level, the concept of communication has, as its basis, an emotional level, which is the sharing of affect. On the linguistic level, there is a two-way flow of information. On the other hand, communication on the emotional level is believed to be much like the sympathetic vibration of two tuning forks of equal pitch, in which when one tuning fork is made to vibrate, the other will resonate in kind. In other words, in the emotional world, it is as if both parties have a constitution capable of resonating with each other simultaneously.

Emotional communication and perception modes

Emotional communication is in part an amodal form of perception, influenced by vitality affect and how things are perceived is readily transformed by the psychological condition of the subject.

Feelings of security and perception modes

Feelings of security cannot be fostered between a child and its caregiver when attachment formation is hindered between the two. Thus, security is not easily nurtured in the autistic child. The absence of security is a condition in which the subject views the environment with strong wariness, and can be called a state in which the mind is contracted. In this state of mind, outer stimuli take on the appearance of a torrent flooding into one's self, which is perceived as menacing or intrusive by the subject.

However, when security is nurtured, outer stimuli take a sudden turn, taking on pleasant hues. Everything in the outer world starts to appear enticing, arousing curiosity. Perhaps this can be called the psychological world of the healthy infant. In this manner, the presence or absence of security is capable of readily transforming the way things are perceived.

Dual function of language in communication: vitality affects and meanings

Words contain the expression of affect, in addition to their function as a tool for conveying meaning. In other words, words have dual functions in the sense that they harbour both meaning and vitality affect.

Thinking over the development of communication between an infant and its caregiver, the primary issue is the deepening of emotional communication between the two. At this level, it is not the meaning of words *per se*, but vitality affect which takes on an important role. Building up a relationship allowing for the mutual resonance of vitality affect is the point of importance in deepening communication at this stage.

In the first case presented, whereas the child K was responding to the vitality affect of words, the caregiver was trying to respond to the meaning of the words, and this discrepancy in communication gave rise to the obsession of his words. Put another way, this state can probably be called the collapse of emotional communication, at the very core of communication.

In the second case, because the subject M and caregivers were able to resonate in terms of vitality affect leading to favourable development of emotional communication, his words did not become obsessive.

When the exchange through vitality affect, i.e. emotional communication is deepened, a sense of security is fostered between the parties concerned. This security lessens the menacing tones shadowing outer stimuli, imbuing them with pleasant overtones instead. When one is no longer overwhelmed by the vitality affect of words, the meaning of the words *per se* rise to the fore, making it relatively easier to communicate via words.

Dual function of perception, communication and language

As stated in the preceding sections, communication is structured from the primitive stage on the emotional level, and a linguistic level of communication, which has been formed as the product of development and differentiation. This dual structure of communication is inherent in words, which is the central theme of this chapter.

The difficulty that autistic people face in the formation of the primitive mode of communication between themselves and their caregivers is inseparably associated with the function of their peculiar primitive mode of perception. In other words, it is seen that mode of perception, level of communication, and the dual function of language are each deeply associated with each other. In short, at the level of primitive communication, the amodal perception is inevitably active, and in that state, it is the vitality affect of words which has the greater power over the literal meaning of words.

Therefore, in constructing therapeutic strategies for autistic subjects, evaluating how we can support the establishment of primitive communication becomes a theme of pressing importance. This is the reasoning behind the author's having focused upon the amodal perception of autistic people.

It is seen that timely responses tailored to their primitive perception modes are of vital importance in establishing communication with these subjects. Taking care to intervene in ways enabling resonance with their flux in affect, and how to go about forging a relationship in which we can hand down to them the culture we have acquired – these become the issues in point. For this, the first step is for us to enter into their world, i.e. the world of primitive, amodal perception. It is only after rich experience has been shared between the therapist and such subjects in their world that the wish to venture into our culture will blossom.

Acknowledgements

The author greatly appreciates the clinical assistance provided by Hiromi Kobayashi, Tokai University School of Health Sciences. This study was supported in part by the Fuji Memorial Foundation Fund and Mitsubishi Foundation Fund.

References

Alvarez, A. (1992) *Live Company*. London: Tavistock/Routledge.

Kobayashi, R. (1996) 'Physiognomic perception in autism.' *Journal of Autism and Developmental Disorders 26*, 661–667.

Kobayashi, R. (1998) 'Perception metamorphosis phenomenon in autism.' *Psychiatry and Clinical Neurosciences 52*, 611–620.

Kobayashi, R. (1999) 'Physiognomic perception, vitality affect and delusional perception in autism.' *Psychiatry and Clinical Neurosciences 53*, 549–555.

Stern, D. (1985) *The Interpersonal World of the Infant*. New York: Basic Books.

Werner, H. (1948) *Comparative Psychology of Mental Development*. Chicago: Follett.

CHAPTER 23

Behaviour Management of Children with Autism

Educational Approach in Fukuoka University of Education

Keiko Notomi

Introduction

Behaviour problems of children with autism are one of the most challenging targets for intervention from a clinical, as well as an educational, point of view. Furthermore they also tend to continue for a long time. Over time they often become worse and hinder the development and learning capacity of the children. Therefore early appropriate intervention is desirable. In this chapter I describe five children with autism and learning difficulty whose behaviour problems have improved rapidly after an approach was introduced using the TEACCH behavioural management, combined with enlisting parents as co-therapists (Schopler and Reichler 1971).

Prior to the case studies, we analyse the TEACCH programme and its application in the Research and Clinical centre of children with disabilities in Fukuoka University of Education and in the community in Fukuoka, Japan.

The TEACCH programme is North Carolina's statewide programme for the *T*reatment and *E*ducation of *A*utistic and related *C*ommunication Handicapped *ch*ildren. It is the only university-based statewide programme mandated by law in the United States. The staff of TEACCH provide clinical and educational services, and research and multidisciplinary training on behalf of children with autism and related developmental disorders (Schopler 1998). Eric Schopler assumes that the reason for this programme's success is the implementation of the TEACCH philosophy into programme structure, clinical research and empirical research. The philosophy is:

1. understanding the characteristics of children with autism

2. parent–professional collaboration

3. improving the child's adaptation through both teaching new skills and environmental accommodation to deficits

4. assessment for individualised treatment

5. use of structured teaching

6. based on cognitive and behaviour theory

7. skill enhancement and acceptance of deficit

8. holistic orientation

9. lifelong community-based service.

After my work as a psychiatrist for several years I realised that autism was an extremely difficult disorder to manage in a single discipline. Therefore I took the initial training of TEACCH in 1989 in Japan. Key steps of TEACCH Behaviour Management are:

1st step: Structuring (or Restructuring), in order to prevent behaviour problems.

2nd step: Iceberg Metaphor; that means seeing behaviour problems from the perspective of an individual with autism, seeking the cause of them and then making intervention based on the understanding of the cause.

3rd step: Applied Behaviour Analysis.

Although it is difficult to introduce all the elements of the philosophy of TEACCH outside North Carolina, I thought that a few of these elements could be gradually introduced in Japan. Until 1999, with a multidisciplinary group of colleagues I provided the following services in Fukuoka Area:

1. TEACCH behaviour management

2. assessment and individualised training of children with autism

3. consultation

4. multidisciplinary training.

Five single case studies

The treatment of five children, aged 4 to 9 years with autism and learning difficulty, will be described. They all had difficulty in communication and inappropriate behaviour in social contexts. The behaviour problems were as follows:

Case 1:   repetitively emptying a toy box

Case 2:   suddenly taking off clothes in the classroom

Case 3:   encopresis

Case 4:   throwing washing from the balcony of a high-rise block of flats

Case 5:   pulling the lid out of a water system in a rice field.

All behaviour problems improved rapidly within a month. All five had the same basic intervention structure.

First, the intellectual ability and level of communication of each child was assessed and the history of a specific behaviour problem was summarised.

Second, the meaning of the behaviour problem was analysed from the child's point of view. In other words I assumed each behaviour problem implied a request or need.

Finally, the individualised home programme was offered to the mother, which included structured teaching, alternative communication, and teaching acceptable behaviour through positive reinforcement.

Case 1

First case was a 4-year-old boy in kindergarten. He was mute, with a severe learning difficulty. His mother informed me he was repetitively emptying his toy box and scattering the toys. Therefore she had to clean up the room many times a day. The mother told me that after scattering the toys he would pick up a specific toy and play with it. My hypothesis of the child's behaviour is as follows: he was attempting to find his favourite toy. However since he was mute, the boy could not ask his mother to pick up a specific toy. This behaviour was his attempt at expressing his wants. According to TEACCH structured teaching, I advised the mother to set up a toy shelf and line up the toys, where the child could see all the toys at once and pick his favourite one.

The outcome of the structuring resulted in the child getting toys from the shelf, playing with them and returning them when he was finished.

Case 2

Second case was a 5-year-old boy in kindergarten. He had no vocal abilities and had severe learning difficulty. His mother was worried because he kept taking off his clothes in the kindergarten classroom. Around the same time this behaviour problem began, he achieved the skill of undressing. My hypothesis of the child's behaviour is as follows: he didn't like to wear specific clothes. Recently research and clinical evidence indicate that many children with autism dislike some textures, fabrics or the design of their clothes. So I advised the mother to let him choose his clothes before going to kindergarten. The outcome was striking. Shortly after the boy started to choose his clothes in the morning he didn't take them off until he came home.

Case 3

Third case was a 5-year-old boy with severe learning difficulty in kinder-garten. He had some words but most were echolalic. He could urinate appropriately at home and in kindergarten, but at home he couldn't use the toilet to pass motions but instead hid away. I asked his mother what she did after his failure. She said she was cleaning up the mess, while her son was pacing around the room. My hypothesis of the child's behaviour is as follows: he thought the evacuation itself was a bad behaviour, therefore he hid himself. So I advised the mother not to scold him but to pick up the stool, bring him to the toilet with the stool, and put the stool into the toilet bowl. Let him sit down on it and flush the stool away. Then construct a chart with stickers or stars to show his improvement. The outcome of this intervention was that he rapidly became capable of having bowel movements comfortably in the appropriate place.

Case 4

Fourth case was an 8-year-old boy in the third grade of elementary school with special educational services for mental retardation. He had limited vocabulary but was accurately echolalic. He suffered from moderate mental retardation. His mother told me he suddenly started throwing their clean laundry from the flat balcony of a high-rise block of flats. At this time I was fully aware that the mother had started teaching him how to fold the dried laundry at home. I asked her when and how the behaviour problem occurred and what she was doing at that time. The first time she noticed this behaviour was when her younger daughter got sick and she left him to care for her. When she returned, washing was scattered all over the room and outside the balcony. My hypothesis is he could not understand why she ignored him. After some trials he finally found the best way he could get her attention was by throwing the washing from the balcony. The mother understood my hypothesis and started to teach him to take the washing from the balcony inside and fold it and praise him for doing so. The outcome of this intervention was that this behaviour problem disappeared and she finally taught him some appropriate house-keeping skills.

Case 5

Fifth case is a fourth grade boy in an ordinary class in elementary school. He could speak very limited simple sentences and had moderate mental retardation. According to his mother, after school he would go for a walk in the countryside and pull out the lids of irrigation systems in the rice fields. His parents had refused to enrol him in special education classes. Being a handicapped student in an ordinary class was very lonely and difficult. He received no special educational support and his social life with his peers was empty and friendless. My hypothesis is that he enjoyed pulling out the lids of the irrigation system and watching the water stream out. This activity gave him a sense of accomplishment and the visual stimulation grabbed his attention. In order to provide the child with the same sense of stimulus and pleasure, I advised his parents to develop an activity that would satisfy his curiosity and his desires.

Our approach was to teach him how to wash the bathroom with TEACCH structured teaching. The mother devised good clear pictures with simple instructions and taught him how to wash the bathroom.

This resulted in him becoming capable of washing the bathroom independently and turning his interests away from the rice fields.

Conclusion

It was found that this clinical intervention was extremely effective, practical, easy to administer and useful for the families of the children.

As I tried to introduce the behaviour management in the early years of my studying the TEACCH programme these interventions were not faithful to the original, but modified by my own clinical experience. However, I confirmed that the effectiveness was prominent.

I focused on the collaboration with the mother, understanding each child from my observations and careful history taking. By giving them visual cues, trying to understand the behaviour from the child's perspective and taking into consideration the characteristics of autism and the limitations of each child's intellectual and communication abilities, I was able to make strong recommendations for a path to removing the problem.

Concerning the designing of an appropriate plan of treatment of autistic children Rutter(1985) indicated that five main goals have to be borne in mind:

1. The fostering of normal development.

2. The more general promotion of the autistic child's learning.

3. The reduction of rigidity and stereotypy.

4. The elimination of non-specific maladaptive behaviours.

5. Alleviation of family distress.

The result of the intervention enabled the mothers to eliminate their children's non-specific maladaptive behaviour and lessen their distress to a certain extent. Moreover the children became capable of obtaining some appropriate skills through visual cues and structured teaching. As my experience was clinical and empirically based, I did not prepare any control group nor had a standard objective assessment tool. If we try to confirm the relative effectiveness of specific interventions, as Sigman and Capps (1997) proposed, more research must be conducted. We have to remember that assessment not only must be done from the perspective of a single discipline but also must include consideration of the quality of life of the clients and their families.

References

Rutter, M. (1985) 'The treatment of autistic children.' *Journal of Child Psychology and Psychiatry 26*, 193–214.

Schopler, E. (1995) *Parents' Survival Manual: A Guide to Crisis Resolution in Autism and Related Development Disorders*. New York: Plenum.

Schopler, E. (1998) 'Implementation of TEACCH philosophy.' In D.J. Cohen and F.D. Volkmar (eds) *Handbook of Autism and Pervasive Developmental Disorders*. New York: V.H. Winston and John Wiley.

Schopler, E. and Reichler, R.J. (1971) 'Parents as cotherapists in the treatment of psychotic children.' *Journal of Autism and Childhood Schizophrenia 1*, 87–102.

Sigman, M. and Capps, L. (1997) *Children with Autism: A Developmental Perspective*. London: Harvard University Press.

CHAPTER 24

Coding of Active Sociability in Pre-schoolers with Autism (CASPA)

Charlotte Hyde, Dawn Wimpory, Susan Nash

Abstract

This chapter describes a video analysis tool for analysing naturalistic interactions. It is known as Coding of Active Sociability in Pre-schoolers with Autism (CASPA). CASPA is currently being developed at the University of Wales, Bangor, in conjunction with North West Wales NHS Trust. It focuses on instances when children with autism are most sociable and aims to highlight the type of interactional styles, patterns and strategies that are most effective for adults to use with these children. It is applied to video recordings of one-to-one interactions between adults and children with autism, in free play or play-based assessment situations. The chapter describes the context and content of the interaction, for example, the effect of directing a child as opposed to taking their lead, using strategies such as imitation, being playfully self-repetitive, and using familiar social routines. The precise results of CASPA's application to play-based assessments are to be published in peer reviewed journals. Therefore, this chapter outlines the purpose and initial findings of CASPA, and its potential for highlighting what facilitates episodes of social engagement in children with autism.

Introduction

Research takes place at the University of Wales, Bangor, in conjunction with North West Wales NHS Trust, as a result of Dr Dawn Wimpory's joint appointment as a consultant clinical psychologist for children with autism in Gwynedd (North West Wales NHS Trust), and a lecturer for autism at the University of Wales, Bangor. Dr Wimpory's work involves evaluating interventions for children with autism as well as advising parents and professionals on how to intervene and work with children with autism. The idea for CASPA developed when it became apparent that differing interactive styles seemed to affect children with autism in different ways, and that a way of measuring this was needed. In developing CASPA, Dr Wimpory is collaborating with Peter Hobson, Professor of Developmental Psychopathology at the Tavistock Clinic in London, Professor Mark Williams, Susan Nash (research officer) and Charlotte Hyde (research assistant) at the University of Wales, Bangor.

CASPA in practice

The idea behind CASPA was to produce a systematic instrument that was capable of analysing children's sociability across different contexts, as well as looking at the effects of different interactional styles on children with autism, when adults are able to interact naturally during a play-based assessment.

CASPA is an observational tool, based on naturalistic interactions. It is designed to identify naturally occurring social engagement in pre-schoolers with autism and to clarify the nature of adult partners' immediately preceding behaviour. CASPA is applied to video recordings of naturalistic one-to-one interactions to determine the context and social conditions that may facilitate instances of social engagement in autism.

These video recordings consist of interactions between an adult and child with autism during a play-based assessment (Newson and Newson 1979). Here, an experienced child development clinician accompanies the child through child-led play with a wide variety of pre-selected toys in a large playroom for one to two hours. The adult ensures that the child has contact with toys available in the play room, in order to determine the child's response to the adult and the equipment being used. This provides an indication of how the child responds to gross motor activities, musical activities, fine motor activities and cognitive tasks.

All the clinicians who played with the children in the research videos were women. They consisted of a variety of professionals who had already spent up to a total of four hours playing with the child on a previous occasion, for example on a home visit. All were members of a child development team and included speech and language therapists, specialist child development nurses and clinical psychologists. The play-based assessments took place prior to or as part of the child's diagnosis, and independent clinicians then confirmed the diagnosis using the Childhood Autism Rating Scale (CARS) (Schopler, Reichler and Renner 1986).

Coding

Coding of episodes of social engagement – child

Ten play-based assessment tapes were selected of 3- and 4-year old preverbal children with autism. All behaviour on the play-based assessment tapes was screened for episodes of social engagement. These were defined as instances where the child looks towards the adult's face, while at the same time displaying one or more other communicative behaviours. These include *body language*, for example a facial expression and gesture, some form of *vocalisation* or a *communicatively motoric behaviour*, for example giving an object or touching someone. Episodes of social engagement are therefore more than a simple glance or noise made by the child, they are instances that often leave parents of children with autism asking why their child can't be like that all the time. Episodes of social engagement can be described as instances when the child is perceived as being genuinely sociable and so it is particularly important that they are rated for reliability.

Previous measures have failed to encompass the social experience of being with an autistic child in this way, and therefore our definition of episodes of social engagement needed to encompass more than straightforward eye contact or looking at the adult's face, in which there may be no genuine sociability. In this sense, it was important that the words 'Active Sociability' formed part of CASPA's title, since we were interested in genuine responses that the adult facilitates in the child, rather than predetermined behaviours which the adult may have previously targeted.

Coding of episodes of social engagement – adult

Following identification of all episodes of social engagement, the adult's 'turn' or what the adult is doing immediately prior to the episode of social engagement was identified. The adult turns were coded according to the following criteria.

Influencing and being influenced by the child

The adult's behaviour was coded as either *continuing* or following the child's focus of attention; *redirecting* or changing the child's focus of attention; or being *silently attentive* to the child's focus of interest.

Activity

The activity was coded as either *pretend play*, for example, dressing up clothes; *musical-motoric activities*, for example, xylophone, climbing frame; or *cognitive assessment activities*, for example, puzzles, blocks or inset board. The activity may also be coded as *adult withdrawal* if the adult was not involved in any activity with the child at that time (the adult may not have necessarily moved physically away from the child).

Interactive strategies

The adult's behaviour was coded as *social routines*, for example, nursery rhymes; *imitation* of the child, for example, motoric, body language, vocalisation; and/or *playful self-repetition*, for example, clapping, patting, tapping, rather than repeating an instruction which would instead be coded as a new turn.

Coding of control points

In order to provide an idea of how the adult was typically behaving during the play-based assessment, each video was also screened at five-minute intervals throughout the tape, a process known as *time sampling*. The point at which the video was screened is known as a *control point*. Control points were identified as the exact point where the fifth minute ended, a method known as instantaneous scan sampling (Altmann 1974). By coding these control points, set at every five minutes throughout the tape, it was possible to obtain a clear idea of how the adult was typically behaving during the session. The control points were coded in the same way as the adult turns described above (influencing and being influenced by the child; activity; interactive strategies).

Results

Content of play-based assessments

This coding of the adult turns at each control point, provided a general idea of how the adult was behaving during the play-based assessment. After completing the coding of all control points for ten of the twenty subjects who will be included in the final study, we found that a large proportion of the adults' time was spent continuing the child's focus of attention. Cognitive assessment and musical-motoric were the most frequently used activities. Playful self-repetition was also quite common during most sessions. Those activities that did not feature heavily in the sessions were silent attentiveness, redirecting, pretend play and adult withdrawal. The use of imitation and social routines was also infrequent.

Adult interactive strategies: preliminary findings

As indicated earlier, results are so far available on only ten of the twenty subjects who will be included in the final study. At present the most important findings are that episodes of social engagement are more likely to occur where an adult follows a child's lead; uses musical and/or motoric activities; imitates the child; engages in social routines with the child; and/or is playfully self-repetitive. Our data so far also indicate that adults attempting to engage the child in cognitive assessment activities is negatively related to the occurrence of episodes of social engagement.

Discussion

Final results from this study will be published in the near future, however the study remains an ongoing project, and has since attained additional funding to look at younger children, and also self-repetition and imitation as separate items within CASPA. In general, characteristics of prolonged and exaggerated preverbal interaction, for example, playful self-repetition, imitation and social routines, were more facilitative of episodes of social engagement. Task-oriented activities were less successful in this respect perhaps partly because of the inevitable shift of attention involved.

CASPA has already been used to investigate the effects of two alternating treatment approaches in North Wales. Treatment One, based on discrete trial training (e.g. Lovaas 1987), and Treatment Two, based on a Hanen Early Language Parent Program (Manolson 1985) were compared for frequency of episodes of social engagement and for the adult behaviour that preceded these episodes of social engagement.

On publication, CASPA's results will allow firm recommendations to be made regarding the strategies and styles that appear to be most effective in helping children with autism to be sociable, as well as providing a sound observational tool which provides reliable data on genuine sociability.

Acknowledgements

The authors would like to thank those families who consented to take part in this research, and to acknowledge financial support from the Wales Office of Research and Development for Health and Social Care.

References

Altmann, J. (1974) 'Observational study of behaviour: sampling methods.' *Behaviour 49*, 227–267.

Lovaas, O.I. (1987) 'Behavioural treatment and normal educational and intellectual functioning in young autistic children.' *Journal of Consulting and Clinical Psychology 55*, 3–9.

Manolson, A. (1985) *It Takes Two to Talk: A Hanen Early Language Parent Guide Book.* Toronto: Hanen Early Language Resource Centre.

Newson, J. and Newson, E. (1979) *Toys and Playthings in Development and Remediation.* London: Allen and Unwin.

Schopler, E., Reichler, R.J. and Renner, B.R. (1986) *The Childhood Autism Rating Scale (CARS) for Diagnostic Screening and Classification of Autism.* New York: Irvington.

PART 5

Services

CHAPTER 25

Editorial

Services

John Richer and Sheila Coates

Three of the four chapters in this part describe services for autistic children in three very different environments. Richard Brooks (Chapter 26) describes the development of the Autistic Service in Oxfordshire, UK. It evolved from small beginnings integrating three autistic children back into primary school. It now has ninety children on roll in six bases set in mainstream primary and secondary schools. An outreach service further supports children in their local, special or pre-school provision. Throughout its history the approach has been eclectic and pragmatic, fitting its therapeutic education to the needs of the child taking into account the development of integration processes within a mainstream school. It has become a model for other services. At its heart lies a respect for the children and an insistence on seeing each child as a child first, who happens to have some autistic behaviour.

Jennifer Cantello-Daw (Chapter 27) describes the work of the Geneva Centre in Toronto. Unlike the Oxfordshire Service for Autism, her institute is not set in schools, nor is it state funded. The service is therefore delivered out of the centre rather than in the child's community, although there is some 'outreach' work. She works within a broad behavioural/learning theory model, but again her work open mindedly embraces a wide variety of useful practical techniques some of which, e.g. Gray's Social Stories, are not particularly behavioural. The essential criterion for deciding and evaluating intervention is what works for each child. This has yielded a rich variety of intervention techniques.

Being behaviourally based the success criteria involve adequate performance. This is as necessary for the treatment of autism as the meeting of minds.

Olga Bogdashina (Chapter 28) works in a very different environment in Ukraine. Not only are services in her country several decades behind those in the UK, but also they suffer additional handicaps of lack of money, outdated diagnostic procedures and a culture where education for disabled children is not a priority. Her brave fight for services for autistic children must be applauded.

Wendy Tucker (Chapter 29) discusses some of the features of a high-quality service for autistic people within the National Health Service, something which is not universally available yet in the UK or, to our knowledge, anywhere in the world.

In the final part of the book on Personal Stories, there are also many references to services from the parent's point of view.

CHAPTER 26

The Chinnor Unit

Richard Brooks

Introduction

In 1971, a 5-year-old boy was suspended from an Oxfordshire primary school. His teachers could not manage him. He fled from the classroom at every opportunity to flush the toilets, shivering ecstatically as the water span. He blocked all the basins, turned the taps on full, and the flood waters began to seep into the classroom. When anyone tried to restrain him, he had wild despairing tantrums, climbed the wallbars and refused to come down. The local doctor was able to make a diagnosis within three minutes of seeing the child because of the way he ran straight into the surgery, ignoring the doctor, and began to dance with the water he set spinning in the basin.

He was given a home tutor who worked with him in her own home. She sought advice from a range of professionals and, intuitively, developed her own techniques and her own mixture of confrontation, negotiation and persuasion to build a rapport with him. They made a Plasticine toilet to sit on the desk beside them while they worked. Whenever the flushing urge came upon him he ran a miniature simulation with fully accurate sound-effects and had no need to leave his seat. Within a few months she felt able to take their mutual trust and his new skills into the classroom for short periods each day and the headteacher, who had always been reluctant to exclude him, welcomed him back.

The boy now has a job, a girlfriend, and a car; he plays in the local silver band and lives independently in his own flat. His time in school was never easy and he always needed support to help him ride out his storms of frustration, make sense of his academic work, nurture his friendships and protect him from bullying. Throughout his time in school he had weekly sessions of music therapy and, while he was in primary school, his two closest friends joined him for the sessions so that his pleasure in music could overflow into his interactions with them.

Almost as soon as his reintegration began, other children with autism began to be referred to the same school so that the same flexibility of programme could be made available to them. Nearly thirty years later, there are now eighty children with autism whose school life is modelled on that initial ad hoc experiment. They come daily from five different counties and are integrated into a network of seven schools. They are always within reach of a base (a room in the school or a separate building) to which they can return whenever the classroom or the playground seems not to be the best place for them.

The role of the base

The Chinnor Unit is now part of a service for autism which provides outreach support for schools which have individual children with autism on their roll. Most of these children have their own learning support assistant for some hours of each day, but very few have a room to which they can retreat from the rigours and stresses of full integration in the school community. They are permanently in the deep end. Some do rise to the high expectations that this places on them but others sink. If they had a sanctuary, they would probably be less fully integrated, but they would have more chance of surviving transitional and crisis periods, remaining in the school, ready for a time when they could return to their previous level of involvement.

Our base offers a place of safety where children can learn at their own pace and go over work they have not fully understood in class; a place where they do not feel that all eyes are upon them and a place where fewer people are doing unpredictable things. It is the base which allows the staff to be flexible about individual children's integration programmes: to take them out of an unsuitable activity, to give them a break when they are suffering a particularly intense anxiety attack or to give them a chance to recover from a tantrum in the taxi on the way to school. Above all, the base is the place where staff can focus most directly on the child's individual needs. The curriculum can be determined by their own level of understanding and gaps can be identified carefully. In an integrated setting, in class, there is always some pressure to paper over the cognitive difficulties of children with autism. Staff know that an autistic child 'off track' can be hard to retrieve and children who are feeling uncomfortable because their incomprehension has been highlighted may become disruptive. This can increase the pressure to keep the child's nose to the grindstone, getting everything down on paper even if it has made no sense. The Unit's first pupil once studied the water cycle of rain, rivers, oceans and evaporation, creating multicoloured diagrams. The geography teacher and the Unit teacher explained the sequence in all manner of ways. The pupil's exercise book was packed with information. Asked to write what he had learned in the previous week, he began: 'The Water Cycle is a picture...'. Whenever autism meets a mainstream educational setting there can be a tension between the pressure to get the work finished and give the child a veneer of understanding and the teacher's awareness of how little real development has taken place. Conformity can be so hard to achieve that it can become the overriding goal. It is not easy to address pupils' underlying difficulties in a place where they are principally being taught to make themselves look as much like everyone else as possible.

The amount of time a child spends in the Unit is often a major area of discussion between staff and parents. It is also a cause of disappointment. Many parents have moved into the area because they want their children to be taught in an integrated setting. They want their children alongside their mainstream peers as much as possible and see the time they spend in class as an indication of their progress towards normal functioning. In some cases this is an accurate judgement – the children are watching and imitating their peers; they are interacting; the work they are doing reflects a real growth of understanding. In other cases, staff feel that they are practising the old naval, cosmetic art of painting everything grey so that nothing stands out. For some children on the autistic continuum academic work is their strong point, a part of their life that brings them pride and social approval. It can boost their confidence and their social standing though not, perhaps, their social understanding. Yet like computer hyperliteracy, it can also become a place to which they retreat to avoid all those parts of life that logic cannot reach.

There are several children who spend little or no time in class because of the severity of their autism or their inability to face such a public space. Their only contact with their mainstream peers comes during playtimes and when ordinary children come to visit them in the Unit. In these cases, we try to ensure that the children's curricula follow that of the mainstream at a level appropriate to their ability and we are able to adapt the resources generated by the host schools. Yet all withdrawal is not for the best educational reasons. We do not have one-to-one staffing and we never send a child into class without support unless we and the class teacher are confident that the child can manage alone. Inevitably, many of our pupils could benefit from more time in class than we can give them.

Innovation

Supported integration is now the norm for autistic children in many countries, but when we began using it in Chinnor it was something of an untried experiment. Since then, we have tried to maintain an overall attitude of optimism, welcoming the reported successes of other parents and professionals and trying to learn from their innovations. When we have come across promising approaches, developed elsewhere, we have sought to give them a positive hearing, examining them theoretically and practically to judge their potential.

Among these, the Waldon Approach has had the most profound influence on the development of the curriculum within the Unit. Dr Geoffrey Waldon, a brilliant theoretician and teacher from Manchester, gave courses at the Unit from 1982 until his death in 1989. He worked on the principle that normal children develop their ability to learn adaptively through the unspecialised nature of their spontaneous, and largely solitary, play. He drew a distinction between General Understanding, learned in this individual and asocial way, and the particular skills that children learn through the shaping processes that different cultures encourage. He assumed that a child with a low level of General Understanding would find it far more difficult to learn particular skills and that, even when these were learned, they were unlikely to be generalised. Teaching or training a child with this weak understanding would actually reduce the child's ability to learn adaptively. The accent, therefore, should be on helping the child to develop a robust General Understanding and learn how to learn effectively. Waldon's ideas have inspired us to try to create lessons that reproduce something of what we see when we silently watch a young child at play: the intensity of effort, the pleasure in activity for its own sake and the focus on the process not the product. His teaching approach is particularly striking and, to some people, perplexing. During his 'asocial' lessons he did not make or respond to any social overtures and used the most direct form of communication possible (usually physical prompts or gestures) to guide the child's activity. He used no form of extrinsic reward or encouragement and relied exclusively on the reinforcement springing from children's own pleasure in movement and activity, allowing them to decide the rightness of their own decisions.

Watching an asocial lesson for the first time, observers are often surprised by the attention span a young autistic child can manage when not interrupted by praise, encouragement or correction. It can seem paradoxical to be teaching children, whose diagnosis stresses the paucity of their social interactions, using a method which is minimally social. Yet it is precisely this quality that helps many children with autism. The approach takes the painful social difficulty temporarily out of the equation in a way that can release the child's capacity to learn. As their confidence and understanding increase, children who are under no pressure to respond socially often begin to experiment with language and social initiation. Yet we have always recognised that such an approach can be only a part of an autistic child's curriculum – just as solitary play is only a part of an ordinary child's day – and that it has to be complemented by an equal amount of social, interactive play. In many ways, the ideal comple-mentary approach may be the Intensive Interaction work (Nind and Hewitt 1994) which has more recently influenced the work of the Chinnor Unit. Although these authors and Waldon would seem diametri-cally opposed in crucial respects, they share an emphasis on detailed observation of normal development and a commitment to recreating its most important elements. Both focus on the process of learning and experience and not on checklists of discreet skills. Both rely on intrinsic motivation.

Those who develop and propound teaching programmes and strategies are usually convinced that, with suitable adjustments, their methods are ideal for all autistic children. Most see their techniques as flowing seamlessly from a philosophical standpoint. Yet in schools the picture is usually less single minded and the concerns of staff are often more pragmatic. There are advantages when one approach is uniformly understood and applied throughout a school, but such consistency can be a force which precludes the development, investigation and absorption of fresh ideas. The autistic spectrum embraces a heterogeneous group of children and some of the most effective teachers are those who are able to draw on a range of approaches, adapting their style to suit different children, and creating further variations as those children mature. From moment to moment, teachers have to make and revise decisions: does this child need to struggle to solve a problem independently or should the child be learning to communicate and ask for help? Do these children need a tighter structure or a space to enable them to initiate, influence others and create their own meanings? Do they need to control their emotions or express and understand them? Should they be given the chance to defend themselves from sensory overload or the encouragement to relinquish their defences? Is now the time to insist or the time to back away? Are children pausing now, on the verge of an idea of their own, or are they lost and desperately needing a suggestion or a clear direction? Like religious faith, a uniform approach gives staff a clear framework for making these decisions, but it may cut out as much light as it sheds and some teachers may feel their own intuition leading them in a different direction.

Innovation can never be undertaken lightly. Investigating an approach carries with it the risk that well-established common sense and good practice will be undermined or jettisoned, swept away by the force of an all conquering new idea. This process can de-skill staff and be damaging to educational provision. We rely on several factors to prevent this. The most important is the experience of the staff – many years of work with autism has helped them to develop an efficient 'crap detector'. They have hunches about what is true and untrue, likely or unlikely to work. And they trust them.

At an autism European conference in 1988, Temple Grandin made the point that all teaching methods and techniques were of secondary importance compared to the personal qualities of individual staff. She said, 'Everyone knows what a good teacher is.' We have introduced new approaches to autism into the Chinnor Unit in order to equip good staff with the tools to help them find a way to help particular children – especially those who have seemed the hardest to reach in conventional ways. Yet, of course, each of these interventions has been only as good as the staff using it. If they were less committed or sensitive in their observations or less systematic in structuring their lessons and the environment, the innovations would not have been of any use to the children.

References

Nind, M. and Hewitt, D. (1994) *Access to Communication*. London: David Fulton.

CHAPTER 27

Help Me Get Started

An Overview of Effective Teaching Strategies to Encourage Initiation and Independence

Jennifer Cantello-Daw

Abstract

The Geneva Centre model is based on the premise that a variety of different techniques and approaches are the most effective way to address the various needs of individuals with Autistic Spectrum Disorder (ASD) and their families. As new and innovative methods of helping people with ASD are discovered and developed, our approaches continue to expand to incorporate the most effective techniques.

The Skill Development Model is designed to promote independence and to teach individuals with ASD to initiate. The individual with ASD is involved in the planning and intervention process whenever possible. The intent of the skill-building strategies is to prevent 'learned helplessness' and to avoid an over-reliance on prompts and cues.

Some of the key strategies include establishing structure and routine, teaching functional skills, the use of visual aids, addressing both receptive and expressive communication skills, helping individuals cope with sensory processing differences, helping individuals to develop better motor planning skills, the use of positive behavioural intervention techniques, teaching specific social skills and teaching self-management strategies to help individuals cope with stress and anxiety.

Introduction

The Geneva Centre for Autism provides a range of services to people with Autistic Spectrum Disorders, their families, other caregivers and professionals. The model involves a flow of knowledge to and from our clients. Through this process, the centre is able to provide families and professionals with essential intervention strategies while remaining flexible, open and sensitive to their needs and wishes. At the Geneva Centre, this exchange takes the form of a range of services that have at their root information, training, skill building and support.

Since the mid-1970s the Geneva Centre has developed a model of intervention which has skill building as its main focus. The main aim is to enhance the skills of individuals with ASD and their caregivers and in this way to encourage initiation of these new skills and therefore work towards increased independence. These teaching strategies are drawn from a variety of sources. As new and innovative methods of helping people with autism are discovered and developed, our approaches continue to expand and grow to incorporate the best practices and most effective techniques

The Geneva Centre model of intervention is based on an assumption of competence. Our approach is based on the recognition of a person's strengths and teaching strategies are designed to build on these strengths while addressing the areas in which each individual needs to develop skills. Each individual is approached with respect and included, with any necessary accommodations, in the intervention planning designed to assist him or her.

Teaching strategies

Establish structure and routine

The use of structured, routine activities and multiple trials as a basis for teaching individuals with ASD has been well documented in recent years (Clark and Rutter 1981; Dalrymple 1990; Mesibov, Schopler and Hearsey 1994; Mesibov *et al.* 1994; Olley 1987). Families and teachers are encouraged to incorporate predictable, structured activities into the daily routine of individuals with autism to enhance their ability to make sense of their environment and to help them to cope and learn.

One compelling argument in favour of the use of structure and routine is the research concerning the neurobiology of autism. Several researchers investigating the neurological aspects of ASD have discovered structural differences in the brains of individuals with autism (Courchesne 1997; Minshew, Sweeney and Bauman 1997). Of particular note are differences in the cerebellum and limbic system. These differences may make it difficult to synthesise information, make comparisons, draw conclusions, be comfortable with novelty and prepare for change and transitions.

By providing structure, familiar routines and the chance to acquire a skill through repeated practice, an individual with ASD should be able to rely on the habit memory system which should be relatively unaffected by these structural differences in the brain. This should make it easier to participate in routines and activities that are well known to the person. Expectations and outcomes should be more clearly understood and in turn, an individual's level of stress and anxiety should decrease.

Using familiar routines and activities should lead to a decrease in behavioural difficulties. While many individuals experience difficulty with novelty and transitions, the use of a routine and the ability to predict the next activity should help the individual experience more success and should decrease behavioural reactions which result from a resistance to change or uncertainty about what will happen next. As the individual develops more adaptive skills, then they may gradually learn to cope with transitions and change.

Teach functional skills

The value of teaching functional skills in the context where they will be used has been researched and documented as an essential part of the skill-building process for individuals with ASD (Donnellan 1987; Donnellan et al. 1983; Scheyer and Falvey 1986). Going back to the idea of familiarity and habit memory, an individual will need the opportunity to practise and use a skill frequently in order to master it.

Most people with ASD have difficulty with generalisation, that is the ability to apply previously acquired knowledge and experience in novel or unfamiliar situations. As a result, there is a need to teach skills which are functional for each individual to ensure that the person receives adequate and frequent opportunities to use and retain the skill in a variety of different settings with a variety of different people as the need arises.

It also may take an individual with ASD longer to learn a skill therefore it is important to select skills which will be of lifelong value to the person. If the person takes a significant period of time to master a task it must still be meaningful once it has been acquired. A self-management technique such as progressive muscle relaxation may take years to be fully learned as a skill but then the individual has mastered a technique that will be of significant benefit for a lifetime.

Once the appropriate functional skills have been determined for an individual, intensive teaching sessions may be an appropriate way to address the need for frequent practice. This method is primarily used to teach pre-school children (Lovaas 1981a, 1981b; Maurice, Green and Luce 1996). A more intensive, sessional teaching approach may be used initially to establish attention, imitation and response to instructions. Sessional teaching is most effective when the targeted skill is also being taught and reinforced in a variety of settings where it will be needed.

Positive behavioural intervention

A combination of positive behaviour management techniques may be required in order to change undesirable behaviour and teach new skills. Techniques that incorporate proactive strategies such as ecological manipulation, positive programming and direct treatment techniques combined with reactive strategies such as redirection and brief time-out from reinforcement when necessary (LaVigna 1988; LaVigna and Donnellan 1989; LaVigna and Willis 1992) are effective methods of intervention.

Difficult behaviours should be approached from the perspective of keeping a scale in balance. If an undesired behaviour is going to decrease in frequency or be eliminated it must be replaced with a positive behaviour which is incompatible with the negative one. Therefore, behavioural intervention must be based on an assessment of the communicative function of undesired behaviour and an attempt to teach a positive way to communicate the same message (Donnellan et al. 1988; LaVigna and Willis 1992).

An essential component of positive behaviour management is the use of individually determined reinforcement strategies to provide additional motivation. This will enhance attention and learning and is recognised as a necessary teaching tool for individuals with ASD (Dalrymple 1989; Koegel and Mentis 1985). While learning to respond to social praise and intrinsic motivation is an important skill, for many individuals with ASD additional reinforcement may be necessary to encourage them to try new tasks or participate in group activities.

Increased motivation and teaching choice making skills (Dalrymple 1989; Koegel et al. 1996) will both have a positive impact on self-control and an individual's ability to learn and use new skills. An increase in a person's repertoire of activities, skills and interests means that more choices are available to him or her and decreases the occurrence of negative and stereotypical behaviours.

It is important to be able to gauge an individual's level of stress and anxiety and behaviour is often a barometer of how agitated someone is becoming. Attention must be paid to environmental and physical antecedents that affect the individual's behaviour in both positive and negative ways. It may then be possible to alter antecedents either to prevent undesired behaviours from occurring or to encourage an increase in positive behaviours.

Self-management skills will greatly enhance the range of activities in which a person with ASD can participate. It is important to begin to teach coping strategies from an early age. Individuals may need assistance with the recognition of what happens to their bodies when they are beginning to get upset or worried. If a person can learn to recognise a variety of physical cues such as the difference between tight and relaxed muscles, that his or her face is becoming flushed, an increase in repeated movements then the person can learn to take positive control in those situations. Progressive muscle relaxation, Cognitive Picture Rehearsal and visual imagery techniques (Groden and LeVasseur 1995; Groden *et al.* 1991) can be taught and used as coping and calming strategies. These can be incorporated into an individual's daily routine and schedule and can also be used both to prepare for stressful activities or transitions and also to calm down once an individual is getting agitated.

Another component of this positive behavioural strategy is to focus on the desired action by the person rather than to place emphasis on undesired behaviour. In other words, tell the person what you would like them to do or what the expected response in a situation may be. This should be more effective than spending a lot of time and attention on an undesired or inappropriate response that has occurred. The individual may have difficulty determining what he or she is supposed to do so it is desirable to demonstrate and talk about what one expects to see as a positive response or action. For example, it is preferable to say 'Walk on the sidewalk' as an instruction rather than 'Stay on the sidewalk, don't run on the road'. This is also useful for individuals who may have receptive language difficulties that cause them to respond to the last words that are spoken or to sentence fragments. It also may prevent unwanted responses that are triggered by hearing an instruction such as 'Don't touch' or 'No hitting'. Some individuals will respond by performing the behaviour you have just asked them not to do so it is more effective to name the positive, desired behaviour instead.

Visual aids

The use of visual schedules and visually cued instruction is an essential teaching technique. The value and success of these intervention techniques has been well documented. Pictorial and written schedules (Brown 1991; Garrison-Harrell and Carter 1991; Hodgdon 1995a, 1995b; Pierce and Schreibman 1994) are an excellent way to provide a person with information about the events in his or her day, who will be participating in those activities and the sequence in which they will occur. At a very basic level, a picture and print representation of 'First —. Then —.' allows the individual to understand what is about to happen. This is most effective if a non-preferred activity is followed by something which the person enjoys. The same theory would apply to a task that is unfamiliar or more difficult followed by a task which the individual has already mastered and can do correctly. Some of the essential reasons for using a visual schedule are to help an individual see a logic and order to the day's events; to provide visual information which can be referred to as often as possible, even when an adult is not available; to aid the understanding of time concepts; to present concisely only the relevant information in a visual manner.

Visual aids provide an excellent strategy to address receptive language difficulties. While spoken language is sequentially coded and temporal, a visual representation of the same information remains fixed in space, constant and provides the individual with more time to process information as the person can refer back to the visual aid when needed. This will in turn promote independence because the necessity for verbal prompts should be greatly reduced as a person is visually guided through the necessary steps. Visually cued instruction (Quill 1995) may also help individuals to cope with transitions, help to decrease anxiety, aid the shifting of attention and allow the person to be more organised.

Positive rehearsal strategies such as Cognitive Picture Rehearsal (Groden and LeVasseur 1995), Social Stories (Gray and Garand 1993; Swaggart *et al.* 1995) and scripting (Kirchner 1991; Loveland and Tunali 1991; Twachtman 1995) are effective strategies. These techniques provide opportunities for people with ASD to receive information about what is about to occur and expected responses in those situations both by hearing a description and seeing print or pictorial descriptions of the pertinent information. They then have an opportunity to practise and prepare for situations before they actually occur which means they are more likely to be successful in that situation.

Communication skills

Communication skills are essential if an individual is going to interact successfully with others. Prior to determining effective intervention strategies for behaviour an evaluation of the communicative functions of the behaviour should be completed (Donnellan *et al.* 1984). Increasing communication skills is frequently an effective method of decreasing inappropriate behaviour and allows an individual to have a positive impact on his or her environment. An emphasis on functional, social-communication skills ensures that what is being taught is meaningful and useful to the individual (Prizant and Wetherby 1989; Rydell and Prizant 1995; Wetherby and Prizant 1992).

Communicative invitations can be an effective way to encourage young children to initiate an interaction and demonstrate communicative intent. An example would be to blow bubbles several times as a child watches and reacts and then pause with the bubble wand placed in front of the adult's mouth. The child will usually then respond with a look, an action or vocalisation to indicate that he or she wants the game to continue. Once a pattern is established then the adult may gently begin to make more demands of the child (such as increased vocalisation) before the desired action occurs.

A variety of augmentative communication systems may be introduced for non-verbal individuals. One method is the Picture Exchange Communication System (Bondy and Frost 1994; Frost and Bondy 1994). This approach teaches an individual who is non-verbal or who has limited speech, that communication requires interaction with at least one other person. A key feature of this approach is that the individual with ASD places a symbolic representation (photograph/word, picture symbol/word or print) in the hand of another person (the communicative partner). This action is a motor movement that involves a contact gesture and may be easier than pointing, which is a distal gesture. Another key feature is that the instructor uses no verbal prompting and instead initially uses a desired item as a visual cue. This teaches the person with ASD that he or she can initiate a request and not wait to be asked.

This technique then advances through several other stages and uses a discrete trial format to teach a variety of communicative functions. Bondy and Frost (1994) have reported that the majority of young children who begin using this technique at age 3 acquire spoken language after successfully using the pictures. This is a structured system with a clear sequence, repeated motor movement and naturally occurring reinforcement and for those reasons would appear to be ideally suited to the learning needs of individuals with ASD.

Other types of augmentative communication system are also frequently used. Word, picture and letter-boards and assistive communication devices are designed and prescribed as needed. Sign language may be used with some children visually and kinaesthetically to enhance spoken language. However, because of the limited understanding of sign by other children and the community in general it may be used as an additional augmentative system and is not likely to be the only system to which an individual is introduced.

Individually designed communication scripts are used as a rehearsal strategy for specific situations where an individual may be experiencing difficulty. A variety of techniques are used to enhance comprehension, change echoed responses, and improve intonation and voice quality. Parents and professionals who support the person with ASD are taught these techniques and encouraged to use them as often as possible to improve communication skills.

Sensory strategies

Recognition of how sensory processing difficulties may affect the behaviour and responses of people with ASD has facilitated creative interventions to help accommodate these sensory differences. Sensory integration practices to accommodate 'sensory seeking' and 'sensory avoidance' behaviours have proved to be an essential part of intervention plans for people with ASD (Cook 1990; Reisman and King 1993). A primary goal of these strategies should be to help the person with ASD become more aware of and cope with their sensory processing difficulties.

It is important to include an occupational therapist who is trained and experienced in sensory integration techniques in the assessment process for an individual with ASD. An assessment of sensory seeking and avoidance behaviours related to each of the five senses as well as the vestibular and proprioceptive systems can provide invaluable insights regarding behaviour. It is then possible to design activities to address specific areas of hypo- and hyper-sensitivity.

Intervention strategies are designed to help regulate arousal levels, maximise the teaching and use of functional skills and decrease anxiety levels. The development of an individual 'sensory diet' (Yack, Sutton and Aquilla 1998) may be used to replace stereotypic behaviours with specific activities designed to increase the organisation of a child's central nervous system. The appropriate combination of strategies and activities can help: to calm an over-aroused child; to increase the activity level of an under-aroused child; to prevent a negative reaction to an upcoming event or transition; to help a child to remain in the calm alert state for longer periods and thereby make him or her more receptive to learning.

Movement and motor planning

When developing teaching strategies for an individual with ASD it is important to consider the implications of difficulty with motor planning. There are many overlaps between the characteristics indicative of movement disturbance and the characteristics commonly associated with ASD (Leary and Hill 1996). Individualised accommodations (Donnellan and Leary 1995) can contribute to the development of self-control and an improved ability to be able to perform a skill in a variety of different environments. Some examples are the use of rhythm, touch, positive self-talk and visual aids.

An occupational therapist can provide expertise in the area of movement and motor planning and may be able to design activities to address difficulties in these areas. A speech/language pathologist may assess oral motor planning difficulties that can make it more difficult for an individual to use speech. Specific exercises can then be individually designed to address these issues.

The Floortime approach (Greenspan and Weider 1998) is designed to improve interaction, communication and play skills while also addressing difficulties related to motor planning. This approach involves strategies such as giving automatic, undesired behaviours new meanings. One example would be a child who lies down on the floor in protest or to avoid an activity. The adult might be instructed to get a blanket, turn out the lights, cover the child and say, 'You're tired? Good night'. Then when the child gets up say, 'You're awake! Good morning', remove the blanket and see what the child does next. Other techniques such as creating obstacles and problems for the child to solve in order to keep them engaged and give them a reason to communicate are an essential part of this process.

Rehearsal strategies (Gray and Garand 1993; Groden and LeVasseur 1995) using visual techniques and/or role playing may help individuals to overcome motor planning difficulties and increase the likelihood that they will be able to access skills in the situations in which they are needed.

Social skills

Social interaction is usually an area of great difficulty for individuals with ASD. A cognitive approach to learning social skills is essential, as these skills are not typically acquired naturally or easily. Social skills for specific situations and environments can be practised individually or in groups (Mesibov 1984). Generalisation of the skills by cueing the individual to use the learned routines in a variety of natural environments is an effective way to ensure that the new skill will be maintained.

Opportunities to spend time observing and interacting with typically developing peers is essential to the development of appropriate social skills. It is also very important to try to teach an understanding of how and why other people are likely to react in a variety of social situations. Social Stories (Gray 1999) are a very useful way to teach this social under-standing while also helping others to understand the perspective of the person with ASD. Social Stories also provide an opportunity to rehearse a social situation to make it more likely that the individual with ASD will be successful when the situation actually occurs. Role playing and scripting can provide an opportunity to practise before the actual situation arises. These can be very useful activities in a group setting to allow a number of individuals to benefit by experiencing a situation and seeing how other people would handle it. It is also helpful to get positive feedback, support and suggestions from the group.

Using video to help prepare for a problematic situation can also be useful. For example, a child can practise a method for dealing with teasing. It might be a sequence such as, 'Stop. Take a deep breath. Count to five in your head. Walk away. Try to tell an adult what happened'. This can be practised and then a role play is videotaped with other children acting the role of teasers. The child then has a video he or she can watch at home and school to help them remember what to do if they are teased. The child can watch the tape as often as needed or at specific times as required such as just before going out on the playground.

Conclusion

This is far from an exhaustive summary of the variety of techniques and strategies that need to be considered when designing individual intervention plans for people with ASD. The Geneva Centre model relies on a team partnership between the individual with ASD, caregivers and consultants to make the implementation of these strategies a success. As new techniques and strategies are developed then they are added to the list of interventions that can help people with ASD to realise their potential and participate fully and more independently in their communities.

References

Bondy, A. and Frost, L. (1994) 'The picture exchange communication system.' *Focus on Autistic Behavior 9*, 3, 1–19.

Brown, F. (1991) 'Creative daily scheduling: a non-intrusive approach to challenging behaviour in community residences.' *Journal of the Association for Persons with Severe Handicaps 16*, 2, 75–84.

Clark, P. and Rutter, M. (1981) 'Autistic children's responses to structure and interpersonal demands.' *Journal of Autism and Developmental Disorders 11*, 2, 201–218.

Cook, D. (1990) 'A sensory approach to the treatment and management of children with autism.' *Focus on Autistic Behavior 5*, 6, 1–19.

Courchesne, E. (1997) 'Brainstem, cerebellar and limbic neuroanatomical abnormalities in autism.' *Current Opinion in Neurobiology 7*, 269–278.

Dalrymple, N. (1989) 'Motivation/choice/control.' *Indiana Resource Center for Autism Newsletter 3*, 1, 4–5.

Dalrymple, N. (1990) 'Teach rather than punish.' *Indiana Resource Center for Autism Newsletter 3*, 4, 1–2.

Donnellan, A. (1987) 'Issues in developing personnel preparation programs.' In D.J. Cohen and A.M. Donnellan (eds) *Handbook of Autism and Pervasive Developmental Disorders.* New York: Wiley.

Donnellan, A.M. and Leary, M.R. (1995) *Movement Differncies and Diversity in Autism/Mental Retardation: Appreciating and Accomodating People with Communication and Behaviour Challenges.* Madison, WI: DRI Press.

Donnellan, A.M., Mesaros, R.A. and Mirenda, P. (1983) 'Developing chronological age-appropriate functional skills in natural environments.' National Conference on Autism, Toronto.

Donnellan, A.M., Mirenda, P.L., Mesaros, R.A. and Fassbender, L.L. (1984) 'Analyzing the communicative functions of aberrant behavior.' *Journal of the Association for Persons with Severe Handicaps 9*, 3, 201–212.

Donnellan, A.M., LaVigna, G., Negri-Shoultz, N. and Fassbender, L. (1988) *Progress without Punishment: Effective Approaches for Learners with Behavior Problems.* New York: Teachers College Press.

Garrison-Harrell, L. and Carter, W. (1991) 'Tips for practitioners: a visual scheduling strategy for integrating students with autism in a general education setting.' *Focus on Autistic Behavior 6,* 4, 19.

Gray, C. (1999) *Teaching Social Understanding with Social Stories and Comic Strip Conversations.* Jenison, MI: Jenison Public Schools.

Gray, C. and Garand, J. (1993) 'Social stories: improving responses of students with autism with accurate social information.' *Focus on Autistic Behavior 8,* 1, 1–11.

Greenspan, S. and Weider, S. (1998) *The Child with Special Needs: Encouraging Intellectual and Emotional Growth.* Reading, MA: Addison-Wesley.

Groden, J. and LeVasseur, P. (1995) 'Cognitive picture rehearsal: a system to teach self-control.' In K.A. Quill (ed) *Teaching Children with Autism: Strategies to Enhance Communication and Socialization.* New York: Delmar.

Groden, J., Cautela, J., LeVasseur, P., Groden, G. and Bausman, M. (1991) *Imagery Procedures for People with Special Needs: Breaking the Barriers II.* Waterloo, Ontario: Research Press.

Hodgdon, L. (1995a) 'Solving social-behavioural problems through the use of visually supported communication.' In K.A. Quill (ed) *Teaching Children with Autism. Strategies to Enhance Communication and Socialization.* New York: Delmar.

Hodgdon, L. (1995b) *Visual Strategies for Improving Communication Vol. 1: Practical Supports for School and Home.* Troy, MI: QuirkRoberts.

Kirchner, D. (1991) 'Using verbal scaffolding to facilitate conversational participation and language acquisition in children with pervasive developmental disorders.' *Journal of Childhood Communication Disorders 14,* 1, 81–98.

Koegel, R. and Mentis, M. (1985) 'Annotation. Motivation in childhood autism: can they or won't they.' *Journal of Child Psychology and Psychiatry 26,* 2, 185–191.

Koegel, L., Koegel, R. and Dunlap, G. (1996) *Positive Behavioral Support: Including People with Difficult Behavior in the Community.* Baltimore, MD: Paul H. Brookes.

LaVigna, G.W. (1987) 'Nonaversive strategies for managing behaviour problems.' In D.J. Cohen and A.M. Donnellan (eds) *Handbook of Autism and Pervasive Developmental Disorders.* New York: Wiley.

LaVigna, G.W. and Donnellan, A.M. (1989) *Alternatives to Punishment: Solving Behavior Problems with Non-Aversive Strategies.* New York: Irvington.

LaVigna, G. and Willis, T. (1992) 'A model for multielement treatment planning and outcome measurement.' In D.E. Berkell (ed) *Autism: Identification, Education, and Treatment.* Hillsdale, NJ: Erlbaum.

Leary, M. and Hill, D. (1996) 'Moving on: autism and movement disturbance.' *Mental Retardation 34,* 1, 39–53.

Lovaas, I. (1981a) 'Behavioral teaching with young autistic children.' In B. Wilcox and A. Thompson (eds) *Critical Issues in Educating Autistic Children and Youth.* Washington: National Society for Children and Adults with Autism.

Lovaas, I. (1981b) *Teaching Developmentally Disabled Children: The Me Book.* Baltimore, MD: University Park Press.

Loveland, K.A. and Tunali, B. (1991) 'Social scripts for conversational interactions in autism and down syndrome.' *Journal of Autism and Developmental Disorders 21,* 2, 177–186.

Maurice, C., Green, G. and Luce, S. (eds) (1996) *Behavioural Intervention for Young Children with Autism: A Manual for Parents and Professionals.* Austin, TX: Pro-Ed.

Mesibov, G.B. (1984) 'Social skills training with verbal autistic adolescents and adults: A program model.' *Journal of Autism and Developmental Disorders 14,* 395–404.

Mesibov, G., Schopler, E. and Hearsey, K. (1994) 'Structured teaching'. In E. Schopler and G. Mesibov (eds) *Behavioral Issues in Autism.* New York: Plenum.

Minshew, N.J., Sweeney, J.A. and Bauman, M.L. (1997) 'Neurological aspects of autism.' In D. Cohen and F. Volkmar (eds) *Handbook of Autism and Pervasive Developmental Disorders.* New York: Wiley.

Olley, J.G. (1987) 'Classroom structure and autism.' In D. Cohen and A. Donnellan (eds) *Handbook of Autism and Pervasive Developmental Disorders.* New York: Wiley.

Ornitz, E.M. (1989) 'Autism at the interface between sensory and information processing.' In G. Dawson (ed) *Autism: Nature Diagnosis and Treatment.* New York: Guilford.

Pierce, K. and Schreibman, L. (1994) 'Teaching daily living skills to children with autism in unsupervised settings through pictorial self-management.' *Journal of Applied Behavior Analysis 27,* 3, 471–482.

Prizant, B. and Wetherby, A.M. (1989) 'Enhancing language and communication in autism: from theory to practice.' In G. Dawson (ed) *Autism: Nature Diagnosis and Practice.* New York: Guilford.

Quill, K.A. (1995) 'Visually cued instruction for children with autism and pervasive developmental disorders.' *Focus on Autistic Behavior 10,* 3, 10–20.

Reisman, J.E. and King, L.J. (1993) *Making Contact: Sensory Integration and Autism.* Peoria, Illinois: Media/Learning Systems.

Rydell, P. and Prizant, B. (1995) 'Assessment and intervention strategies for children who use echolalia.' In K.A. Quill (ed) *Teaching Children with Autism: Strategies to Enhance Communication and Socialization.* New York: Delmar.

Scheyer, M. and Falvey, M. (1986) 'Functional academic skills.' In M.A. Falvey (ed) *Community-Based Curriculum.* Baltimore, MD: Paul H. Brookes.

Swaggart, B., Gagnon, E., Jones Bock, S., Earles, T., Quinn, C., Smith Myles, B. and Simpson, R. (1995) 'Using Social Stories to teach social and behavioral skills to children with autism.' *Focus on Autistic Behavior 10,* 1, 1–16.

Twachtman, D. (1995) 'Methods to enhance communication in verbal children.' In K.A. Quill (ed) *Teaching Children with Autism: Strategies to Enhance Communication and Socialization.* New York: Delmar.

Wetherby, A. and Prizant, B. (1992) 'Facilitating language and communication development in autism: assessment and intervention guidelines.' In D.E. Berkell (ed) *Facilitating Language and Communication Development in Autism: Assessment and Intervention Guidelines.* Hillsdale, NJ: Erlbaum.

Yack, E., Sutton, S. and Aquilla, P. (1998) *Building Bridges through Sensory Integration: Occupational Therapy for Children with Autism and Other Pervasive Developmental Disorders.* Toronto: Print Three.

Further reading

Bambara, L.M., Koger, F., Katzer, T. and Davenport, T.A. (1995) 'Embedding choice in the context of daily routines: an experimental case study.' *Journal of the Association for Persons with Severe Handicaps 20,* 3, 185–195.

Frost, L. and Bondy, A. (1994) *PECS: The Picture Exchange Communication System Training Manual.* Newark, DE: Pyramid Educational Consultants.

Morton, K. and Wolford, S. (1994) *Analysis of Sensory Behaviour Inventory (Revised).* Arcadia, CA: Skills with Occupational Therapy.

Newman, B., Buffington, D., O'Grady, M., Poulson, C. and Hemmes, N. (1995) 'Self-management of schedule following in three teenagers with autism.' *Behavior Management 20,* 3, 190–196.

Schopler, E., Mesibov, G. and Hearsey, K. (1995) 'Structured teaching in the TEACCH system.' In E. Schopler and G. Mesibov (eds) *Learning and Cognition in Autism.* New York: Plenum.

Willis, T., LaVigna, G. and Donnellan, A. (1989) *Behavior Assessment Guide.* Los Angeles: Institute for Applied Behavior Analysis.

CHAPTER 28

The State of the Problem of Autism in Ukraine

Olga Bogdashina

Introduction

Although much progress has been made in research, services, under-standing and recognition of autism in western countries, the problem of this disability in Ukraine still remains rather a virgin land. The experience of our psychiatrists in the field of diagnosis and treatment of autism leaves much to be desired. Probably, it is not their fault, or not only theirs. For many decades the totalitarian regime in Ukraine forced psychiatrists to be occupied with questions which were unrelated to medical treatment. Willy-nilly the lag behind the world level was created.

The attempt to answer the question: 'Why don't we recognise and diagnose autism despite availability of diagnostic criteria (ICD-10) and positive experience of other countries in early intervention?' leads us to the analysis of the research literature on autism in the former USSR (until recently Ukraine was a part of USSR) in order to see the development of understanding of the disability.

Situation in Russia

Russian researchers still use the term 'early infantile autism' (EIA), probably because the interest in this disorder has arisen quite recently and they focus their research on children, hence 'early infantile', while autistic adults, being misdiagnosed, still carry the label of 'schizophrenics'.

In general, in Russian medical literature EIA is described as a schizophrenic process (Bashina 1975, 1980, 1986; Lebedinskaya and Nikolskaya 1993; Sukhareva 1972), sometimes as brain pathology (Kagan 1979; Mnukhin and Isayev 1968, 1975). There are still controversies in the definition of EIA in Russian medical literature. Thus, the two kinds of disorders in the clinical-psychological picture of EIA, distinguished by Lebedinskaya and Nikolskaya (1991) – leading professionals in the field of autism in Russia – are first, autism ('autism proper': Nikolskaya *et al.* 1997), and second, stereotyped activities, i.e. they consider autism as one of the symptoms of EIA.

Though, as we can see, there are some controversies regarding understanding of autism among Russian researchers (that can be accounted for by the fact that EIA has been studied there for a few decades), one can see the desire to move forward, and a lot of work dealing with education and treatment of autistic children is being carried out in Russia.

1. Characteristic features of EIA and some possible ways of treatment of this disability have been described.

2. Under the leadership of K.S. Lebedinskaya a complex of medical-psychological-educational ways of rehabilitation of EIA was worked out.

3. A chart for identification of EIA in children of up to 2 years of age was made.

4. An introductory course on the problems of EIA has been read in the Moscow Open University.

5. Research work is being carried out in some research institutes.

Though in Russia there is still no state special educational institution for autistic children, the professional support for these children can be obtained through some special institutions, such as Dobro Association for autistic children care, Russian Research Centre of psychological welfare in Russian Institute of Psychiatry and some others.

Situation in Ukraine

In Ukraine the situation in the field is much worse. Although some Ukrainian high-rank professionals claim their deep knowledge of autism/EIA, non-professionals (i.e. parents of autistic children) cannot agree with that. For example, the Chief Child Psychiatrist of Ukraine considers that if a child is hyperactive, he or she cannot be autistic (personal communication, 1996). Another professor thinks that a verbal child is not autistic as autism is applied only to non-verbal children. Some psychiatrists in Kiev (capital of Ukraine) and some other large cities do diagnose autism; however, in other regions of the country the situation is very difficult for the parents of autistic children as autism in not recognised and, consequently, not diagnosed there. For example, in Donetsk region, eastern Ukraine (population of about 5 million people) there were no officially recognised children with autism until 1995 when only one boy was diagnosed autistic (under the pressure of his mother). The pace of recognition of Autistic Spectrum Disorders in this region is very slow: since 1995 in Gorlovka (population of about 350,000) chief specialists (medical and educational) who determine the fate of Gorlovka children have diagnosed autism in only three children. All the other disabled children examined by them (there are thousands of disabled children in special institutions for mentally retarded people) have been diagnosed as unteachable and written off as hopeless. It is a very convenient position: no autism – no problems concerning it. What makes the situation even worse is that Ukrainian specialists insist on isolation of 'hopeless' children in special institutions without any training. If the parents refuse, the educational authorities 'forget' about these children and deny their right to education. Thus, in Ukraine autistic children are not allowed to attend any kindergarten or school; they are kept at home without any professional support.

According to the data of epidemiological studies (Ehlers and Gillberg 1993; Wing and Gould 1979) a prevalence rate for children within autistic spectrum is estimated as 91 per 10,000. Clinical practice suggests that the number of autistic people in Ukraine might be higher, though as the majority of Ukrainian specialists fail to recognise autism, hence they claim there are no autistic children in Ukraine.

Assessment procedures in Ukraine

I should explain the situation in Ukraine regarding children with special needs in general. These children are assessed by a panel of 'experts' for 5–10 minutes each. They are told to do some tasks. If the children do not finish the tasks they receive the diagnosis of mental retardation and are offered a place in an institution. If the parents – whose wishes are not taken into account – refuse, the child is forgotten by the education department and the parents do not receive any professional help.

The process of assessment itself is very humiliating for the parents and stressful for the child. The 'specialists' (members of the assessment panel) do not take into account the most elementary thing.

A child who has spent the first six to eight years of their life at home, within four walls, surrounded by two or three very close people, all of a sudden is placed in an unfamiliar room with five or six unknown men and women, who ask the child questions. The parents feel uneasy, to say nothing of the child, especially an autistic child. To tell the truth, our specialists did not recognise autism in 1995 as seen from the official letter signed by the head of Donetsk Region Education Department:

> The lack of children with autism was testified by the session of the psychological-medical-educational consultation. Of six children examined, only one child, Bogdashin Alexey, was given the diagnosis, together with the main disease (?), of autism syndrome. The diagnosis of autism was not confirmed in the rest of the children.

Here are two vignettes to illustrate the work of this psychological-medical-educational consultation:

> A 6-year-old boy who could already read (though his speech was very limited) was offered by one of the 'experts'…to assemble a pyramid, the task he coped with when he was 2. Naturally, the boy did not pay any attention to her, clung to his mother. The 'experts' exchanged significant glances. So, what was their conclusion? Well, nobody was going to tell you that. To write their conclusion, to put their signatures under the diagnosis (by the way, the parents are not told the diagnosis given to their child) – not on their lives.

> The mother of another 6-year-old boy, non-verbal, asked them to appoint a speech pathologist to work with her son and help him to develop communicative skills. The answer was: 'Why do you think that a speech pathologist should work with him? He doesn't talk. How can we teach him to talk? Come to us when he starts talking, then we'll work with him.' (We understand it as: Let him learn how to swim and we'll pour water in the swimming-pool.)

These situations took place in 1995 in Gorlovka, in Donetsk region, but they are very typical for Ukraine. And this happens not because the existing legislation regarding disabled children is too bad (though none of the laws concerning children includes the category of 'autistic children'), but rather it is possible for the authorities not to fulfil their duties enumerated in the legal documents. Thus, the full procedure of the sessions of psychological-medical-educational consultation is described in the Legislation Acts of the Ukrainian Ministry of Education according to which parents have the right to know the diagnosis of their child and to expect the appropriate professional support from the state; however, this procedure is only on paper and is not fulfilled in reality. Moreover, the main law of the country – the Constitution of Ukraine – guarantees for every child the right to education, but again, it is merely declarative, and thousands of Ukrainian children with disabilities are kept at home because their parents cannot persuade the educational authorities to allow them to be educated.

It is known that social, psychological and medical support for autistic children in Ukraine lags three or four decades behind clinical support abroad. The officials to whom parents appeal for help either have no idea about autism or regard children with autism as mentally diseased. As a result, the parents lose any hope, they are driven to despair in their vain attempts to solve the problem themselves; the children, in the end, are lost to society through the fault of the society itself.

Economic conditions

I must stress that the economic conditions in Ukraine are very bad nowadays. The main task for everybody is to survive. Teachers, doctors, miners and others have not been paid for months. Kindergartens are closing because there is no money to buy food for children. We are having to argue our case for proper treatment for our children when there is a general lack of resources available for all public services. However, despite all present difficulties the parents do not want to lose their children.

Autism Society of Ukraine

On 6 July 1994 a group of parents of autistic children in Gorlovka founded the first Autism Society of Ukraine 'From Despair to Hope'. The Society has achieved the following:

1. In September 1995 a small school for children with autism was opened.

2. With the help of Charity Know How Fund and the National Autistic Society (NAS), two representatives of the NAS visited Gorlovka school for autistic children (in 1995 and 1997) in order to support the activities of the Autism Society of Ukraine, and three representatives of the Autism Society of Ukraine were able to visit Storm House School for children with autism in England (in 1996) in order to learn about the treatment of autistic children there.

3. On 6–7 December 1996 the first training seminar for doctors, teachers, social workers and parents of autistic children 'Autism: Yesterday, Today, Tomorrow' was organised.

4. On 5–7 May 1997 the first International Autism Conference in Ukraine 'Autism Does Not Know Any Boundaries' was held.

5. To promote awareness of autism and draw the attention of the public to the problems and needs of children with autism the leaflets 'What is Autism?' (1996) and 'Could You Recognise Autism?' (1998) were published; many articles concerning these children were published in the newspapers.

6. The most important documents concerning people with autism (such as, for example, Charter for Persons with Autism, the European Written Declaration on the Rights of People with Autism), other materials dealing with diagnosis and treatment of autism have been translated from English into Russian and distributed among specialists and parents of autistic children.

7. A book *Autism. Part 1: Definitions and Diagnosis* (Bogdashina 1999) was published.

8. In October 1998 the Diagnostic and Rehabilitation Centre for children with autism was founded in Gorlovka on the basis of the Autism Society of Ukraine, where up to the time of writing more than ninety children from more than ten regions of Ukraine have been examined and diagnosed.

9. Research work in the field constantly is being carried out dealing with the problem of autism and appropriate methods of treatment.

Having described the state of the problem of autism in Ukraine, it is appropriate to touch upon the approach to the problem in the Autism Society of Ukraine.

The approach is based on my own experience as a teacher of children with autism and the mother of an autistic son. As there is a scientific evidence that deficit in information processing that is both perceptive and executive, is found in all people within the autistic spectrum, I am inclined to believe that one of the core features in autism is abnormal perception of sensory stimuli.

Unusual sensory experience has been observed in people with autism for many years and is listed as an associated feature of autism in many classifications. The personal accounts of high-functioning autistic people confirm that one of the main problems they experience is their abnormal perception (e.g. Grandin 1984, 1988; Williams 1992, 1994, 1996, 1998) the direct symptom of which is unusual responses to sensory experience. Some authors think it is justifiable to include the unusual responses of children with autism to sensory stimuli as a new criterion into the diagnostic criteria.

Returning to the definition of autism I would start with a (probably, unscientific and simplified) traditional description of a person with autism as 'living in a world of his own'. But I would distinguish not two 'worlds': 'theirs – autistic' and 'ours – non-autistic', but three: 'theirs – autistic', 'sensory (visual auditory/tactual/gustatory) distorted (different?) world perceived by people with autism' and 'ours – non-autistic world'.

In the Autism Society of Ukraine we start with the assumption that while working with autistic children, what we are dealing with, at any time, is a reflection of sensory dysfunction, the adjustment to it, the compensatory strategies (voluntary and involuntary) the child has acquired, that particular child's strengths and weaknesses, the child's personality, the learning and family environment and the interaction of all these factors.

Bearing this in mind we consider the possible ways of alleviating their perceptual difficulties first. To achieve this means to 'enter their autistic world' in order to see/hear/feel/smell/taste through their senses, understand and reconstruct that 'second/distorted world' and then find appropriate methods to remove distortions, thus, leading the children to our world. And only then we can work with other problems.

We follow Donna Williams's recommendation of the way to help people with autism: 'If you've got a camel which is finding it hard to walk under the weight of all the straws on its back, the easiest way to make it easier for the camel to walk is to take as many straws off its back as possible' and not to train 'the camel to walk or appear to walk while carrying the straws' (Williams 1996, p.87). As Temple Grandin confirms, all the behaviour modification in the world will not teach a child to tolerate a noise that is overloading and damaging the nervous system (Grandin 1988). Returning to Williams's allegory: 'To take the straws off the camel's back, you have to do two things. One is to identify them and the second is to know how to remove them' (Williams 1996, p.87).

Special therapies and methods should be used to help to normalise the sensory experiences of people with autism. The problem is that, on the one hand, people with autism have a lot in common, on the other hand, each of them has their own unique problems of perception. It is we who have to identify them and find appropriate methods of correction.

Theoretical models of abnormal perception

We can create several theoretical models of cases of abnormal perception.

According to the number of senses working at a time

People can be classified into 'Multi-Track' versus 'Mono' processing (Williams, 1996). Most people use all their senses simultaneously. When they are hearing something, they still continue to make sense of what they see and feel emotionally and physically. They know what their body is doing while they are speaking or what their face is doing while they are using their hands. They can do all these things because they are 'multi-tracked'. For people who work in 'mono' to process the meaning of what they are listening to while being touched may be to have no idea where they were being touched or what they thought or felt about it. To process the location or special significance of being touched while someone is showing them something means that they saw nothing but meaningless colour and form and movement (Williams 1996, pp.95–96). For example, Williams's inner-body sense, like everything else, was mostly mono: if she touched her leg she would feel it on her hand or on her leg but not both at the same time; her perception of a whole body was in bits: she was an arm or leg or nose (Williams 1994, p.228).

According to what channel (or channels) is deficient

One of the reasons that children with autism cannot deal with the stimulation coming into their brains from the outside world is because one or more intake channels (sight, sound, feel, smell or taste) is deficient in some way. To find out which one(s) are deficient and to what extent is a very difficult task as all the senses are integrated and deficiency in one may lead to disturbances in the other(s).

Probably, this can account for the fact that some treatments – such as Auditory Integration Training (AIT), Irlen method, etc. – are beneficial for some people with autism and do not bring much improvement in others. The right problem (deficient channel) appropriately treated leads to improvements of other perceptual problems. A widely known example is described by Annabel Stehli (1990) concerning her daughter Georgiana, who suffered from extremely acute hearing: after undergoing AIT her hypersensitivity to sound diminished and this enabled her to cope with her other perceptual problems to such an extent that she is no longer considered autistic.

Another example to illustrate this deals with correction of vision by means of Irlen filters. A boy with autism (Gorlovka, Ukraine) at the age of 8 was also diagnosed as suffering from Irlen Syndrome (in this case, fragmented vision). After screening and selection of appropriate filters (Irlen glasses) and after having worn them for a few months one can see not only that his hypersensitivity to bright light has reduced but also that his speech has considerably developed, his social interaction and motor coordination have significantly improved.

According to the intensity the senses work

We can distinguish hyper- and hypo-sensitivity of any of the senses or a combination of the senses. Carl Delacato (1974) classifies each sensory channel as being hyper, hypo, or disrupted by 'white noise', or interference within the system. Each sensory channel can be affected in a different way, e.g. a child could be hypo-visual, 'white noise' auditory, hypo to tastes and odours and hyper-tactile. We add another category to those listed above – fragmented vision/hearing, etc. Each child is considered on an individual basis. Evaluation is complicated by the interaction of the five sensory channels.

According to the (in)consistency of perception

One of the most baffling features of autistic children is their inconsistent perception of sensory stimuli: a child who appears to be deaf on one occasion may react to an everyday sound on another occasion as if it is causing acute pain; visual stimuli that may appear so bright on one occasion will on another occasion appear very dim. Similarly, reaction to pain may vary from complete insensitivity to apparent 'over-reaction' to the slightest knock (Jordan and Powell 1990).

Freeman (1992) describes this phenomenon as perception of the world by people with autism 'like an FM radio that is not exactly tuned on the station when you are driving down the freeway. Sometimes the world comes in clearly and at other times it does not' (Freeman 1992, p.5).

People with autism contribute to the explanation of this phenomenon. VanDalen (1995) terms it as 'sudden falling out of' autism and describes his personal experience of this process as: 'the stay in the non-autistic condition lasts only a few minutes...the exit-procedure occurs instantaneously, the return is gradual' (VanDalen 1995, pp.13–14).

Williams experienced the perceptual problems of deafness, dumbness and blindness as very real. She thinks that they are caused by shutdown caused by extreme stress, brought on by an inability to cope with incoming information (Williams 1992). She compares autism with a seesaw: when it is up or down she cannot see a whole life; when it is passing through in the middle she gets to see a glimpse of the life she would have if she were not autistic (Williams 1994, p.233).

According to the child's development

One should take into consideration that children with autism are developing, their symptoms are changing. One of the explanations of this might be that to survive in our world (foreign to them) they have to work out adaptations and compensations, voluntary and involuntary (Williams 1996). They may be beneficial or may hinder treatment.

After drawing a profile of each particular child with autism we choose the methods and therapies for that particular child.

Conclusion

We never fail to see little personalities in these strange 'hopeless' children who live near us. They are neither better nor worse than we are. They are different. And it does not mean that they have no right to live in our society. We have to do our best to prevent the 'two worlds' from clashing.

References

Bashina, V.M. (1974) 'Kanner's syndrome of early infantile autism.' *Zh Nevropatol Psikhiatr Im SS Korsakova 74 (10)* 1538–1542.

Bashina, V.M. (1980) 'Course and prognosis of childhood schizophrenia in the light of follow-up information.' *Zh Nevropatol Psikhiatr Im SS Korsakova 80 (10)*, 1507–1510.

Bashina, V.M. (1986) 'Features of the relation between preclinical dysontogeny, the Kanner syndrome of early infantile autism and early childhood schizophrenia (according to the results of catamnestic examinations).' *Zh Nevropatol Psikhiatr Im SS Korsakova 86 (3)*, 413–418.

Delacato, C. (1974) *The Ultimate Stranger: The Autistic Child.* Noveto, CA: Academic Therapy.

Ehlers, S. and Gillberg, C. (1993) 'The epidemiology of Asperger syndrome: a total population study.' *Journal of Child Psychology and Psychiatry 34*, 8, 1327–1350.

Freeman, B.J. (1992) *Diagnosis of the Syndrome of Autism: Questions Parents Ask.* Los Angeles: University of California.

Grandin, T. (1984) 'My experiences as an autistic child and a review of the literature.' *Journal of Orthomolecular Psychiatry 13*, 144–174.

Grandin, T. (1988) 'Teaching tips from a recovered autistic.' *Focus on Autistic Behaviour 3*, 1, 1–8.

Jordan, R. and Powell, S. (1990) *The Special Curricular Needs of Autistic Children: Learning and Thinking Skills.* London: Association of Heads and Teachers of Adults and Children with Autism.

Kagan, V.E. (1979) 'Nonprocess autism in children: Comparative etiopathogenetic study.' *Zh Nevropatol Psikhiatr Im SS Korsakova 79 (10)*, 1400–1403.

Lebedinskaya, K.S. and Nikolskaya, O.S. (1991) *Diagnosis of Early Infantile Autism.* Moscow (in Russian).

Lebedinskaya, K.S. and Nikolskaya, O.S. (1993) 'Brief report: Analysis of autism and its treatment in modern Russian defectology.' *Journal of Autism and Developmental Disorders 23 (4)*, 675–679.

Mnukhin, S.S. and Isayev, D.N. (1968) 'Psychosis in oligophrenics.' *Vopr Psikhiatr Nevropatol 13*. 149–157.

Nikolskaya, O.S., Baenskaya, E.R. and Libling. M.M. (1997) *An Autistic Child.* Moscow (in Russian).

Stehli, A. (1991) *The Sound of a Miracle.* New York: Doubleday.

Sukhareva, G.E. (1972) 'Diagnostic criteria for oligophrenia in children.' *Zh Nevropatol Psikhiatr Im SS Korsakova 72 (9)*, 1342–1347.

VanDalen, J.G.T. (1995) 'Autism from within: looking through the eyes of a mildly afflicted person.' *Link 17*, 11–16.

Williams, D. (1992) *Nobody Nowhere.* London: Doubleday.

Williams, D. (1994) *Somebody Somewhere.* London: Doubleday.

Williams, D. (1996) *Autism: An Inside-Out Approach.* London: Jessica Kingsley.

Williams, D. (1998) *Autism and Sensing: The Unlost Instinct.* London: Jessica Kingsley Publishers.

Wing, L. and Gould, J. (1979) 'Severe impairments of social interaction and associated abnormalities in children: epidemiology and classification.' *Journal of Autism and Developmental Disorders 9*, 11–29.

CHAPTER 29

Quality Management and Staff Training throughout Health Services

Meeting the Health Needs of Clients within the Autistic Spectrum

Wendy Tucker

The search for coherence: finding a balance

Growing families are faced with joys, difficulties and changes within the home as each new child is born. Throughout times of adjustment, family members define roles and responsibilities for themselves and for one another, feeling reasonably confident in seeking advice and support from services in health and in education. Juggling this is never easy; however, confirmation that a child has a disorder on the autistic spectrum tests everyone to the full, family, friends, plus the services normally there to offer support. It further stretches the ability of everybody when the young person is already known to have a complication such as cerebral palsy or Down Syndrome, to name just a couple of many possible conditions.

For the person with autistic tendencies, meeting specific health needs involves changes to routines and unwanted attention from more people, bringing additional anxiety and stress. Simple procedures may be regarded as invasive and unacceptable. This may happen during a home visit by a health visitor, or when going to the dentist, doctor, hospital, etc. Being the focus of attention is sufficient to raise alarm and anxiety for this person, often followed by physical reaction and a need to escape. As a parent said recently, 'Some children who are admitted to a large, open ward may find it easy to "escape", or harm themselves or others in their attempt to get out of their stressful situation.' It becomes clear that for everyone to work in partnership, it is necessary to value, understand, enjoy and love the autistic personality.

Until one tests a service it is not possible to know how it will work for you

Alex, our son, is 14 years old and has a heart defect which will mean increasing hospital visits, eventually leading to periods of hospitalisation. We know many other families caring for people who share the same combination of health needs as Alex. With medical support, it should be possible for many non-autistic peers to live into their third decade, but will our children with autism have the same chance of life? We ask this question in the knowledge that if clients like Alex are to become less anxious and willing to cooperate within changing situations and programmes of treatment then everybody involved should feel positive and confident in their knowledge of autism, with a clear focus towards successful treatment for this person. Feedback through parents and carers of others with autistic tendencies indicates that negative situations happen when people to whom we turn for help do not understand the autistic personality and do not know how to work with it. Often intentions are good, but responsible people, including managers, often lack the training and the experience to establish trust, partnership and positive outcomes for those with autistic tendencies. Setting national standards in health care and linking these with ongoing staff development, so raising awareness of the autistic spectrum for all medical teams and support staff, would aim to establish the same levels of awareness for everybody, in all areas of the UK. There is a desperation in the way carers express the need to be confident that in seeking treatment, they will find the same, consistent standard of care wherever they go. Further networking would target consistency within British and European standards.

Trust

With services as they are, carers say:

> I hope that when we have any new hospitals that there will be guidelines for when a patient is identified as having 'special needs'.

Our hospital did not seem to know how to handle a child like Jack.

We are anxious that another hospital may offer better treatment.

We must be ever vigilant and become experts.

We continually check with others and shop around for the best service.

We cannot trust that hospital treatments and attitudes of staff will be as good where we live as they are in London and Middlesex.

No one seems interested.

Families attending clinics across the UK often communicate with one another through membership of charities such as the National Autistic Society and when autism exists with other conditions such as Down Syndrome, also the Down's Heart Group. They communicate on the internet and use the net as a worldwide source of information. For carers, learning more of possible treatments within centres in other parts of this country and other parts of the world identifies lack of consistency in approach, advice and treatment. Very confusing for families who already have low expectations of receiving competent levels of health care.

Valuing autism

Carers worry continually that their dependants may be undervalued, 'not worth treating', seen as 'difficult', 'a nuisance' and 'expensive', leading to a cut-off point and reduction in care and resources routinely offered to others. We develop a protective role becoming increasingly concerned with equality of care and recognition of equal rights for each individual. This highlights the need for professional clarity and transparency regarding the value of the autistic personality. Clearly, inclusion in the Strategic Plan towards budgeting resources to enable staff training and appropriate approaches to treatment is long overdue. Fortunately, we do find many instances of good practice within the health service and know that many providers work extremely hard to provide relevant standards of care. New centres are opening and staff development is taking place.

Good practice

Good practice happens, but is this consistent within a total quality management strategy or is good practice random, happening through actions and knowledge of a sensitive individual, team or unit? Clearly, there is a need to recognise where this is happening and to build on existing good practice, making it available to everybody as a matter of routine within nationally recognised standards of care. Carers express good fortune in having such valuable support and anxiety at the thought of any changes to the service, particularly when moving from paediatric to adult services. 'How will an adult unit support our young person with autistic tendencies? We feel a paediatric approach is still needed for all of us.'

'They tell me I'm the expert'

A cry from the heart from carers whose aim is to find and to relax in the care of the true experts with the full knowledge that at last they can trust the advice given and have confidence in resources and care provided. To tell carers that they are the expert in the treatment of health matters is not what they wish to hear, destroying trust and shaking confidence in the ability and the intentions of the service.

Recent press coverage, including reported comments by the prime minister, confirms fears and raises questions from ministers concerning quality management structures within health services. There are concerns about the ability to self-assess, accountability, monitoring, audit and of failure in a number of hospitals to comply with recognised standards of care, or to maintain the standards upheld in other parts of the country. The prime minister is reported to say that this must change and that a total review of the National Health Service will happen.

To effect change

The opportunity is here now for change to be effective and happen quickly to benefit those with autism, through looking at ways to move forward, clarify policy and have the resources we need. We must not miss this opportunity and find ourselves at the back of the queue. Changes to be managed methodically within a national strategy which builds on present good practice and draws on the skills of people both inside and outside the health service today.

Liaison

Ask the experts who know autism to liaise within staff training programmes and standards committees, so informing national standards of health care. At this point there is a need to know what is happening at the moment and how this is working as a possible basis for further developments. If an advisory team or advisory groups are to form, then further questions are generated. The conference, 'Autism in Oxford' in September 1999, brought together a wealth of people, the expertise of whom would greatly enhance and inform an advisory process. Similarly, we have huge expertise within the membership, managers and coordinators of the National Autistic Society.

Standards

Standards which are desirable, achievable and measurable should recognise the user as the primary client with the provider as the secondary client. It is important to recognise that the client or the person with autistic tendencies is the prime client with distinct needs to be met as part of the contract with the NHS. The contract is made clear within the client charter and made available in all health centres. Carers should be aware that these are recognised criteria towards setting standards, as are the answers to the following questions:

1. Who are our clients?

2. What are their needs?

3. How are these needs to be met?

Client satisfaction, customer care

Feedback of client satisfaction is essential, with systems in place to invite regular feedback from people with autism, resulting in action to bring about changes and to continually improve services. Improving the service for people on the autistic spectrum and looking at resources to meet individual needs improves services for all.

PART 6

Personal Stories

CHAPTER 30

Editorial

Personal Stories

John Richer and Sheila Coates

The usual view of autism is from the outside, from the professionals providing the services and from the scientists researching the phenomenon. But there are two other stories to be told.

One story is the families' stories, particularly the parents'. Julia Stuart (Chapter 31) tells of her journey with her son James to find ways to help him out of his autism. She plots with great sensitivity those factors which led to improvement and those which led to deterioration, sometimes a catastrophic regression after an apparently small incident. She notes the vital importance of honest, open, spontaneous communication, of emotional support and security, of physical factors such as food intolerance. She develops a sense of the coherence of the diversity of factors affecting her son. This chapter exemplifies the importance of close prolonged observation of a child with autism and of open-mindedly trying reasonable approaches, whether medical, educational or psychological, all within a framework of love and respect for the child.

Rachel Tams, a clinical psychologist, has surveyed and summarised the range of parents' views about their autistic child, about having such a child in the family and the change in views over time. In Chapter 32 she contrasts the position of 'fighting' autism and looking to 'breakthrough' to the child, with a greater acceptance of the likelihood that the condition is lifelong and accommodation to it needs to be made. The former position marked the early stages, the latter the later stages of having an autistic child.

Alan Watkins (Chapter 33) describes his family's experience with the Lovaas programme, their reasons for choosing it, their energetic pursuance of it, the recognition that it is not for everyone, and the fact that it goes alongside other therapies (they also treated their son physiologically).

John Lubbock's son also benefited from a Lovaas programme but in Chapter 34 he points to the importance of knowing when to stop a programme as well as when to start. This emphasises the importance of understanding how various programmes fit into an overall therapy programme and what changes are to be looked for at each stage (Richer, Chapters 2 and 3 in this volume). Julia Stuart, like many parents, was able to develop this with her son.

Parents, being on the receiving end of many different therapeutic approaches, are well placed to look for some coherence among those on offer. It is understandable that many parents become very enthusiastic about one approach, perhaps one has particularly helped their child, or one they feel it will do so, thus their enthusiasm is necessary to maintain their commitment to the programme. However, as the experience of John Lubbock's family shows, a child is best served by loving parents taking what seems best for their child and their family from the various approaches on offer, energetically following those that seem to serve their child's long-term benefit, but not forgetting the centrality of the child's experience.

The latter experience is revealed in the other type of personal story, that of autistic people themselves. By the very nature of autism, the difficulty in the meeting of minds, this story is not often told. Now it is told by more people who have made sufficient progress to be able to communicate their subjective world to others: Temple Grandin, Donna Williams, Gunilla Gerland, Wendy Lawson and many others. The publisher of this book, Jessica Kingsley, has made a great contribution in publishing so many of these authors. In Chapter 35 in this volume, Marc Fleisher, diagnosed as having Asperger Syndrome when a child, gives a clear, engaging and illuminating account of some of his experiences. His personal story of family misfortune and the effort required to sustain his integration into school are a testament to his courage and determination, a fitting conclusion to this book.

Further Reading

Grandin, T. (1996) *Thinking in Pictures*. New York, NY: Doubleday.
Williams, D. (1992) *Nobody Nowhere*. London: Jessica kingsley Publishers.
Williams, D. (1994) *Somebody Somewhere*. London. Jessica Kingsley Publishers.

CHAPTER 31

Coherence from the Fragments

An Assessment of Home Programmes and Other Influences on a 14-year-old Boy with Autism and its Implications

Julia V. Stuart

Despite the variety of programmes introduced and the range of symptoms or manifestations of autism demonstrated by my son James since 1987, the thesis of this contribution will be that there is an underlying coherence both in how autism manifests itself and how it is affected for good or ill. That coherence is dramatically illustrated when a number of factors come together in a single moment, precipitated by a single trigger, but equally attributable to the convergence of many predisposing factors. Some possible implications will be explored for ways of developing the potential of children with autism.

James' fourteen-year-history has been a chequered one with several *peaks and troughs* as I have tried to show in Figure 31.1. The outstanding peak which has thrown the most light on his condition happened during a period of three weeks in September 1989 when he was 4 years old and had been diagnosed as autistic one year previously though treated as hyperactive with many allergies for over a year before the diagnosis.

In early September 1989 James was a very active child who never slept for more than two or three hours at a time, swinging daily from great good humour to frequent prolonged tantrums, with a vocabulary of several hundred words and phrases mostly stereotyped, drawn from nursery rhymes and television programmes, though he rarely spoke unless

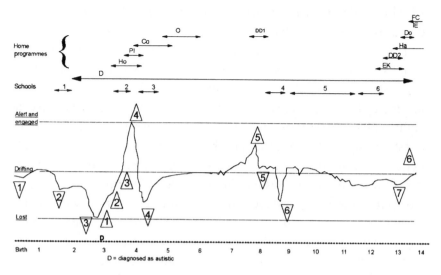

Figure 31.1 James' progress 1985–99

someone prompted him. His day consisted of family breakfast, mornings alone with his mother including lots of cuddles, 'talking' and some relaxed pre-school work on reading, writing and numbers, lunch waiting for us downstairs, afternoons in the park with his grandmother followed by more, different reading and number work with her or else a twice-weekly visit to an informal indiosyncratic *play-therapist*, fairly relaxed family evenings, prolonged books and games in his room and cuddles before – and between – periods of sleep. He was following a *restricted diet, without sugar, eggs, cow's milk products or wheat.* He was waiting to take up a place at an assessment unit the following January.

This was his situation when, following a friend's recommendation after her daughter's asthma was much reduced, I started to take James to a *cranial osteopath* in the vague hope that it might ameliorate his allergic reactions. He disliked being touched, so I had to imprison him on my knee, holding his arms and legs throughout each session. At home after the first session he stopped screaming when he woke up from his daytime naps; after the third session he started to make a few comments spontaneously; ten minutes into the fourth session he relaxed in my arms but stayed sitting unmoving and looking tranquilly into the eyes of the osteopath during several minutes. She advised me to take him home, be very gentle with him and not put any pressure on him, to cancel the next appointment but keep the one after that.

For the next few weeks I had a different child. James showed no traces of autism other than a lack of the experience and expertise, particularly in language, which would be normal in a 4 year old but he seemed to be making up for lost ground at an accelerating rate. We began to hold six and eight sentence conversations with him. He began to comment and ask questions about the world around him. There were no tantrums and I began to take for granted that I could go with him anywhere. When I took him to noisy places or dressed him in clothes with zips and buttons, he would give me a quizzical look then take stock and get on with the next adventure. He began to dress himself and insist on going to the toilet alone and with the door closed. His bearing and facial expression changed and it seemed that even the shape of his face was different, less symmetrical with a crooked grin and a squarer chin. He rode his tricycle for the first time and began to kick and throw a ball. He approached other children and, usually by following and copying boys' games, was accepted by them. Every day someone would comment in surprise on some new small achievement.

Three weeks after that turning-point at the osteopath's, my daughter was home during her half-term holiday coinciding with our au pair's absence for ten days. Both children developed slight colds. The home-made bread season started and, urged to let James have some for once, I thought he was 'solid' enough to try and gave him one bread roll. In retrospect he 'plateaued' and was a little quieter; other people's daily exclamations at his progress stopped. However, I was encouraged and four days later I gave him another roll at teatime.

The next day he regressed completely, with fiercer tantrums than at any time before and his new-found language turned to endlessly repeated singsong phrases, always to himself. He refused to return to the osteopath or to his play-therapist, refused to wear anything but pyjamas or tracksuits, opted for a range of inappropriate receptacles in place of the toilet and showed no interest in anything else around him. He quietened and became more amenable during the next few months and we returned to the osteopath, but that radical change never happened again. He has since had other periods of progress and others of regression but he has never regained, other than briefly, the alertness and skills he attained during those weeks.

Autism is not, in any child, 'cured' by cranial osteopathy nor is it 'caused' by a bread roll. Both were triggers and illustrate just how dramatic can be the effect of beneficial treatment at just the right time with a good support structure and, in the absence of that support, just how devastating can be the straw that breaks the camel's back.

James' response to cranial osteopathy was similar to Georgie's response to *auditory integration therapy* (Stehli 1991) or to Billy Tommey's response to *secretin*. Georgie had a supportive family who followed up the effects of therapy by expecting and getting better behaviour and fighting for a normal education for her, and Billy Tommey's family are following a Lovaas programme.

Other small *breakthroughs* happened:

1. After spending hours one warm evening throwing pebbles into the Thames James drew his first self-portrait.

2. Having ignored the class craft project for several days he constructed the straw and paper boat in minutes while the teacher's back was turned.

3. James proved to be as able as his companions when introduced to horse-riding and crab-football.

4. Once or twice he has produced perfect language that registers a mature understanding of his own and others' feelings and rights, such as the time when after deliberately, for the umpteenth time, inverting the contents of a toy beaker he had taken to using in place of the toilet, he suddenly came up to me and said 'I'm sorry Mummy. I won't do it again' (and didn't) or, at the age of 2 with almost no non-echolalic language he looked quietly at me after, in exasperation, I smacked his bottom and said 'Don't hit me, Mummy'.

Other parents have given similar examples. One of the most striking is that of a friend's teenage daughter whose speech consisted of a few concrete phrases – 'Go home', 'Go in car', 'Cup of tea' – but who produced two abstract pictures, one of which she labelled 'Conscience' and the other 'Freedom'. Another father working late in his study heard the door open and his mute autistic daughter popped her head in and said, for the first and last time, 'Hello Daddy'. One is reminded of Mary McCracken's book *Lovey* when a profoundly unhappy angry and mute child reveals fluent language after the whole class is taken, on the spur of the moment, to have a picnic by the river (MacCracken 1977).

What all these breakthroughs have in common were, I think, three things:

1. They were unselfconscious, and *spontaneous*, in an atmosphere free of expectations.

2. The adults were *emotionally honest*, whether happy, exasperated or just there, they were responses to situations, not to direct approaches.

3. The *child* took the *initiative*.

What seem to be common to the *triggers* that can precipitate regression or even the apparent onset of autism are the following:

1. Loss of expected support such as James experienced when I took over the running of a toddler group; other children experience this at the birth of a sibling (or even in one case three months into his mother's pregnancy).

2. Heavy-handed approaches such as James' all-or-nothing behaviour modification programme; the experience of being subjected to unreasonable demands to perform or conform as happens all too often in public places such as parks, shops and schools.

3. Feeling ill and disoriented, whether from an allergic reaction, a cold, vaccination, the effects of anaesthetic, especially if others do not realise the severity of the reaction and its possible distorting effects on the child's perceptions and understanding; sensory distortions are far more common – and susceptible to treatment – than is commonly realised.

4. Above all, failure on the part of adults to recognise and respond to small signals. Ours is not a child-friendly society. Just a few children experience early on the mixture of guidance, security and unconditional love leading to a 'great sense of freedom' as described in one woman's account of life in the nursery with a traditional, but nevertheless exceptional, nanny (Smith and Grunfeld 1993).

Autism can readily be seen as a consequence of genetic inheritance, an unpropitious environment and a series of great or small, temporary or long-lasting 'assaults' as described above. Each *fragment of the process* is a *random* occurrence but the *convergent* whole is *coherent* and inexorable.

It would be useful to find a similar coherence in the varied approaches and techniques that have been devised to help children with autism overcome their handicaps. The *approaches* used to help James which appear in Figure 31.1 can, ostensibly, be divided into three groups: *physiological/neurological, psychological* and *educational* in the sense of facilitating the imparting of information. In fact they are all based on *psychological* factors: the way in which the approaches are implemented is more important than the techniques and this is because every technique should be used to uncover and develop what is already present but hidden by the autistic person's reactions to what are, to that person, physical and psychological traumas. If the language were not already present, the sudden uses of it described above, and also in *Facilitated Communication*, could not occur. Some exceptional skills reveal an awareness – access to a way of thinking and working – which is lost or returns only fleetingly the more a person is absorbed into the ways of this world (Williams 1998). This of course is an argument for the value of autistic strengths, borne out by their continued presence in the gene pool and also for the benefits that would accrue to us all if those skills could be retained (Selfe 1977).

As well as some of those whose histories have been published (Stehli 1995), I have known personally three children and one adult whose lack of communication and challenging behaviour was moderate to severe as young children and whom one would barely recognise as autistic today and, more importantly, for whom life poses none but commonplace problems. I know of a dozen or more others who, after equally serious problems when young, now lead independent and interesting lives but for whom a sense of belonging and friendships remain unattainable. The tactics employed were different in every case: *Holding, Doman-Delacato, Lovaas* and *role modelling* by siblings or friends, often simple insistence on *acceptable behaviour and participation,* using a more intensive version of the same mixture of bribery and sanctions used for the family's other non-autistic children. Common to all these instances, however, was the *commitment* of two people, usually the mother and a teacher or another family member and an unswerving belief in the child's ability.

Given the will and open-mindedness to *experiment,* the chance for all children to develop in the same way as these few could be explored in numerous ways:

1. by creating an environment in which the needs of children with autism – *as indicated by the children* – would be met before introducing gradually the demands of everyday life

2. by looking at the successes achieved by different *approaches* with a view to bringing them into the public domain so that access is not denied to all but those with the considerable resources in funds, personnel and energy that are presently required

3. by funding experiments and serious research to be chosen and controlled by parents and teachers and autistic people themselves, in the home, in the classroom, in other centres

4. by using existing successful approaches to explore options in the educational system such as *one-year special schools* aimed at paving the way for integration into the mainstream, comparable with at least one existing school for dyslexic children; or after-school clubs dedicated to both *differentiated school work* and *creative activities* chosen by the child

5. or, my own fantasy, all schools everywhere would devote morning sessions to an identical *national curriculum* to be attended by every child in the catchment area: afternoons would be devoted to various sports and structured physical activities including specific *neurological training techniques*, organised cooperatively by the schools; and late afternoons would be the right time for one-to-one or selected small group work geared to the child's strengths and *creative abilities*.

All of these suggestions are ways to explore approaches that combine respect for the child with respect for mainstream practice and a belief that they can work together to the benefit of each. They also reflect an abiding principle to which we all agree but which is rarely invoked in school and medical contexts, although over the years and off the record we have been told by a paediatrician, two psychologists and even a hard-nosed psychiatrist that the most important thing we could do for James is to love him, 'provide a loving home for him', give him 'guidance, modelling and love'. However, to focus on love is to risk being trapped in saccharine aimlessness. Love in action is *empathy* and it is empathy that both provides a *coherent strategy* in our explorations of how best to help those with autism and alerts us to those critical *moments of coherence* which can transform their and our lives.

References

MacCracken, M. (1977) *Lovey: A Child Reclaimed.* London: André Deutsch.[1]

Selfe, L. (1977) *Nadia: A Case of Extraordinary Drawing Ability in an Autistic Child.* London: Academic Press.[2]

Smith, N. and Grunfeld, N. (1993) *Nanny Knows Best: How to Bring Up a Happy Child.* London: BBC Books.[3]

Stehli, A. (1991) *The Sound of a Miracle.* New York. Doubleday.

Stehli, A. (ed) (1995) *Dancing in the Rain: Stories of Exceptional Progress by Parents of Children with Special Needs.* Westport, CT: Georgiana Organization.[4]

Tomney, J. (2000) 'The testing times are here.' *The Autism File 2,* 4–11.

Williams, D. (1998) *Autism and Sensing: The Unlost Instinct.* London: Jessica Kingsley Publishers.

Further reading

Grandin, T. (1996) *Thinking in Pictures: And Other Reports from My Life with Autism.* New York: Random House.

Sacks, O. (1995) *An Anthropologist on Mars: Seven Paradoxical Tales.* London: Picador.

Waterhouse, S. (1999) *A Positive Approach to Autism.* London: Jessica Kingsley Publishers.

1   See also M. MacCracken (1974) *A Circle of Children.* London: Gollancz.

2   Another case is that of Stephen Wiltshire, described among other prodigies and *savants* in O. Sacks (1995) *An Anthropologist on Mars: Seven Paradoxical Tales.* London: Picador.

3   Further information on these approaches will gladly be supplied, on request, by the author: Julia Stuart, 23 Warbeck Road, London W12 8NS; juliastuart@lycos.com

4   This book, together with S. Waterhouse (1999) *A Positive Approach to Autism.* London: Jessica Kingsley, is guaranteed to lift the morale and increase the determination of anyone who feels that children with special needs have potential that is rarely acknowledged.

CHAPTER 32

Parents' Perceptions of Autism

A Qualitative Study

Rachel Tams

Abstract

This qualitative project aimed to explore parents' experiences of having a child with autism. Grounded Theory was used as a framework for collecting and analysing the data. In total twelve parents of ten children were interviewed.

Findings highlighted the extensive impact of autism on the family and the stresses associated with diagnosis. Subtle differences in how parents perceived their child and the condition emerged. For example, a number of parents viewed autism as an 'emotional disorder', making a clear distinction between children with autism and those with 'learning disabilities'. Linked to this perception was the central theme of 'breaking through' to their autistic child. Other parents reported a change in perceptions with time, stating that they had previously hoped for the breakthrough of their 'normal child' but now viewed autism as a pervasive and enduring disorder. Parents' understanding of their child's disability influenced their subsequent behaviour toward their child.

Drawing on recurrent themes that emerged throughout analysis, a potential typology was proposed. This distinguished between those parents who were 'fighting' against autism and those who 'accepted' the disability. Parents who were 'fighting' were optimistic about a cure and were actively involved in the 'autistic culture'. These parents described attempts to change their child's behaviour – 'we try to make him normal'.

In comparison, parents in the second group were less actively involved in the autistic culture. They viewed autism as an integrated part of their child and described 'allowing' difficult behaviour – 'we let him be autistic'. It was tentatively hypothesised that these two positions marked the ends of a gradual continuum of change, although many factors (e.g. contact with other parents and an involvement in research) influenced parental perceptions.

Introduction

Extensive research has been conducted to examine the effects that children with learning disabilities have on their families. In particular, parental distress and stress mediators have received considerable attention (see Beresford 1994 for review). Studies have also adopted models of coping (e.g. Lazarus and Folkman 1984) to examine factors associated with successful adaptation by families. In general, the available studies have served only to demonstrate the complexities that exist within this area and consequently few conclusions have been drawn.

There has been limited systematic exploration of the impact that a child with autism has on the family. Although negative effects have frequently been documented by researchers (e.g. Dumas et al. 1991), there is also evidence that many parents cope adequately with their circumstances. In general, findings are contradictory and inconclusive (e.g. Gray and Holden 1992; Konstantareas and Homatidis 1989), highlighting the heterogeneity between families. Existing literature therefore throws little light on to how individual families adapt to their experiences and the kinds of problems they encounter in the process (Davis 1993). The need for further studies exploring how families 'make sense' of, and deal with, their special circumstances has been highlighted (Beresford 1994; Tunali and Power 1993).

This study aimed to address some of the existing shortcomings in the literature by adopting qualitative methodology. Qualitative methods explore systematically a small number of participants' subjective experiences, in order to yield rich insights into the phenomenon under investigation. Parents of ten children with autism were therefore interviewed in depth about their experiences.

Procedure

Parents of children aged 3 to 12, who had received a diagnosis of autism at least six months previously, were contacted via the local parents' support group or through professionals working with the family. Altogether ten mothers and two fathers were interviewed in a total of ten interviews. Two parents had children who fell outside the initial sampling criteria (their children were aged 17 and 18) and were interviewed towards the end of the research process in order to test out emerging themes. The age of children within the sample therefore ranged from 4 to 18 (mean age of 7). Nine of these children were male, and eight lived with their parents (the two oldest children were in residential placements).

A flexible semi-structured interview was developed which focused on such areas as day-to-day experiences and the impact of their child's disability on the family. Each interview was recorded on audio-tape and transcribed. Grounded Theory (Glaser and Strauss 1967) was used as the principal method of data collection and analysis. Guidelines described by Henwood and Pidgeon (1995) and Strauss and Corbin (1990) were followed.

Results

Some of the key themes to emerge from parents' descriptions of autism are described below.

Heterogeneity

There was general recognition that children with autism present in very different ways. When describing the condition, however, a number of common features emerged. These included normality of appearance, vulnerability, communication difficulties, and behavioural difficulties.

Real life versus media portrayal

Parents perceived children with autism as more affectionate and less withdrawn than typically portrayed:

> I don't know any child that's typical in Kanner's way, you know, switched off.

> They're not traditionally perceived as being affectionate. But within their families I think they're very affectionate.

Parents also discussed the stereotypes held by others. Many felt that the film *Rain Man* had helped raise public awareness, but had left people with an unhelpful perception of autism:

> People always say 'Has he got any major talents yet?', and I feel like saying 'Not everyone's bloomin' Dustin Hoffman, you know'.

Emotional disorder versus learning disability

The theme of the 'disturbed' nature of autism was expressed by a number of parents:

> Autistic children seem to be very disturbed, their minds are complicated.

Two parents made a distinction between autism and 'mental retardation', stating that children with autism were 'more normal':

> It's not that they are slow, you can't regard them as retarded in any way, really... It's not like a learning disability... I wouldn't say any of them are retarded in the way some mentally handicapped children are. I think it's different.

Ability versus compliance

A usual distinction was drawn between what their children were capable of doing and what they actually would do:

> He's not daft by any means, you know, but obviously it's if he wants to do it. If he doesn't, forget it. You may as well not bother you know.

Transient illness versus enduring disability

Some parents perceived autism as unstable and external to their child. Consequently, they hoped for 'breakthrough':

> Something comes over her and takes her away... You can't reach her until it passes over her again. That's the way I think about autism.

> I believe there's a normal, bright little boy in there, definitely... I hope there will be a way, whether it's through the research or through teaching methods, that will be able to get him out.

Most parents of older children reported a change in expectations with time.

> *I used to wonder what would be the key. But I don't think there is a key. I think you could have a million keys and spend forever trying to unlock him into normality, I think it's too complex.*

From retrospective accounts, it was hypothesised that hopes of 'break-through' characterised a stage that parents passed through. Further analysis revealed two cases that did not fit this pattern, however. These parents reported that autism had always been thought of as a stable and integral part of their child. In contrast to other parents in the sample, they believed that their child had been affected with autism at an early stage of development.

Early versus late-onset autism

Most parents believed that their child developed normally as a baby then deteriorated at approximately 18 months:

> *He'd got marvellous eye contact, he was talking, everything was great. But by 18 months, just nothing. He'd gone backwards, he stopped talking, he stopped looking me in the eye.*

Parents made subtle distinctions between early and late-onset autism. For example, one parent who perceived her child's autism as late-onset stated:

> *I know a lot of autistic children – you know there's something wrong from the beginning, but I think there's a distinction between early and late onset. Late-onset are apparently more normal.*

Two children, however, were believed to have been affected at a very young age:

> *I wouldn't have said he developed normally until he was 12 months old, until he had this injection and then his behaviour went, because he didn't. I mean it was something with him from an early age.*

Causal explanations of autism

The majority of parents expressed confusion as to why their child was autistic although they tentatively proposed one or more explanations (such as unspecified biological causes or emotional trauma). Four parents felt that the triple MMR (measles, mumps and rubella) vaccine was linked to their child's autism. This causal explanation was closely associated with perceptions of onset:

We really felt that his vaccine had a lot to do with the way he became. And although you do get some people who will say that it's because of the timing of when autism is more evident, and it coincides with the time of the vaccine, and the typical things like the loss of speech and that sort of thing, but he was perfectly and utterly normal as a baby.

Even within the MMR-blaming subgroup, however, there was a lack of consensus in opinion. Some parents perceived their child as falling into a distinct subgroup, viewing their children as quite different from others with autism:

Another reason that they think it might be MMR related is that he's not autistic in the classic sense. MMRs are apparently more normal.

Others felt that MMR was the widespread cause of autism. This highlights subtle distinctions in causal beliefs.

Autism versus other disabilities

Autism was construed as a difficult and demanding condition to live with. Most comparisons made with other types of disability were negative. Parents drew on features such as appearance, vulnerability, communication problems, the need for constant supervision, and others' lack of understanding:

It's the lack of understanding of danger, it's just so worrying. Maybe children with other disabilities wouldn't have that total block.

With Down Syndrome and other things you've got the physical appearance, so when they misbehave when you're out, you haven't got the disapproving looks.

Own child versus typical autism

All parents saw their own child as unique or different from the typical child with autism. In particular, this was related to their perceptions of their child's affectionate nature:

Unlike a lot of autistic children, he's a very loving child, he's very affectionate and very warm and loving.

Perceptions of parental role

During interviews, parents discussed the stresses of living with autism. Very common themes emerged, including battling for diagnosis, battling for services, dealing with their child's difficult behaviour, other people's lack of understanding of autism and subsequent insensitive reactions to their child. Parents also discussed the major restrictions imposed on their lives. These stresses have been frequently documented in the literature and are not replicated here.

Parents' perceptions of their role and management style emerged from their descriptions of common stresses. Parents discussed acting as *initiators* to access services and *battling against the system*. They described becoming involved in parents' support groups, actively searching for answers/cures (attending conferences, reading latest research) and becoming experts on the condition.

Perceptions of management style

When discussing their child's difficult behaviours, parents stated that few management strategies had been successful. Most parents negatively perceived their management style, viewing it as a sign of weakness:

> *I give in more than I should. I know I shouldn't but I think, is it worth it?*

Two parents, however, conceptualised how they dealt with difficult behaviour differently (although strategies adopted were no different from those of other parents). This was strongly related to their perceptions of autism. They viewed problem behaviour as an intrinsic part of the condition, not amenable to change. Consequently they 'allowed' the behaviour:

> *Autistic people in their autistic world are fine, they are happy. It's when you try and take them out of that, that they get stressed and unhappy. So we let Henry be autistic. We used to try and stop him being autistic all the time, but we don't do that now. We let him be him.*

> *I feel that the autism is an important part of him and if there are times in the day when he needs to fiddle or flick lights on and off, or flick the TV, then that's just as important. It's part of the way he is.*

The first quote ('We used to try and stop him being autistic all the time') indicates that at one time this parent 'battled' against autism. This response is suggestive of a developmental process that they had passed through. The parents of the oldest children also discussed testing a range of therapies when their children were younger. This idea of an initial 'battle' is also consistent with the views of parents of younger children:

I'm constantly trying to make him normal, to normalise him.

'Battling against' versus 'integrating' autism

There was evidence that some of the above perceptions altered with time. Findings suggest that some parents had become less actively involved with autism over time, they were less actively searching for a cure, autism was seen as an important part of their child and 'autistic behaviour' was allowed. From the pattern of results, a potential typology was proposed. This drew on the recurrent themes emerging throughout analysis, of changes in parental perceptions and behaviours with time. It distinguishes between those parents who are 'fighting' against the autism and those who 'accept' the disability. The idea of passing through stages is not prescriptive or age-bound, however, and many other factors were influential. These included perceptions of onset and contact with other parents. A tentative hypothesis would be that these two positions mark the ends of a gradual continuum of change.

Summary

Although sharing a number of views, the parents interviewed had developed unique constructions of autism and subtle distinctions were frequently made. Emerging themes supported the view that many parents pass through stages in viewing autism, initially hoping for a 'breakthrough' but later feeling that autism is an integral part of their child. Perceived stability of autism was found to be related to reduced efforts to fight autism, reduced hopes of breakthrough, and an allowance of autistic behaviour. Parents who perceived their child's disability as unstable generally made more exerted efforts to normalise their child. This idea of progressing through stages did not apply, however, to the two parents who believed their children had been affected by autism early in their development. These parents viewed the condition as stable and held fewer expectations of cure. This highlights the complex relationships between variables.

Conclusion

This study aimed to explore parents' understanding of their child's autism. Making sense of a situation is critical for coping, and these parents have the difficult task of 'making sense' of a condition where much uncertainty exists. Parents differed subtly in their perceptions of autism, which suggests that professionals working with families should determine personal belief systems before suggesting strategies for change. Parents who are attempting to 'break through' the autism, for example, will have different aims and objectives from parents who feel that disruptive behaviours are an important part of the condition. These views may also influence parental involvement and identification with others.

The study, although limited in its generalisability, provides some insight into what autism meant to the parents interviewed. It is hoped that increased knowledge of these 'insider accounts' may improve service delivery for other families who have a child with what remains a perplexing condition.

Acknowledgements

Many thanks to Neil Frude and Gill Green, who provided comments, guidance and support through all stages of the research. Special thanks are extended to all of the parents who were interviewed, for giving up their time and talking so openly about their experiences.

References

Beresford, B.A. (1994) 'Resources and strategies: how parents cope with the care of a disabled child.' *Journal of Child Psychology and Psychiatry 15,* 1, 171–209.

Davis, H. (1993) *Counselling Parents of Children with Chronic Illness and Disability.* Leicester: British Psychological Society.

Dumas, J.E., Wolf, L.C., Fisman, S.N. and Culligan, A. (1991) 'Parenting stress, child behaviour problems, and dysphoria in parents of children with autism, Down's syndrome, behaviour disorders, and normal development.' *Exceptionality 2,* 97–110.

Glaser, B.G. and Strauss, A. (1967) *The Discovery of Grounded Theory.* Chicago: Aldine.

Gray, D.E. and Holden, W.J. (1992) 'Psychosocial well-being among the parents of children with autism.' *Australian and New Zealand Journal of Developmental Disabilities 18,* 2, 83–93.

Henwood, K. and Pidgeon, N.F. (1995) 'Grounded theory and psychological research.' *The Psychologist 3,* 115–118.

Konstantareas, M.M. and Homatidis, S. (1989) 'Assessing child symptom severity and stress in parents of autistic children.' *Journal of Child Psychology and Psychiatry 30,* 3, 459–470.

Lazarus, R.S. and Folkman, S. (1984) *Stress, Appraisal and Coping.* New York: Springer.

Strauss, A.L. and Corbin, J. (1990) *Basics of Qualitative Research: Grounded Theory Procedures and Techniques.* Newbury Park, CA: Sage.

Tunali, B. and Power, T.G. (1993) 'Creating satisfaction: a psychological perspective on stress and coping in families of handicapped children.' *Journal of Child Psychology and Psychiatry 34,* 6, 945–957.

CHAPTER 33

A Home-based Applied Behavioural Analysis (ABA or Lovaas) Programme

A Personal View

Alan Watkins

Introduction

My interest in autism started when we realised that our middle son, Sam, was autistic; we have three boys aged 7, 6 and 5. I want to present the thinking processes that we went through as a family and what led us to start Sam on a home-based Applied Behavioural Analysis (ABA or Lovaas) programme. My own training is in medicine. I qualified in the mid-1980s and my area of interest is clinical trails and clinical trial methodology, so I am a researcher. I also have a degree in psychology and I am just finishing my PhD in immunology, thus I speak a few languages scientifically.

Once we realised, at the age of 2.5 years, that Sam was autistic we immediately set out to review all the treatment options and read everything we could find on autism. We quickly became quite knowledgeable about the subject, particularly about treatment options. Our review of all the research on treatment options led us to the conclusion that the best approach for Sam was a home-based Applied Behavioural Analysis programme first developed by Dr Ivor Lovaas at University College of Los Angeles (UCLA).

The ABA programme now forms the main part of our approach to Sam's education but we recognise that there are many other educational approaches that may have value and that can complement what we do. For example, Sam has been on an ABA programme for three years, but we also have a speech therapist who comes in five times each year to advise and support what we are doing to encourage spontaneous speech and communication.

It is also very clear that gut function is critical in autism. When gut function is disturbed, then attention and concentration are impaired and self-stimulatory behaviour increases. We noticed, for example, that Sam had gluten intolerance (not allergy) and tended to constipation. So he is now on a gluten free, low sugar, low casein diet. We have supplemented his diet with dimethyl glycine (DMG) and we did try to supplement with *Supanuthera* but he did not like the taste and he would not drink anything we put it in. At times he also requires glycerine suppositories to help clear his constipation and mebendazole for recurrent pinworm infection. More recently Sam has started on secretin injections but we are still not entirely sure that they are helping. We manage Sam's gut function quite carefully because it improves his ability to learn but I really want to describe how we teach him to communicate and engage with others.

One of the amazing things I have learnt though meeting hundreds of parents with autistic children is how much their own personal lives have opened up as a result of having an autistic child. Autism really is the most incredible gift. It is very easy to focus on what we are teaching our child, i.e. to speak, to pay attention, to help themselves, to play, to interact and to manage themselves, but what we must also recognise is how much our children are teaching us. Sam teaches us a lot about compassion, love, tolerance, understanding, creativity, flexibility, to be organised and to manage ourselves. It is important to remember that interacting with an autistic child is a two-way process: we are teaching these children but they are also teaching us.

There are many challenges in autism: the deficits of language, attention, play skills, self-help and social interaction. In addition, there are the excesses of aggression, self-stimulation, tantrums and non-compliance and these are the challenges faced daily by those working with autistic individuals.

Early intervention

What led us to make Lovaas the mainstay of our treatment approach? The first thing we did when we realised that Sam was autistic was (with me being a scientist) to look at all the research, to see what we could learn about what we should be doing, particularly the research on learning and the brain, also memory and brain function. It was pretty clear that one of the most significant understandings that has come through in neuroscience since the late 1970s is how brain structure follows function, i.e. follows experience. That is why, I think, that it is critically important to intervene early with these children. If you wait for late diagnosis at 5 or 6 or 7 years, you've missed a golden opportunity to teach autistic children when the brain is still developing connections and patterns. I think it is vital to start teaching in the pre-school years. Fortunately, as more educationalists become aware of the research on brain development, early intervention is becoming much more commonplace.

Karl Pribram's data (personal communication) illustrate this point well. There is a massive increase in connectivity between the brain cells of a new-born baby, a child of 3 months, a child of 15 months and a child of 24 months. So, when you are born, the brain is unfinished. What happens in those first few years is crucial in determining brain function for the rest of your life. You lay down the crucial key connections and this really emphasises the importance of intervening earlier and earlier.

Many 'experts' will tell you that it is difficult to diagnose autism before the age of 4 or 5 years. But my experience, certainly with our own son, was that we knew from 15 months. In addition, nearly all parents of autistic children I have ever spoken to knew there was something wrong between 15 and 20 months of age; the earlier that teaching begins, the better the long-term results.

ABA/Lovaas: theoretical assumptions and basic principles

We all learn, whether we are autistic or non-autistic, through experience; we then generalise that experience to other circumstances. One of the things that autistic children particularly struggle with is the whole generalisation process. Marc Fleisher (Chapter 35 in this volume) has said that knowing how to tie shoelaces does not necessarily enable you to know how to untie them. It's almost as if you have to teach every single small minutia of behaviour. One of the main theoretical assumptions of an ABA/Lovaas programme is that we must teach through repeated experiences. This is called drills in Lovaas terminology, constantly repeating experiences until they are learned. Once a behaviour is learnt it is then necessary to teach an autistic child how to generalise a learned behaviour.

This emphasis on generalisation is very much at the heart of a Lovaas programme.

The other thing that is quite clear from learning research is that positively reinforced behaviours reinforces the brain circuitry. This is again true for all of us, autistic or non-autistic. Thus if you are laying down a new pattern in your brain, a new memory trace, it will become more established in your network if it is rewarded or reinforced, and it will be easier to remember. So success breeds success in learning terms. In addition, it is important to create a positive emotional environment in which to learn, since this increases adrenaline and DHEA[1] levels and reinforces the memories laid down. So, it is very important to generate a positive emotional learning experience for the child because that actually affects the memory traces in the brain. The whole learning environment has to be a very positive emotional experience.

The other crucial factor is consistency. We can often undo learning by being inconsistent or having two or three approaches that don't connect together, or two or three teachers who give contradictory messages. This can undermine the learning in a normal child but it really undermines learning for autistic children.

Another cornerstone of an ABA or Lovaas approach is a constant analysis of the responses to adjust the teaching accordingly. This approach is really summed up by this quote:

> *If a child is not learning in the way that you're teaching them, then you must teach them in a way that they can learn.*

This is at the heart of the Lovaas approach, constantly to change and adjust what you are doing to make sure that the child can learn. So if the child is not learning, our view is that the fault is with the tutor who must change what he or she is doing in order to teach. Autistic children find it very difficult to change; variety and flexibility is not their strong suit, so it is up to us as teachers and tutors to change what we are doing. I think this really is a critical point. We must have a process but then be open to evaluate constantly whether that process is working or not and if it is not working then change it.

---

[1]   Dehdroepiandrosterone (DHEA) is an adrenal precursor of steroid biosynthesis and centrally acting neurosteroids.

So those are the main theoretical assumptions and basic principles behind an ABA/Lovaas programme and they are based on 50 or 60 years of behaviourism, which started with B.F. Skinner. Interestingly Lovaas himself was originally a psychotherapist, from almost the opposite school to behaviourism, but he learnt very quickly that psychotherapy did not help these children communicate so he jumped ship.

Research literature

Having read very extensively about research on learning in general and autism in particular we came to the conclusion that the Lovaas programme was the most thoroughly researched treatment currently available and the only treatment with a significant amount of outcome data suggesting that this approach could make a difference to the future of an autistic child.

I am not saying that all autistic children should be put on the Lovaas programme. Lovaas is clearly not the best approach for all children and it is not the best approach for all families. Each child and family needs to be evaluated on an individual basis in determining whether a child should start a Lovaas programme as it is currently delivered in the UK.

For Sam, I came to the unequivocal conclusion that Lovaas was the best option. This was my conclusion having examined all the research studies that had been published, on the main treatment methods that we could pursue in Hampshire, namely TEACCH,[2] Higashi,[3] Options,[4] Sensory Integration[5] and Portage.[6] The clinical trial research was overwhelmingly in favour of Lovaas.

Again I am not saying that there aren't real methodological problems with the research database on Lovaas programmes. But compared to the methodological flaws in the research on the other interventions, the flaws in the Lovaas research were much less significant. In Hampshire where we

2   Mesibov, G.B., Schopler, E. and Hearsey, K.A. (1994) 'Structured teaching.' In E. Schopler and G.E. Mesibov (eds) *Behavioural Issues in Autism*. New York: Plenum Books.

3   Roland, C.C., McGee, G.G., Risley, T.R. and Rimland, B. (1987) 'Description of the Tokyo Higashi Program for autistic children.' Publication N17, Autism Research Institute, 4182 Adams Avenue, San Diego, CA 92116 +(619) 281-7165.

4   Kaufman, B.N. (1981) *A Miracle to Believe In.* New York: Ballantine Books.

5   Sensory Integration Network, UK and Ireland, 26 Leopardstown Grove, Blackrock, Co. Dublin, Ireland. www.iol.ie/~headon/si/

6   White, C. and Cameron, M. (1987) *Portage Early Education Programme.* Windsor: NFER-Nelson.

live, the main option advanced by the local educational authorities (LEAs) is TEACCH. My view was that the research advocating TEACCH as a treatment option was very patchy indeed. The evidence just wasn't there that it would help.

Why Lovaas?

I tabulated the main factors that pushed us towards Lovaas rather than TEACCH (Table 33.1).

Table 33.1 Comparison of Lovaas and TEACCH		
	Lovaas	**TEACCH**
Data	Plenty	Scarce
Goal	Unlimited Speak	Limited Communicate
Work on	Areas of weakness	Areas of strength
Deficits	Overcome	Adapt to
Outcome	Normalise	Vocational
Method	Intense 1 to 1	1 to 1 and group
Problems	Pragmatic	Theoretical

Evidence of benefit

The primary consideration was the data. The clinical trial outcome data for both treatments differed widely. I could find plenty of evidence outlining the benefits of Lovaas in terms of what it could do, although there were methodological issues. However, the amount of outcome research for TEACCH was paltry and the methodological flaws were much more significant.

Future potential

As Marc Fleisher has highlighted (Chapter 35 in this volume) we wanted to take the approach that did not see Sam as limited. We wanted to start with a very optimistic view, a very hopeful view, that his future may be potentially unlimited rather than take the limited view and limited hope that TEACCH advocates.

Speaking not just communicating

We wanted to teach Sam to speak to us rather than to communicate with us through signs or symbols. I am not saying that it is wrong or bad to learn to communicate with sign language or pictures but we wanted Sam to talk to us and spontaneous speech is very much a key goal of the Lovaas programme.

Overcome difficulties not accept limitation

Our view was that there was no limit to what Sam might be able to do and we wanted to teach him to speak to enable him to fulfil his potential. Our understanding of TEACCH was that communication was its goal and TEACCH tended to focus on an autistic person's strengths rather than their weaknesses. We wanted to work on Sam's weaknesses and try to overcome those weaknesses and the deficits, rather than adapt to them and work round them. The goal for us was to try to integrate Sam as much as possible into a normal life. So we wanted to try to get him into a normal school rather than an autistic special needs school. We wanted to try to teach him the skills he would need for a normal life rather than lower our expectations and teach him to accept less and follow some limited vocational path.

Pragmatic daily help

But the thing that really clinched it for us was just the pragmatic solutions on a daily basis that Lovaas offered compared to TEACCH. One of the things my wife used to find most stressful in interacting with our son was she did not know what to do and when something went wrong she did not have a plan, a process to go through. TEACCH offered a theoretical outline and some guiding principles but it required us constantly to problem solve. What Lovaas offered were answers. If this does not work, try that. We did not have to spend all our time thinking about how we could help Sam, we could just get on with the programme and spend our time actually teaching rather than thinking about the teaching.

One of the things that people who follow Lovaas programmes find immensely helpful is that it gives you an almost blow-by-blow account: here is what you do if this happens, here is what you do if that happens, a support structure. Most families who are working with Lovaas find that invaluable. So, it was a really pragmatic, nuts and bolts, incredibly detailed way of going about things. If the teaching was not working, that convinced us to start a Lovaas programme. Lovaas provided lots of different options that had already been tried and tested by other people. For us TEACCH was too theoretical.

Available support of highly qualified professionals

Another thing we found very useful with the Lovaas approach was its hierarchy of professionals with a very rich experience of the treatment approach. There is always somebody to ask when things get difficult who has already solved the problem you face.

Speed of learning

A most striking advantage of the Lovaas programme is the speed of progress. One of my wife's friends, who she had known when she was at school, also had an autistic child who started a more TEACCH-based approach at a special needs school at the same time as Sam started his Lovaas programme. The children seemed pretty much the same in terms of IQ and their ability prior to the programmes. After a year on Lovaas, our son was out of nappies, toilet trained and taking himself to the toilet, and had a vocabulary of maybe 400 words having started with none. Our friend's child was still in nappies, was learning to sign and had five or six signs. It was this speed of progress that convinced me that, for our own child, we were going down the right path.

To be involved daily

Finally another factor that persuaded us to pursue a Lovaas programme was that we particularly wanted to take control of our own child's future rather than surrender control to another authority or agent. If Sam was going to make progress we wanted to be involved in driving that to help him learn. We felt very strongly that we wanted to be closely involved with his care and his future. I think that in some families it is not the way that they want to go, which is why Lovaas is not suitable for all.

There were other obvious differences between Lovaas and TEACCH that influenced our decision and which made it obvious why Lovaas is not suitable for all children. For example, Lovaas is clearly very intensive, 35 to 40 hours per week one-on-one teaching. That degree of intensity places different demands on families. In contrast, TEACCH, as practised in Hampshire, is mainly group work with some one-on-one time.

Lovaas myths dispelled

There are a few myths that are frequently rolled out whenever people discuss the Lovaas programme. Like most myths they stem from ignorance and are usually offered by people who do not have any first-hand experience of a Lovaas programme and have not studied it in any detail. Perhaps the classic myth, which sadly was believed by a community paediatrician in our own area, was that Lovaas involved electric shocks and other aversives. That people still believe this might sound surprising but it is still a quite commonly held view and simply reflects how out of date many people are. It is true that when Lovaas first started working with autistic children in the late 1960s, he did use electric shocks to try to inhibit self-mutilating behaviour. In fact at that time such approaches were common in psychological research (as in smoking cessation programmes for example). But Lovaas soon stopped using electric shocks and the most aversive thing Sam ever gets is for us to say 'No' to him. In fact, he probably gets less aversive input than our other two boys receive. So this concept of aversives and punishment does not exist any more within the Lovaas programmes.

Also I've heard people say that Lovaas is really dog training, which is an interesting comment to make to a parent who is concerned about trying to help their child. Because autistic children struggle to generalise, teaching them new behaviours is a little bit like building a cathedral out of matchsticks. There are so many things that an autistic child needs to learn you really do have to teach inch by inch and build behaviours up gradually in order to get these behaviours. The fact that there is a detailed structure to the programme and there are positive rewards for success make a Lovaas programme no more dog training than teaching a class of normal school children.

Another remark that is often thrust at parents is that Lovaas children become automatons: they all learn to respond in the same way. Again this really shows ignorance and anyone who has spent time with enough children taught through a Lovaas programme will realise that they are all unique with their own individual personality. If your assessment is shallow and superficial then you may fail to notice their depth and uniqueness. These children do not even respond in the same way to the same drills.

Another myth concerning Lovaas programmes is that it fails to generalise what is learnt. This is often the mantra of educational psychologists at tribunals. It is a particularly interesting accusation because generalisation is the central plank of the Lovaas programme. There really is no point in teaching a child a behaviour that he or she can do extremely well in one room of your house if the child cannot do that behaviour anywhere else. What would be the point of that? You would then be trapping your child in that room. The whole point of doing this kind of teaching process is to get the child to generalise those skills out into the big wide world. Again, the goal is to try to integrate your child as much as possible: of course you want them to generalise in every single setting so that they can integrate into the wider world. Generalisation is central to a Lovaas programme.

Costs of running a Lovaas programme

It is often argued that Lovaas is expensive and costs about £20,000 per year on average. I think that this is a somewhat fallacious argument. The Mental Health Foundation recently reported that the lifetime cost for an autistic person with associated learning difficulties is nearly £3 million or £40,000 per year for 70 years (Knapp and Jarbrink 2000). Since the goal of Lovaas is to integrate the child and reduce the reliance on external services the potential savings are huge over a lifetime. As the Mental Health Foundation states: 'Evidence suggests that even moderate increases in educational provision could potentially result in major savings in later living costs' (Knapp and Jarbrink 2000).

Even in direct comparison to special educational needs provision, running a Lovaas programme is not expensive. At tribunal many LEAs have estimated the cost of special needs education to be £6000 to £7000 per year. However, this calculation is normally spurious since it does not include the transport and all the hidden fixed costs of running a special educational facility. If you were to include all these costs you would probably arrive at a figure of at least £20,000 per year.

In the cases of the nine families who have to date gone to tribunal in Hampshire, the costs of the Hampshire LEA's proposals were as expensive and in some cases, particularly our own, more expensive than the home-based Lovaas programme. So it seems that cost is not the reason why most LEAs insist on going to tribunal.[7]

---

7   What is the state of Lovaas in the UK now? In 1996 there were five families who brought Lovaas into the UK and set up a parents' support group called PEACH. There may have

Which families, which children?

Families

Which families is Lovaas suitable for? Organising 40 hours per week of teaching requires you to be very well organised. This is not everyone's skill and you have to be incredibly committed to what you are doing to achieve this.

Starting a Lovaas programme often has financial implications because, unfortunately, most parents are still having to go to tribunal to obtain funding. This means that most families will have to be self-funded initially and that is a major inhibitor on people getting going on a Lovaas programme.

It clearly has social implications, in that you have to organise the rest of your family and your other siblings around your child's home-based programme. Running a Lovaas programme also has emotional implications, in that you have to be much more robust emotionally, because you are part of the therapy team whereas if somebody else is doing the therapy with your child there is in many ways less day-to-day emotional burden.

Children

Which children does Lovaas help? The earlier you start the better, so the younger the child the better, although Svein Eikeseth in Norway has produced data when they began with 7 year olds, having not previously been started with Lovaas, showing that significant gains can still be made.

been families doing Lovaas before that, but I am not aware of them. In 1999, there were 350 families, according to the PEACH database, running home-based programmes. Although PEACH started as five families, it now has about a thousand members. There is a trend among parents towards Lovaas and at present there are now 73 separate LEAs funding Lovaas programmes, that is virtually half of all the LEAs in the UK funding programmes. Of those 73 LEAs now funding Lovaas programmes, most fund them fully although some only partially. Out of 109 tribunals which have gone to court where the LEAs have refused to support the parents' desire to run a Lovaas programme the parents have won in 100 of those cases and the LEAs have won just 9. Fighting tribunals is, I believe, one of the biggest disasters that happens to these children. Forcing parents into combat is, I feel, one of the most unworthy activities that LEAs engage in. Combat is a waste of money, a waste of time and very stressful on both sides. If LEAs could understand that many parents are highly informed about the educational options, often more so than many educational psychologists in my experience, and go into a Lovaas programme with their eyes open, we will have moved forward. If we could simply stop the battling that is sadly initiated by many LEAs and get away from this tribunal process, I think we will have made a great step forward in helping autistic children.

Starting at the age of 7 is probably not as successful as if you started at the age of 2½ or 3.

The auditory learners seem to do better than the visual learners although there are programmes being devised by Eva Lovaas specifically to address those children who learn visually and have a much harder time than learning through the auditory channel.

The Lovaas programme also seems slightly better for normal IQ children rather than lower IQ children. Although according to research, lower IQ children still seem to benefit.

Lovaas also seems to work somewhat better with children who have some verbal ability as opposed to children who are mute when you start. But, again, my son was fairly mute, he had three or four words randomly unrelated to his environment, and now he has 400 words. Mute children can do very well but generally Lovaas seems to work a bit better if there is some pre-existing verbal ability.

Professional resources

Who are the people you need to get involved? You clearly need a hierarchy of professionals.

Consultants

In the UK, these are either independents from Norway, the USA or home-grown. You may be able to obtain some from PEACH[8] itself or two organisations called CARD[9] and LEAP.[10] The consultant is the most senior person in the team, usually somebody with a PhD or at least ten or fifteen years' experience with Lovaas programmes. The consultant should be familiar with all the different aspects of the programme and all of the different ages of the children and different stages of the programme. Consultants should visit four times per year and provide advice on the general direction as well as trouble-shooting problem areas.

---

8   PEACH: Parents for the Early Intervention of Autism in Children. www.peach.uk.com
9   CARD: Centre for Autism and Related Disorders. www.cardhq.com
     card@mbi.ufl.edu
10   LEAP: London Early Autism Project. Leap House, 699 Fulahm Road, London, SW6 5UJ

Supervisor

The same authorities that supply a consultant can provide a supervisor. Supervisors should be in contact with your child every two to six weeks depending on the stage of the programme.

Tutors

Tutors really are just anybody you can get who is willing and robust enough to do this work. They may be psychology students or special needs teachers or just friends and family. Relatives are often useful but they have to be very emotionally robust because it can get quite tough. Previous professional experience is no guarantee of quality or ability. Friends, families, other people doing Lovaas programmes or PEACH itself might be able to find you some tutors.

General principles involved in Lovaas drills

Functional appropriateness

It is no good teaching language unless the language is going to be used and going to be relevant to that child's life. Every drill that gets done and everything we teach Sam is with a view to helping him interact with those around him. We are working towards the goal of helping Sam become independent and self-supporting.

Maintainance

Another principle is to maintain the skills Sam has learnt. Part of the programme is spent reviewing what we think he has mastered to make sure he still retains this learning.

Generalisation

This is a central plank and the goal is to go outside the home to mainstream integration in nursery or school. Sammy now currently goes to mainstream school 50 per cent of his week. One of the most wonderful things to see about mainstream integration is the learning that the school and the other children in Sam's class have gained from having Sam with them.

Discrete trial methodology

I want to say a brief word about the actual mechanics of Lovaas teaching or what is called discrete trials methodology. Discrete trial methodology requires you to give a command or an instruction and then to wait for a response. So, you make a request of your child and see what they do. After the command they do a number of things: they may give you the exact response you wanted, so you might say 'come here' and then they come here. If that occurs you strongly reward the child with cheering, shouting, clapping, cuddling, tickling or whatever they love.

Or the child may give an incorrect response or a non-response. For example, you might say 'come here', and either the child completely ignores you or goes and does something else. In this case you then prompt the correct response. In the early stages, the prompt may be a physical prompt or it may be some reward to try to entice the correct behaviour. You give the command up to three times and on the third trial success will be achieved, even if it has to be forced initially. So the child achieves a successful outcome and is then rewarded.

After a while the child learns that the reward is actually contingent on some sort of behaviour and once they understand that, they tend to be a bit more attentive, particularly if you're offering them great rewards. The rewards may be primary, food and drink, or secondary, such as tickles or cuddles.

Programme structure

The first three things you teach on a Lovaas programme are 'come here', 'sit down' and 'look at me'. Those are the first three drills the children have to master because, unless you can get them to come to you, to sit down, to look and to engage eye contact, it is very difficult to teach anything else. So, those are the first three goals and then you get into non-verbal imitation, matching and sorting, objects and behaviour labelling, verbal imitation, teaching abstract concepts, sentence construction, descriptions, pre-academic skills, and so on. The programme flows with a view to integrating into mainstream school. The early part is really to do with the receptive language, reducing the disruptive behaviour, the non-verbal imitation and the matching and sorting, 3D to 2D, and then non-identical.

It is an extremely detailed programme and that's one of the things that we found very valuable. It is always clear what to teach each day, and what the teaching goals are for the week and month. There is always a plan and you know where you are going. If people work to the plan and can see a demonstrable success on a daily, weekly and monthly basis, that is very encouraging.

The shadowing process, where the child is shadowed into school, also goes through a phased process. First of all every activity may need to be prompted but gradually you fade the prompt and start to promote language, and you start to target independent functioning until they are fully independent. Sam, aged 6, is already in mainstream school 50 per cent of the time. The goal is to get him there full-time.

References

Knapp, M. and Jarbrink, K. (2000) 'The cost of Autistic Spectrum Disorder.' *Mental Health Foundation Updates 1*, 17.

CHAPTER 34

In the Balance

The Lovaas Experience

John Lubbock

I am writing this having pursued the Lovaas programme for two and a half years with my son.[1] I want to emphasise that I would not be writing this if I were not a huge advocate of the Lovaas programme in general and of our team in particular. I think the fundamental tenets of the programme are extremely valuable and the mechanisms devised to help children to learn are brilliant; in our son's case the programme was extremely successful in breaking through what seemed like an impenetrable barrier to communicating and learning.

My purpose in writing is to highlight what I and, as I am learning, many other 'Lovaas' parents have found to be an inherent and ultimately extremely damaging situation. Because I am such a fan of the programme I am sad that it is creating for itself such negative feelings in some parents.

The problem arises when the programme fails to run smoothly. It seems that many of the Lovaas therapists have very little experience or knowledge to fall back on when problems arise. There is always a tendency in new approaches for those who practise them to be evangelical and inflexible; this is bound to limit their response to problems.

Our son is very able and intelligent. After about eighteen months he started to show considerable resistance to the pressures inherent in the

---

1   This experience was the subject of a film *Raising Alexander*, broadcast 22nd May 2000 on Channel 4 Television in the UK.

programme. This resistance eventually took the form of screaming with almost every therapist. It seemed fairly obvious to us, as parents, that he had got to a point where he was angry and insulted by having repeatedly to answer questions which he had already answered correctly the first time. We felt that his intelligence was not being respected and he did not like having 'no' shouted at him a few inches from his face when he failed to answer correctly or was not compliant.

I come to the point of writing this. The advice we were given was that there was absolutely no question that the only solution was to inflict on him more strict Lovaas for more hours. This attitude threw up many thoughts for us and highlighted what we have come to see as an inherent weakness in the programme.

The programme is taught by enthusiatic people who are nevertheless amateurs. Even some supervisors, however well versed in Lovaas techniques, have very little, if any, wider training in children's psychological problems. This is the obverse of a strength of the programme, namely that a family can get going in a matter of weeks after one consultant's visit, as we did. But the movement has to acknowledge the weaknesses which accompany this. The fundamental lack of wider knowledge and experience will tend to make people inflexible, as they have no response to problems other than 'more Lovaas'. This is perhaps exacerbated by the nature of the Lovaas approach itself, which emphasises complete control of the child's behaviour and restriction of the child's autonomy. To misquote Henry Ford, 'You can do any behaviour you want, as long as it is the one I want'. This 'control mentality' can reduce flexibility and appreciation of a child's growing autonomy.

It took a team meeting, at which my wife became hysterically upset in response to the pressure to do more hours, for us to get across that we were not prepared to go on with the programme at the same intensity. The level of distress in our son had become intolerable and lasted long after the therapists had left the house. Very senior and professional outside opinion gave us to believe that we were in danger of seriously alienating our son.

It is interesting that after nearly three years we still have one therapist, who has children of her own, who has never lost sight of the fact that the most important thing in all this is our son's well-being. Her flexibility has ensured that for her, he has never objected to work. Sadly this is not always the case, particularly when the programme became a career for a therapist: we observed the Lovaas theory slowly taking precedence over the needs of our son. We felt that he had become a pawn in the Lovaas movement, and he could be abandoned rather than the programme adapting to his needs. At the end, what we were doing, by backing off the programme, was disparagingly described as babysitting and that this was no part of a Lovaas therapist's career.

With the little I know of autism, I cannot believe that any programme can be applied with such inflexibility when the problem is so complex and the manifestations as diverse as the many children who are autistic.

Throughout the programme and from when our son was first diagnosed, we have had tremendous support from senior child experts; one remark made to us I found both extremely apposite and a very sad indictment. He said that the Lovaas programme is not a service to children, it is a product, take it or leave it. Such a clear observation, which in my personal experience is absolutely right, saddens me greatly.

The inability to deal with our problem in an inclusive, gentle and caring way, turned a problem into a trauma which lasted months instead of weeks, was very upsetting for our son and produced enormous anxiety, guilt and stress for us.

I keep emphasising my support for the basic Lovaas approach – our son has benefited enormously – and it is these positive thoughts that make the weakness of the response to problems so sad to see.

We know many parents who have had very similar experiences with other Lovaas people and I have a strong feeling that if this is not addressed very seriously, the resulting negative publicity will do much damage to the movement. I cannot honestly say that I would use the word 'bullying' to describe how we were treated, but I know several families who would certainly use that word. Any therapy for a problem as complex as autism, which is run almost entirely by amateurs, must have the humility to recognise that the tendency to rely on a narrow field of knowledge and experience is not enough to deal with the many problems which almost certainly will arise in the majority of cases. Some system of expert referral either within the movement or outside it should be devised and be available to parents who find themselves in our situation.

I know that consultants exist and in fact we had only one visit at the beginning of the programme to get it going. We did not have further visits because we were entirely satisfied with our supervisor, as we were with the rest of the team. When the problem arose we were not offered the option of a greater authority or second opinion and the strength of the inflexibility did not encourage us to seek a solution from within the movement. We know other families who, despite regular visits from their consultant, encountered the same problems as ourselves.

I beg those running the Lovaas programme to address this problem. It is happening to many families who are encountering very similar problems to ours and we have evidence that in our area there is a noticeable decline in the numbers taking up Lovaas as a result.

I personally would still advocate the programme to any parent who came to me for advice but along with my undoubted enthusiasm, I would give them a strong warning to be very vigilant when the programme hits a problem, to trust their instincts and to insist on a more flexible response than that which we encountered.

As a postscript there has recently been a conference[2] about a new Applied Behaviour Analysis (ABA) therapy which is similar to but on much gentler lines than Lovaas. Several families who were at the conference have as a result changed to the new system, which is in fact very similar to what we were advocating for our son.

Finally there is, it seems to me, a danger that the general autistic world will throw the baby out with the bathwater, rather as it did in the late 1960s for other reasons, if this problem is not addressed. Lovaas is brilliant when it works but recognition and acknowledgement must be given when it has achieved what it can and when we need to move on.

2   London, July 1999.

CHAPTER 35

Autism

An Inside View

Marc Fleisher

I am a 32-year-old man who suffers from Asperger Syndrome, a form of autism. For many years people of all types, including friends and family members, have been asking me exactly what autism is. One of the problems is that there is no one right answer to the question. Like the common cold, there are so many different varieties and degrees of severity that even the professionals are often baffled. This is why it is worse than someone with an obvious disability. An autistic person often looks normal to an outsider in terms of physical appearance. It can make people forget that while we can do incredibly well in some areas we are struggling to do everyday things that people take for granted.

I was told many times when I was younger that the first step in solving a problem is to understand what the problem is. Often with autism unless it is diagnosed early, people do not know exactly what the problem is that needs to be solved. Suppose that you are having car trouble – it is a burst tyre. You can see the problem. If instead, there is something wrong with the engine unless you are a trained mechanic you probably will have no idea how to proceed, since there may be no obvious physical signs as to what has happened.

There is a tendency among many to shy away from what we do not understand, or to feel embarrassed as to how to react; this can breed isolation among autistic people, the depth of which is often underestimated. To get a feel of this intensity, imagine there was a member of your family (or you) who has been shipwrecked but had escaped on a life raft with the shore in sight, with the rest of the family waving at you. Trouble is, the tide is really strong, and every time you almost get to shore, you are swept out further to sea again. Although you can reach out, you can never quite reach your family. Unless the autistic individual can get help, he may be destined to remain as if in that life raft, with a feeling of helplessness, for years.

One of the key reasons for lack of confidence socially is the autistic person's inability to understand social idiosyncrasies. A feeling of embarrassment (or dread in extreme cases) would be felt while attempting to ask for help. We need to remember that this sense of dread, or exaggerated worry, can be present 'all the time' in the autistic person's life, and not just in isolated moments. Misreading social sayings can sometimes lead to serious, but more often embarrassing results. I once went to a pub where a friend wished to buy me a drink, but didn't say so in as many words; he simply remarked 'It's on the house'. It was only an hour later, after I had been trying to figure out why anyone would put a drink on the roof of the pub, and everyone had burst out laughing, that I found out the true meaning of the phrase.

One particular understanding of an autistic person, often overlooked, is the depth of feeling that some worries can make.

1. You are in a room with an autistic individual and you are trying to give a maths lesson. On the table, and among other items, you have a wooden ruler. At one particular instant, you unintentionally brush your arm against the ruler so that it now is only just balancing on the table edge with almost half its length in the air with no support. Provided there is no draught the ruler will probably still remain, but shove it any more, and it will certainly fall, making a loud clatter on the stone floor.

2. You get a phone call at home one day with tragic news: a member of your family or loved one has had a terrible accident at the seaside a hundred miles away and has been thrown out of the car on top of a cliff. You are responsible for getting help to them.

How can we link (1) and (2) when on first sight they have nothing in common. In (1) you probably would not even have been aware that you had moved the ruler. Many autistic people are very susceptible to noise. Suddenly their whole world is focusing on that ruler – all other objects in the room seem to dim. The ruler! The ruler! That's all that matters. If it falls it will make a loud clatter on the floor. How much is our individual worrying? Well, this may be hard to believe, but he is worrying just as much as you are in (2) about your loved one in distress.

The idea is hard to grasp for an outsider, but it is true for some. I speak as a sufferer. This is not to say that every autistic person is as supersensitive. Others can avoid the extreme effects with professional help. But it does happen to people like us. So next time your friend (or son or daughter) with autism says something to you that appears to be totally trivial, it's worth considering for a moment how deep the worry might be.

In my first years of education I attended a normal primary school. I had many experiences, both good and bad, that a 'normal' child may have, i.e. happy memories of Christmas and opening presents, or falling in the nettles, a bad moment. However, I always have a sense of isolation, having no desire to mix in with the other children and feeling like an outsider, but at this time, although my parents suspected that something was not quite right with me, they couldn't quite pinpoint what that something might be.

On one of those long forgotten warm and sunny English summer afternoons, my primary school class was sitting outside under a big oak tree being told a story of 'Icarus the bird' who, it is argued, flew up too close to the sun. His feathers were falling off. Suddenly, right in the middle of this story a loud voice interrupted, shouting 'STOP! STOP! 'THIS STORY IS STUPID – DON'T BOTHER READING IT ANYMORE – HOW COULD A BIRD FLY ANYWHERE NEAR THE SUN. BY THE TIME IT GOT ABOVE THE TROPOSPHERE IT WOULD HAVE FROZEN AND DIED OF LACK OF AIR.' Of course the teacher said 'Be quiet' and continued, but that voice was me! Unknown to the teacher I had been reading a book beforehand about the layers of the atmosphere and had memorised every single detail. This illustrates two important concepts, not only my intense factual and scientific knowledge, but also my inability and lack of social sense to wait till after the story to express my views. I was unable to distinguish between myth, fiction and fact and took everything literally.

At the age of 10 I was involved in a car accident where my sister was killed. I was badly injured, my parents still alive but walking in a daze as to what had happened. It would take far too long to explain how I managed to cope with not only the obvious grief of the whole family, but also my autism too, which intensifies worries. My education suffered, I moved schools about ten times, I was hit, bullied and victimised. Once I hid in the bathroom all day. The positive thing to come out of these bleak years of my life is that I believe they toughened me up and helped me become a survivor and ready for anything later in life.

When I was about 11 I saw a brilliant doctor in London who at once diagnosed Asperger Syndrome. She knew this after about five minutes, whereas my parents spent a lifetime wondering what the problem was. It was a great relief for them to know exactly why I acted as I did. I also had a new sister (Po-Ling), an adopted Chinese girl who brought me a great deal of happiness. At the age of 13 I started attending the Chinnor Resource Unit for autistic children. This turned out to be a crucial turning-point in my life. The idea of this unit was to integrate pupils with autism into the mainstream school, but always with the support and back-up of the trained staff to step in and help when the need arose. As the autistic person's confidence grew, support could be slowly but surely withdrawn.

In addition to this support, the Unit also assigned a certain number of hours a week away from the normal classroom environment for specialised tasks. These included shopping, cooking and a social skills group where pupils' knowledge of social situations was enhanced by acting out 'role play' of different social events. They challenged the ability of the pupils, and pushed them to make progress; tasks were never set 'beyond reach' of the ability of each pupil at the time. There is a tendency for parents either to overprotect their young ones and do everything for them for fear of uncontrolled behaviour or panic or to try to make them do almost everything at once, fearing otherwise that a very lazy layabout child will result. Neither approach works. In reality, the problem is usually too complex for the parents to expect to handle themselves and they should always be able to contact organisations with professionals who know about the condition of autism. There is a fine balance between not pushing enough, and trying too hard.

The crucial role of unit support was continued throughout my teenage years. I started to make great strides in my academic studies, and as my confidence increased I was able to 'fill in' many of the gaps from my troubled schooling earlier. I had confidence in my ability academically, but I had no real friends. I withdrew in to my own makebelieve world of planes and war – I saw my exams as battles of will and strength that demanded great perseverance to get through. Passing those exams felt like winning the war for me.

My teenage school years emotionally were easily the worst time of my life. I felt a real outcast and the laughing stock of the school. I also had a horror of physical violence, having been threatened, and hit, on numerous occasions. I felt that most people hated me, because they couldn't understand my condition. I was so shy that I was unable to express my views properly, so I felt that if I did they would not take me seriously. I did have a crush on one girl in the year above me at school who appeared to be friendly, but she left to work in a local supermarket. I was then frightened away from talking to her again by a boy who warned me to stay away from her. Another boy threatened me with a large barge pole and said he was going to 'get me' when no one else was looking. After these two incidents I hardly talked to the other pupils at all.

My problems did not end when I left school. At 18 I managed to get work in an accounts office of a transport firm for over three years. This was rather nice for emotional support because my mum worked in the same place. However, I was still suffering from excessive anxiety and with the Unit support now gone I had to rely upon social services and my parents to help me. Normal office deadlines made me ill with worry. Then in an awful twist of fate my mum fell very ill through cancer. Realising the potential dangers, my parents sent me to a special hostel for young people with learning difficulties to improve my independent living, as they were still doing nearly everything for me. I hated it at the time, but it had a crucial role to play in my learning independent skills.

My mum finally died in 1991. Then, somehow, I was able to summon up inner strength. I said, 'OK, my parents have spent a lifetime trying to help me. Now it's my turn'. With the crucial role of the social services, I was able to turn my misfortune round to my favour, and achieve, in a few short years, the following:

1. My own rented accommodation: I now live almost completely independently, with only occasional visits from a very good social worker and rehab officer.

2. I have appeared on national television several times, including QED on BBC1, discussing my condition.

3. I have had some of my writings about autism published (including this one!).

4. I have become an established speaker on autism covering all levels of talks, up to international level e.g. Leeds and more recently Christ Church, Oxford.

5. I have developed a passion for tennis, and have coached other mentally handicapped people in the sport.

More recently I set myself a challenging goal, having mastered my essential basic living skills. I began a quest to learn to become a mathematician. I had to aim high and achieved a degree and postgraduate qualification. I thought I would never finish, yet I did because failure was unthinkable – it was not an option. When they finally told me I had passed, it felt like winning Wimbledon. Now at last I feel content, that I have done enough.

I still get caught out with my autistic tendencies. But I am now able to take them in my stride and accept myself for who I am. The hardest part of my maths exams came right at the end, where you had to thread some string though the holes in the papers to tie them together so they don't get lost. This caused me untold grief – it was much harder than the questions! I was just no good at tying string – I lost sleep over this seemingly trivial thing. I continue to try to overcome these phobias to this day. I am currently doing some teaching of maths. It seems really strange that just a few years ago I was the laughing stock of the school, and totally stupid; now I may very well end up helping the same sort of people. It makes me happy. I feel that I am giving something back for all the help I have been given.

How, then, can we help others on the long road to success? In order to answer this I have to think of what the main reasons were that I have done so much. Upon reflection I realise there were three main factors:

1. The crucial role of help from the Chinnor Resource Unit throughout adolescent years, both academically and emotionally.

2. Supportive family and parents who never gave up faith in my ability to make progress.

3. Good support later in life from social services.

The most important fundamental rule is to get help from professional people who are trained in autism, and to get a diagnosis as soon as possible. The earlier this is done, the more help can be given, thus making things easier later in life. This is of crucial importance. People who do not know about the condition can unwittingly make things much worse. Parents must trust their instincts if autism is suspected, and should not be fooled by inexperienced people who don't know what they are talking about, and will never know a son or daughter as well as a parent does. It is not always easy to recognise autism, but parents must check with someone who is thoroughly trained in the condition and *not* anyone else, as a general rule.

There is plenty else that the family can do to help in the name of autism. We must believe in our child's ability to do more. This is not always easy, but if we set small goals as part of a larger aim and take things slowly but steadily, we will have a firm foundation to build on. Remember who won the race of the tortoise and the hare. I also believe we should try to spread the awareness of the condition through the general population though regular media coverage via television, radio and the press.

Continued good support from social services later in life was just as crucial, because once I left the Unit this was all I had apart from my family to support all my needs. Without them I never would have got my own home, learned how to be independent, or go to university. I am not just talking about the obvious physical resources such as hostels and trained staff, but also back-up, the financial support from local governments without which the former can never begin.

One more crucial factor, perhaps less obvious, cannot be ignored. The final 'push' and determination have to come from within the individual. No matter how much anyone helps an autistic person, in the end they need to believe in themselves and have at least some confidence. Even a small task accomplished properly is progress.

I have given you only a brief insight into my life as an autism sufferer, but I hope it has been enough to convince you that breakthroughs can and do occur, even with disability. One of my biggest hopes is that I can be remembered as someone who did spread the awareness around and that the time has come for a universal recognition that autistic people have the same rights and potential as the rest of the population.

I shall finish this chapter with one of my favourite summing up phrases to describe what having this condition is like.

Autism is like you are climbing a very high mountain with really heavy shoes on. But you can climb really high mountains with heavy shoes on. It may take a bit longer. But you can reach your goal at the summit.

CHAPTER 36

The Search for Coherence from the Fragments of Autism

Summary of the Workshops

Sheila Coates

One aim of the Christ Church, Oxford conference was for all participants, not just speakers, to share their experiences and knowledge. This was motivated by the knowledge that at many conferences there resides as much knowledge in the audience as in the speakers, that many participants get as much from discussions with each other as from presentations, so that an attempt to structure these discussions might increase their value to participants.

During the conference eight simultaneous workshops were held. Eight live issues within autism were developed and participants chose which group they wanted to take part in. The issues were:

1. Early detection, early treatment and provision.

2. Being social and communicating, reading minds, reflective self-function, being 'one of us'.

3. Mainstream education or separate education. The benefits and costs – to whom?

4. What are we educating people with autism for? Our goals, their goals *plus ça change?*

5. Do autistic children learn differently, if they do what are the implications?

6. What are the effects of having a person with autism on the family?

7. Emergence into adulthood – letting go or not.

8. Preparing the young person. And how prepared is the community?

The methodology was borrowed from that of focus groups in that the moderators had prepared a list of issues related to the main issue, and had some idea of how the discussion might start and be structured. In fact, most groups quickly generated these and more. It would be difficult and repetitive to summarise each group discussion in turn; instead I have extracted some of the key ideas which emerged. Many will be known, but they reflect the current thinking of many of the participants.

Is it possible to 'teach' or facilitate people with autism to be 'one of us'? Donna Williams describes the difference between 'our world' and 'their world'. We should all try harder to generate a shared understanding, not all ours or all theirs. We are beginning to learn about the internal state of autism from young people themselves, which was not possible before. The information is powerful and needs to be heard, told and acted upon.

For the non-verbal person with autism we need to find more ways of describing and understanding what separates us, sensory, perceptual disturbances, or distortions of the input and output systems which change reality and confuse.

It is for all of us to understand and finds ways to accommodate. The degrees and depth of variation across the Autistic Spectrum Disorders adds to the need for greater flexibility in addressing needs and providing useful services. Great emphasis was placed on the lack of cohesion among all aspects of service provision for children and adults with autism. There are very few good studies describing how, why and where children with autism are educated. There is little evaluation of how different groups of children fare in different settings. There are very few written descriptions of examples of good practice, across the UK and abroad.

Attitudes and belief systems need challenging in the light of new initiatives exploring the effects of a small adversity on the young developing child. What are the potential triggers for the autistic spiral?

Teacher training for children with autism, until recently, has remained poor, if available at all. For parents and professionals, there still remains a great deal of confusion, which many struggle with in their work or parenting. There is a great need for more networking, better continuity of provision. Education for us as well as the children must be more flexible between the approaches used, and the systems in place.

Great concern was expressed about the tension between providing a curriculum which addresses autism and the child's pedagogical needs on the one hand and on the other one that has to adhere to an inflexible imposed system. There is the question of what education means for the child with autism. Is it to fit in, to join society, or to be accepted for themselves, or to conform? Is it to moderate extremes of behaviour or to enhance quality of life? Does it concern the fulfilment for the individual or control by society? Is there acknowledgement of the gifted and the child with significant interests? Is education for independence, or belonging, or attachment? What is the most appropriate education for a particular child? It often rests on expedience, funding and fads. There is a pressure to measure progress but not development.

The above questions were debated with similar outcomes. We need to raise awareness in all communities. We need to educate society still – in spite of all that is being done, autism is not well understood. Multi-agency approaches to education and provision of services are essential. This needs to tie in with families, their culture and their needs. Normalisation is not a realistic goal, mutual accommodation may be. The debate did not underestimate the challenges and time scales involved in creating change. We have moved slowly.

The implications for all of those included in the education/caring debate were highlighted in the discussion around learning styles. The strength and interests of the person with autism can be used to their advantage. We have to acknowledge the problems incurred for those with sensory overload, motor planning problems, other physical or biological complications. We now know that anxiety-dominated states, frustration, stress and confusion, pervade the lives of many with autism.

It is necessary to provide multimodal ways of accessing ideas, thoughts and feelings. It is also essential to remember that social skills, understanding social relations and other cultural tools usually need to be taught, they are not caught. It remains important to challenge the relevance of certain aspects of teaching, to design progress at the child's pace, to embrace creative ways of teaching, of facilitating change, without preconceived judgements about outcomes. There are some clear motivating triggers to learning for children with autism – we should use them!

More questions were posed than answered. This is the dilemma for all of those struggling with the route through to each individual with autism. How do children with autism learn? What is motivation when learning with or from another seems not to be experienced in any way as interesting or fun? How important is it to build a relationship before trying to teach? There is a comfort and danger in rote learning. This can be safe but meaningless. Self-esteem and confidence are crucial – how do we build them? Can we make some learning enjoyable for the child with autism too?

For teachers/carers and parents there are great frustrations. Children show fragments of building blocks for learning. The children can de-skill the best teachers and render them helpless. When children with autism appear upset by new ideas or new ways of thinking, de-skilling can also turn to depression especially for parents. The professionals are always in danger of projecting their anxiety on to the child/person with autism.

For many there is an urgency as the young person with autism reaches 16. Community care has not extended sufficiently to accommodate the person with autism. School remains a relatively safe place, even if not satisfactory. Adulthood is problematic. Parents wish for their young adult to have a fulfilled life, with entitlements to continue developing skills. Supported living, employment schemes, extended education and opportunities are still sparse, poorly organised and underfunded.

Though most parents experience the conflict of letting go, most want their youngster to have an independent lifestyle, with as little institutionalising as possible. To create more family and person centred choice in the community, there has to be a greater awareness among the community, appropriate resources and networks to support the young person, with support for parents to let go safely. As a society we are still far away from this possibility for most youngsters emerging into adulthood. The pockets of good practice emerging need to be highlighted. Parents still feel that they have to fight for quality provision for their child. Barely adequate is not good enough. The ideal should be striven for because currently, the youngster moving into adult services remains a traumatic experience in most cases.

There is a burden of care for all families. There are long-term effects on brothers and sisters who have different perspectives and expectations about their future goals. Their private lives can become public with an autistic brother or sister. Their need for respite, counselling and nurturing is often swept aside in the chronic need to attend to the child with autism. The guilt in some family systems inevitably leads to collapse and depression. Yet in spite of these adversities, many families persevere and achieve a good outcome.

Listen to parents, hear their story and their stress. Bureaucracy, prevarication and inadequate financing of support, all cripple the energy of struggling families. Family breakdown, depression and illness occur too often. Is normality for the family a realistic goal?

Where are equal opportunities for children and young people with autism and their families?

Summary

1. Facilitate more networking and exchange of ideas between agencies.

2. Be more flexible in providing individually tailored programmes for teaching and care.

3. Include the whole family. Work with the family.

4. Work to the strength of the autistic person.

5. Don't reject new and creative ideas and approaches without exploration.

6. Raise awareness everywhere.

7. Help the person with autism reach out for contact rather than avoid or reject it.

8. Realise that if we are to provide places in the community for children and people with autism, we have to enable them without prejudice.

Contributors

Ann Alvares is a psychologist at the Tavistock Centre, London.

Olga Bogdashina is a psychiatrist and President of the Autism Society of Ukraine.

Ralph Brooker works at the Adult Development Centre of the Hampshire Autistic Society.

Richard Brooks is Deputy Head of the Oxfordshire Autism Service.

Jennifer Cantello-Daw is a psychologist at the Geneva Centre for Autism, Toronto, Canada.

Sheila Coates is a headteacher at the Oxfordshire Autism Service.

Linda Crawford is a clinical psychologist at the Oxfordshire Learning Disability NHS Trust.

Edward Danczak works at the Centre for the Study of Complementary Medicine, BMI Victoria Park Hospital, Manchester.

Marc Fleisher is a mathematician and speaker on autism.

Iain Garner works in the Psychology section, Sheffield Hallam University, Sheffield.

David Hamilton works at the Department of Psychology and Intellectual Disability Studies, RMIT University, Bundoora, Victoria, Australia.

Francesca Happé is Senior Scientist in Cognitive Psychology, Social, Genetic and Developmental Psychiatry Research Centre, Institute of Psychiatry, King's College, London.

Lalli Howell is a counsellor and play therapist with the Oxfordshire Autism Service.

Charlotte Hyde is a psychologist at the University of Wales, Bangor and North West Wales NHS Trust.

Sibylle Janert is a psychologist working in London.

Ryuji Kobayashi is Professor of Psychiatry, Tokai University School of Health Sciences, Kanagawa, Japan.

Anthony Lee is a scientist at the Tavistock Centre, London.

John Lubbock is a parent and orchestral conductor in Oxfordshire.

Emma Masefield is a teacher at the Oxfordshire Autism Service.

Sophia Mavropoulou is a psychologist at the In-Service Training Unit "D. Glinos", Thessaloniki, Greece.

Susan Nash is a psychologist at the University of Wales, Bangor and North West Wales NHS Trust.

Elizabeth Newson is Professor of Psychology at the University of Nottingham, now at the Early Years Diagnostic Centre, Ravenshead.

Keiko Notomi is a psychiatrist at the Fufuoka University of Education, Japan.

Lydia Otter is a teacher at the Oxfordshire Autism Service.

Sue Reid is a psychologist at the Tavistock Centre, London.

John Richer is a consultant clinical psychologist at the John Radcliffe Hospital, Oxford.

Dermot Rowe is a consultant psychiatrist at the Oxfordshire Learning Disability NHS Trust.

Dave Sherratt is from Mowbray School, North Yorkshire.

Marian Sigman is Professor of Psychiatry at UCLA, USA.

Rachel Stuart is a parent from London.

Rachel Tams is a clinical psychologist at the Department of Psychology, Llwyneryr Unit, Bro Morgannwg NHS Trust, Swansea.

Wendy Tucker is Quality Manager of the Charity Executive Committee, Nottinghamshire.

Auriel Warwick is Senior County Music Therapist with the Oxfordshire Education Authority.

Alan Watkin is a father and medical researcher at the University of Southampton.

Dawn Wimpory is a psychologist at the University of Wales, Bangor and North West Wales NHS Trust.

Nurit Yirmiya works at the Department of Psychology and School of Education, Hebrew University of Jerusalem, Israel.

Michele Zappella is Professor of Psychiatry, Azienda Ospedaliera Sienese, Siena, Italy.

Subject Index

Author Index

Ainsworth, M.D.S. 53, 54
Altmann, J. 238
Alvarez, A. 134, 138, 140, 179, 183, 221, 334
Aquilla, P. 259
Arnold, N. 153
Asperger, H. 73

Bailey, A. 65, 95, 118
Baird, G. 49
Balla, D. 191
Baron-Cohen, S. 16, 17n, 37, 49, 76, 84, 91, 146
Bashina, V.M. 265
Bauman, M.L. 111, 253
Beeghly, M. 146
Beresford, B.A. 295
Bettelhiem, B. 55
Beyer, J. 33, 149
Biklen, D. 154, 163
Bishop, D.V.M. 102
Blackman, L. 164
Block, D. 47
Blurton Jones, N.A. 26b
Bogdashina, O. 244, 334
Bondy, A. 257, 258
Boucher, J. 146
Bouvard, M. 66
Bowlby, J. 53, 54
Briggs, D. 164
Briggs Myers, I. 18
Brinbrauer, S. 99
Brooker, R. 334
Brooks, R. 243, 334
Brown, F. 256
Brown, J.D. 39
Bruner, J. 86, 140
Bryson, S.E. 75
Buitelaar, J.K. 24n
Burford, B. 42, 50

Cafiero, J.M. 110
Cameron, M. 109
Cantello-Daw, J. 243, 334
Capps, I. 58, 60, 233
Cardinal, D.N. 163
Carter, W. 256
Chandler, S. 215, 219
Charlesworth, W. 40
Charman, T. 146, 212
Chaves, E. 118
Chess, S. 103
Christie, P. 33, 211, 213, 219
Chugani, D.C. 103
Cicchetti, D. 146, 191
Clark, P. 252
Coates, S. 131, 334
Cook, D. 258
Cooke, R. 69
Corbin, J. 296
Courchesne, E. 75, 253
Cowen, M.A. 119
Crawford, L. 19, 334
Crossley, R. 159–61
Crossley, S.A. 57
Crowson, M. 147

Dalrymple, N. 252, 254
Danczak, E. 10, 32, 96, 334
Davis, H. 295
Dawkins, R. 23–24
Day, R.A. 83
De Bona, C. 106
Delacato, C. 272
DeLong, G.R. 102, 103
Deonna, T. 102
DiLalla, D. 57, 99, 114
Dissanayake, C. 57
Donald, G. 149
Donne, J. 46–47
Donnellan, A.M. 163, 253, 257, 259
Dumas, J.E. 295

Eggar, J. 118, 122
Ehlers, S. 106, 266
Eikeseth, S. 313